FLOWER TYPES

SPIKE RACEME CORYMB PANICLE UMBEL CYME

COROLLA SHAPES

ROTATE CAMPANULATE FUNNELFORM URCEOLATE SALVERFORM

TREE AND SHRUB SHAPES

LOW TRAILING ROUND COMPACT HORIZONTAL SPREADING

ERECT ARCHING UPRIGHT

CONE COLUMN WEEPING GLOBE FASTIGIATE

indoor
gardening

General Consultants:
Robert Bowden, Harry P. Leu Botanical Gardens, Orlando, Florida
Deborah Lalumondier, Missouri Botanical Garden
Julie Morris, Blithewold Mansion and Gardens, Bristol, Rhode Island
Jerry Parsons, University of California Botanical Gardens, Berkeley
Francisca Planchard-Coelho, The New York Botanical Garden

Botany Consultant: Dr. Lucile McCook, former taxonomist,
Missouri Botanical Garden

indoor gardening

Chicago Botanic Garden

by
Kate Jerome
Horticulturist, Writer

Meegan McCarthy-Bilow
Horticulturist, Plant Information Supervisor

Wanda Supanich
Education Greenhouse Supervisor

Series Editor: Elvin McDonald
Principal Photographer: Cliff Zenor
Preface: Dr. Roy Taylor

Pantheon Books,
Knopf Publishing Group
New York
1995

Acknowledgments
This book was created with the help, expertise, and encouragement of a great many people. We would like to thank all the consultants who contributed so much to it, and Cliff Zenor who took magnificent photographs. We appreciate the help of Dr. Roy Taylor, Beth Buchsbaum. Dr. Thomas Antonio, and Kris Jarantoski at Chicago Botanic Garden. We are grateful to several nurseries that provided plants for photography: Geimer Greenhouses, Rentokil Tropical Plants, Orchids by Hauserman Inc., Jamaican Gardens, and Oakhill Gardens. Thanks also to Kurt Piepenburg, Paul Wilkinson, Beth Castellon, Keith Lloyd, Susan Ralston, Kathy Grasso, Altie Karper, David Prior, Alan Kellock, Jay Hyams, Eric Marshall, Chani Yammer, Etti Yammer, Susan Lurie, Michelle Stein, Shirley Stein, and Deena Stein.

Project Director: Lori Stein
Book Design Consultant: Albert Squillace
Editorial Director: Jay Hyams
Associate Art Director: Chani Yammer

Library of Congress Cataloging-in-Publication Data
Jerome, Kate
    Indoor gardening / writer, Kate Jerome.
       p.   cm.   -- (The American garden guides)
    "Chicago Botanic Garden."
    includes index
    ISBN: 0-679-75828-3
1. Indoor gardening. 2. House plants 3. House plants--Pictorial works I. Chicago Botanic Garden II. Title III. Series.
SB419.J47 1995
635.9'65--dc20   94-29988
                                   CIP

Manufactured in Singapore

First edition

9 8 7 6 5 4 3 2 1

Opposite: **The Education Greenhouse at Chicago Botanic Garden.**

contents

Cattleya orchid.

Note: Common names are provided only for plants most widely known by those names; some of these common names refer to only one species of the genus listed.

Homalomena sulcata (Drop Tongue)

the american garden guides

The network of botanical gardens and arboreta in the United States and Canada constitutes a great treasure chest of knowledge about plants and what they need. Some of the most talented, experienced, and dedicated plantspeople in the world work full-time at these institutions; they are the people who actually grow plants, make gardens, and teach others about the process. They are the gardeners who are responsible for the gardens in which millions of visitors exclaim, "Why won't that plant grow that way for me?"

Over thirty of the most respected and beautiful gardens on the continent are participating in the creation of *The American Garden Guides.* The books in the series originate with manuscripts generated by gardeners in one or several of the gardens. Drawing on their decades of experience, these originating gardeners write down the techniques they use in their own gardens, recommend and describe the plants that grow best for them, and discuss their successes and failures. The manuscripts are then passed to several other participating gardens; in each, the specialist in that area adds recommended plants and other suggestions based on regional differences and different opinions.

The series has three major philosophical points carried throughout:

1) Successful gardens are by nature user-friendly toward the gardener and the environment. We advocate water conservation through the precepts of Xeriscaping and garden health care through Integrated Pest Management (IPM). Simply put, one does not set into motion any garden–indoor or outdoor–that is going to require undue irrigation, nor apply any pesticide or other treatment without first assessing its impact on all other life—plant, animal, and soil.

2) Gardening is an inexact science, learned by observation and by doing. Even the most experienced gardeners often develop markedly dissimilar ways of doing the same thing, or have completely divergent views of what any plant requires in order to thrive. Gardeners are an opinionated lot, and we have encouraged all participants to air and share their differences–and so, to make it clear that everyone who gardens will find his or her own way of dealing with plants. Although it is important to know the rules and the most accepted practices, it is also important to recognize that whatever works in the long run for you is the right way.

3) Part of the fun of gardening lies in finding new plants, not necessarily using the same ones over and over. In this book and others in the series, we have purposely included some lesser-known or underused plants, Wherever we can, we call attention to endangered species and suggest ways to nurture them back to their natural state of plenty.

This book originated at Chicago Botanic Garden, where Wanda Supanich provided plant portraits; Kate Jerome and Meegan McCarthy Bilow added the introduction, design, techniques, and special conditions chapters, and worked the whole thing up into a lucid manuscript. It was reviewed and added to by Robert Bowden at Harry P. Leu Botanical Gardens, Francisca Planchard-Coelho at The New York Botanical Garden, Deborah Lalumondier at Missouri Botanical Garden, Julie Morris at Blithewold Mansion and Gardens, and Jerry Parson at The University of California Botanical Gardens at Berkeley.

Elvin McDonald
Houston, Texas

director's preface

There is perhaps no group of plants as well remembered and beloved as
our houseplants. Each of us has specific memories of plants in our home, in
our grandparents' home, and in our neighbors'. For those of us in the
northern climes, nothing is more satisfying than a bright cheery geranium
in the middle of winter while outside snow swirls around the house.

The diversity of plants available for culture in our homes in enormous.
Many require little care, but others are more demanding and specific about
their care. The authors of this book have much practical know-how and
experience to guide the inexperienced and the experienced grower of
houseplants. Common-sense ideas abound to provide simple but effective
ways of dealing with mineral deficiencies and pests and diseases as well as
the propagation and culture of our best-loved houseplants.

No one book can answer all questions and define all plants available to
the indoor grower. The list of specific plants for trial is both rich in species
and practical for the beginner and "non-green thumb" gardener. The
choice of plants made by Kate Jerome, Meegan McCarthy-Bilow, and
Wanda Supanich for this volume will be generally recognized by most
indoor gardeners, but there are some new and interesting challenges for
those willing to try something new.

The importance of houseplants is best exemplified by the great care that
has been taken through many family generations to keep the favorite family plant propagated and thriving. Some of these clones go back many generations and in some instances arrived here with the early immigrants to
this country. Houseplants represent a wonderful legacy to our past and to
the future. This volume will help us to maintain the stewardship of these
important plants from the past and insure their success in the future. The
book is a key to good gardening of houseplants.

Roy L. Taylor, Ph.D.
Director
Chicago Botanic Garden

INTRODUCTION

An indoor garden–whether it consists of a few African violets (above), an extensive arrangement of windowsill plants and hanging baskets (opposite bottom) or exotic orchids (opposite top) brings a little bit of nature to our living and working environments.

Whether in a home, workplace, or public space, plants enhance our indoor environment with varying shades and textures of foliage and colorful, fragrant flowers. Plants speak reassuringly to our senses and positively affect our mental well-being. Gardening gives us the opportunity to interact with a bit of nature–a rewarding experience that allows us to nurture, partake of the natural world, and give back a little something in return for the benefits plants give us.

The people-plant relationship is a critical part of our natural world since we are not distant observers but rather part of that world. Having plants in our indoor environment and preserving the outdoor habitats where these plants originate reflects a heightened appreciation for this relationship with the plant world. In our homes we can capture our heritage and create cozy, pleasant surroundings with plants to soften the nonliving, man-made elements common to our living spaces.

Plants appeal to every one of our senses and often bring to mind distant lands and peoples. A lush Boston fern draped over a basket hanging in the foyer or a blooming orchid on the dining table remind one of the mists and mysteries of a rain forest. A weeping fig bathed in morning light in the breakfast nook or three sweet pots of blooming African violets on the bedroom windowsill elate the spirits instantly and bespeak of sunny, lush countries. A fragrant calamondin orange or clove-scented jasmine twining around a Victorian willow basket hints of the bustle of a spice market in an Asian city. The tastes are tantalized with pots of sage, chives, and French tarragon perched on the windowsill waiting to be tossed into the evening's gourmet meal, and a spiky aloe from desert Africa waits patiently for its leaves to be pinched and render their soothing salve to the skin.

Studies show that plants improve the physical indoor environment by removing pollutants from the air and producing oxygen. Also, the mental environment is fortified because working with plants lowers blood pressure, gives one a sense of control in life, and improves the quality of life by providing beauty and useful products.

CHOOSING A PLANT The plants that can be grown successfully indoors are those whose native habitat resembles the conditions of common indoor settings and which show extreme tolerance and adaptability to varying light and temperature. Although plants have not evolved specifically to survive under indoor conditions, their physical characteristics allow many to survive, adapt and even thrive indoors.

Origin and habitat are indicators for determining a plant's ideal growing situation. Almost every type of natural ecosystem in the world has a specific plant community perfectly adapted to it. Time and evolution dispersed plants into areas according to their ability to grow in the temperature, light, soil, humidity, and moisture available at each physical site. These five limiting factors are the basis of a plant's ability to survive in any location. Generally, plants of tropical or subtropical habitats are best suited to indoor growing since these environments do not have the extremes found in temperate regions.

Previous pages: The arid collection in the Education Greenhouse at Chicago Botanic Garden

Houseplants should be obtained from suppliers specializing in growing houseplants, not by collecting from the wild. Collecting from the wild damages the ecosystem, endangers the survival of other elements of the community, and depletes natural plant stands. Each gardener must take the responsibility, when purchasing, to make certain that the nursery propagates the plants from cultivated stock instead of collecting from the wild.

INDOOR GROWING CONDITIONS Indoor gardening shares basic similarities with outdoor gardening in regard to basic plant growth and response to light, humidity, temperature, and water. However, indoor gardening involves artificial manipulation of conditions rather than gardening according to nature's whims of rain, sun, and wind. This allows the gardener to enhance the growing conditions by changing them as necessary, although there are built-in limitations, particularly concerning light.

At the highest technical level, full-scale greenhouses with computer controls can recreate nearly any growing environment. It is impossible to recreate the intricacies of a complete ecosystem, but in many cases we can mimic the basic growing conditions in order to grow a plant out of its habitat.

In the average home, some conditions can be manipulated, but a smart gardener will evaluate the existing conditions and select plants accordingly. Although we will give some tips on manipulating the environment, long-term success depends on selecting the right plant for a specific location instead of trying to adapt the indoor site to the needs of the plant. The result of poor choice is often a pathetic looking plant under constant stress, a situation that is frustrating to the gardener and a struggle for the plant.

HISTORICAL NOTES

Potted and container-grown plants have graced outdoor living spaces for millennia. From the Hanging Gardens of Babylon to the extensive conservatories of Victorian England and modern greenhouse rooms, our houseplants are the products of over 3500 years of tradition. Sumerian and Egyptian art give us the first evidence that plants were grown for ornament in stone pots or planters.

Perhaps most important in the evolution of houseplant culture was the development of the first hothouses by the Romans. They built structures with windows made of thin sheets of mica, talc, and eventually crude glass in which to cultivate exotic plants and roses for winter enjoyment.

With the fall of the Roman empire, many ornamental horticultural practices were lost, leaving pot culture apparently restricted to medicinal and culinary plants in monasteries. Pot culture reappears in the signature courtyards of the Moors and moved into Europe with the Moorish conquest of southern Spain.

As the Renaissance dawned, horticulture reemerged as an art form and interest in exotic plants resurfaced. This was a time of world exploration, and explorers returned to Europe with not only spices and textiles, but also with exotic cactus and tropical plants. Wealthy merchants and royalty often kept elaborate plant collections. Throughout the 16th century, the French and English aristocracy favored flowering exotics, probably to brighten the dreary winters of northern Europe. Of necessity, glass houses had to be built and perfected in order to keep the tropical plants through the winter. As Renaissance gardens grew in size and complexity, the privileged Europeans copied Italian gardens, growing Mediterranean plants indoors. Citrus of all types were perhaps the most popular plants of this time, leading to the development of the orangerie in the mid 16th century. One of the most famous orangeries was built by Louis XIV at Versailles in 1683.

By the mid-1700s, glass production techniques had improved drastically, making glass houses affordable to the upper middle class. Technologic advances during this time resulted in movement of people from rural areas into cities and gave them an unknown possession–leisure time. Women of the upper middle classes had technology to help with the household chores, leaving them time to cultivate themselves and beautiful growing things. Technology also changed heating systems from coal, with its fumes, to cleaner steam heat. Whole houses could now be heated easily, eliminating the need for closed off, cold rooms that were heated only when necessary.

Indoor gardening became a rage with every household possessing at least a plant or two. The first books on house plant culture appeared in the 1820s, teaching the Victorians how to force bulbs and flowers from the garden such as geranium, primrose, roses, and violets. Flowers became a focal point of society as they were given special sentiments involving all aspects of life. Victorian parlors soon held a myriad of tropical plants in combination with knick-knacks, hair art, and lace doilies. Also, since glass-house construction was somewhat affordable, many upper-middle-class houses were being graced with atriums, conservatories, and glass morning rooms.

A worldwide search for exotics was fueled by the desire to fill these glass structures with orchids, camellias, and exotic begonias. Plant collecting expeditions fanned out across Africa, Asia, New Zealand, Australia, and South America, and British gardens such as Kew became renowned for their exotic collections.

In the home, flowering plants were gradually replaced with foliage plants, popular because of their easy culture and usefulness in decorating. Some of the most favored species, many of them new to Europe, were ivies of all types, peperomia, philodendron, sansevieria, aspidistra, dracaena, ficus, and Norfolk Island pine. Ivy trained onto topiary frames and draped around windows became the one item found in almost every Victorian home. Another specialty craze included the collection of cycads, bromeliads, and proteas.

Toward the end of the century, palms became a staple of decorating. In order to force winter hardy plants into bloom indoors, gardeners also began to put plants such as arborvitae, barberry, honeysuckle, mahonia, and peony in cold storage in the cellar for needed dormancy, only to be brought into the atrium or summer room in March and forced into leaf or bloom. Flowering plants came back into favor, with parlors and conservatories filled with cactus, flowering maple, fuchsia, passionflower, stephanotis, and jasmine.

Although most modern trends in house plant culture originated in Britain and Scandinavia, they quickly crossed the Atlantic to become American passions as well. Wealthy Americans and Europeans traveled to exotic places and wanted to bring back the unusual plants they saw.

In the 1930s, architecture and landscape architecture began to connect indoor and outdoor spaces. Although this style began in California where the climate lent itself to using the same plants indoors and out, as the trend moved across the United States, houseplant culture became firmly entrenched in most households. Frank Lloyd Wright advanced the unity of indoor and outdoor space by using glass walls on his buildings.

The indoor and outdoor nursery industry burgeoned after World War II. During the 1950s, people again had the leisure time to spend on gardening. After the necessity of vegetable gardening for sustenance during the war, many people focused their energy on houseplants cultivated strictly for their beauty.

Houseplant popularity grew steadily but slowly from this point until the 1970s when it boomed in Europe (especially in Scandinavia and Holland) and the U.S. As society as a whole became more urban, crowded spaces, close quarters, increased stress, and lack of touch with the outdoors encouraged people to bring plants indoors for a touch of green and a tie to nature. Houseplants are a multibillion dollar industry, and scarcely a home exists without at least one or two plants.

UNDERSTANDING PLANT FUNCTIONS A caller to the Chicago Botanic Garden Plant Information hotline expressed distress because all of his house plants were dropping leaves, shriveling, and dying. While prodding for more information, we discovered that he had put them into storage with no light or warmth for several months. He considered them accessories to his furnishings–it never occurred to him that they were living things. An understanding of how plants function and their specific needs turns any type of gardening into a matter of common sense. A green thumb is nothing more than adequate understanding of a plant's needs as a living organism.

Plants must have a growing medium, light, water, and nourishment. The variation and manipulation of all these elements will dictate whether a plant will thrive, merely survive, or fail.

Plants need light to perform photosynthesis, the process of turning light energy into sugars or food for plant growth. Plants also need a place where their roots are anchored and they can absorb water and nutrients essential to growth. A basic tenet of gardening is that a plant is only as good as its soil or growing medium. This medium must provide water, air, and nutrients and must be strong enough to anchor the plant securely. Growing media range from soil-based to soil-less potting mixes to pure water in a hydroponics system. In hydroponics, air and nutrients are bubbled into water that constantly bathes the plant roots.

Water, another essential element, is absorbed through the roots and used in photosynthesis, to hold a plant firm and upright, and to cool the plant. Water in the form of vapor surrounding the leaves (humidity) is also critical to many plants, particularly those of rain forest origin. Sufficient water vapor in the air decreases the amount of water lost by the plant during its normal process of respiration. Although water is critical, too much water can easily drown a plant. Therefore, it is necessary to maintain a delicate balance of air and water for maximum plant health. Carbon dioxide and oxygen, critical to photosynthesis, are drawn from the air surrounding the plant and also from the root zone where water and air share the spaces between soil particles.

Nutrients, usually obtained from the soil, are used in basic chemical processes to build leaves, stems, and flowers. The three elements that are used in the greatest quantity are nitrogen, phosphorus, and potassium, abbreviated as N-P-K and given as numerical quantities on fertilizer labels such as 30-10-10.

PLANT CLASSIFICATION Formally, plants are grouped taxonomically by characteristics they share, such as flowers or fruits, and are named according to this scientific classification. Informally, though, plants are grouped by habitat similarities, whether they are grown for foliage or flowers, according to light requirements, or whether they are grown as disposable plants. For example, palms are usually included in one group because of their physiological structure even though they come from all different types of habitats, all over the world. Epiphytes, such as bromeliads and orchids, are grouped together because of their unusual growth habit of using trees and other plants for phys-

From top to bottom: Aroid (spathilphyllum); bromelliad (cryptanthus); cactus (gymnocalycium).

A BRIEF LESSON IN BOTANY

Plants are living things and share many traits with animals. Plants are composed of millions of individual cells that are organized into complex organ systems. Plants breathe (take in and expel gases) and extract energy from food; to do this they require water, nutrients, and atmospheric gases. Like animals, plants reproduce sexually, and their offspring inherit characteristics through a genetic code passed along as DNA and, unlike animals, some plants reproduce asexually.

Plants, however, can do one thing that no animal can do. Through a process called photosynthesis, plants can capture energy from the sun and convert that energy into compounds such as proteins, fats, and carbohydrates. These energy-rich compounds are the source of the energy for all animal life, including humans.

THE IMPORTANCE OF PLANTS

Because no living animals can produce the energy they need to live, all their energy comes from plants. Like other animals, we eat green plants directly, in the form of fruits, vegetables, and grains (breads and cereals), or we eat animals and animal products that were fed green plants.

The oxygen we need to live on Earth is constantly pumped out of green plants as a byproduct of photosynthesis. Plants prevent the erosion of our precious soils and hinder water loss to the atmosphere.

Plants are also an important source of drugs. Fully one-quarter of all prescriptions contain at least one plant-derived product. Aspirin, one of the most commonly used drugs, was originally isolated from the bark of the willow tree. Today, scientists are screening plants from all over the world in search of new compounds to cure cancer, AIDS, and other diseases.

THE WHOLE PLANT

Basically, a plant is made up of leaves, stems, and roots; all these parts are connected by a vascular system, much like our circulatory system. The vascular system can be seen in the veins of a leaf, or in the rings in a tree.

LEAVES

Leaves are generally flattened and expanded tissues that are green due to the presence of chlorophyll, the pigment that is necessary for photosynthesis. Most leaves are connected to the stem by a stalk, or petiole, which allows the leaves to alter their position in relation to the sun and capture as much energy as possible. Plants that have leaves year-round are often called "evergreen," while plants that lose all their leaves at one time each year are termed "deciduous."

Leaves come in an astounding variety of shapes, textures, and sizes. Some leaves are composed of a single structure, or blade, and are termed simple. Other leaves are made up of many units, or leaflets, and are called compound (see endpapers).

STEMS

Technically, a stem is the tissue that supports leaves and that connects the leaves with the roots via a vascular system. Stems also bear the flowers on a plant. Therefore, a stem can be identified by the presence of buds, which are the unexpanded leaves, stems, or flowers that will develop at a later time.

Plants that send up leaves in a rosette or clump may have stems so short that they are difficult to distinguish. Other plants, like the iris, have a stem, called a rhizome, that travels horizontally underground. Many plants of arid regions have very reduced leaves or have lost their leaves altogether in order to avoid loss of water to the atmosphere. The barrel cactus is an example of a plant that is almost entirely stem.

ROOTS

Although out of sight, roots are extremely important to the life of the plant. Roots anchor a plant in the soil, absorb water and nutrients, and store excess food, such as starches, for the plants' future use. Basically, there are two types of roots: taproots and fibrous roots. Taproots are thickened, unbranched roots that grow straight down, taking advantage of moisture and nutrients far below the soil surface. Taproots, such as carrots, store carbohydrates. Fibrous roots are fine, branching,

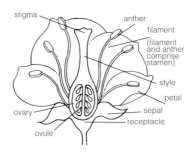

and generally more shallow. They often form dense mats of roots, making them excellent agents of soil stabilization. Fibrous roots absorb moisture and nutrients from a shallow zone of soil and may be more susceptible to drought.

Roots obviously need to come into contact with water, but they also need air in order to work properly. Except for those adapted to aquatic environments, most plants require well-drained soils that provide them air as well as water.

VASCULAR SYSTEMS

Plants have a well-developed vascular system that extends throughout the plant body and that allows movement of water and compounds from one part of a plant to another. Once the roots absorb water and minerals, the vascular system funnels them to the leaves, where they are used in photosynthesis. Likewise, energy-rich compounds that are produced in the leaves must travel to the stems and roots to provide nutrition for further growth. The vascular system also strengthens plant tissues. Although much of the vascular system is part of the internal anatomy of a plant, some parts can be seen.

PHOTOSYNTHESIS

A green plant is like a factory that takes raw materials available in the environment and converts them into other forms of energy. In a complex series of energy transfer and chemical conversion events called photosynthesis, plants take energy from the sun, minerals and water from the soil, and gases from the atmosphere; these raw materials are converted into chemical forms of energy that are used for plant growth. These same energy-rich compounds (proteins, sugars and starches, fats and oils) can be utilized by animals as a source of food and nutrition. All this is possible because of a green pigment, chlorophyll.

Photosynthesis is an extremely complex series of reactions that takes place in the cells of leaves, the byproducts of which are connected to other reactions throughout the cell. The most basic reactions of photosynthesis occurs like this. Energy from the sun strikes the leaf surface, and electrons in the chlorophyll molecule become "excited" and are boosted to a higher energy level. Excited electrons are routed through a chain of reactions that extracts and stores energy in the form of sugars. As a byproduct of electron loss, water molecules (H_2O) are split; hydrogen moves in to replenish the electrons lost from chlorophyll, and Oxygen is released, finding its way into our atmosphere. In another photosynthetic reaction, carbon dioxide from the atmosphere is "fixed," or converted into organic compounds within the plant cell. These first chemical compounds are the building blocks for more complex reactions and are the precursors for the formation of many elaborate chemical compounds.

PLANT NUTRITION

Plants require mineral nutrients from the soil, water, and the atmosphere in order to maintain healthy growth and reproduction. Macronutrients, those nutrients needed in large amounts, include hydrogen, oxygen, and carbon so essential for photosynthesis. Other macronutrients are nitrogen, phosphorus, potassium, sulfur, and calcium. Nitrogen is an important component of chlorophyll and of proteins, which are used to construct DNA, cell membranes, and other vital compounds in the cell. Phosphorus is also used in building DNA and is important in cell development. Potassium is important in the development of tubers, roots, and other storage organs. If macronutrients are in limited supply, growth and development in the plant will be strongly curtailed. Micronutrients, such as iron, copper and magnesium, are required in smaller amounts and are of variable importance to different kinds of plants.

LIFE CYCLE

Higher plants (except for ferns) begin life as a seed. Given the right set of conditions (temperature, moisture, light), a seed will germinate and develop its first roots and leaves using food stored in the seed (humans and other animals take advantage of the high-quality food in seeds when we eat wheat, rice, and corn, just to name a few). Because of the presence of chlorophyll in the leaves, the small plant is soon able to produce its own food, which is used immediately for further growth and development. As the seedling grows in size, it also grows in complexity. The first, simple root gives way to a complex root system that may include underground storage organs. The stem is transformed into an intricate system of vascular tissue that moves water from the ground upward into the leafy part of the plant, while other tissues transport energy-rich compounds manufactured in the leaves downward to be stored in stem and root systems.

Once the plant reaches maturity, flower initiation begins. Flowers hold the sexual apparatus for the plant; their brilliant colors and glorious odors are advertisements to attract pollinators such as insects or birds. In a basic, complete flower, there are four different parts, given below. However, many plants have incomplete flowers with one or more of these parts missing, or the parts may be highly modified.

1. Sepals. The outermost part of the flower, the sepals cover the young floral buds. Although they are often green, they may be variously colored.

2. Petals. The next layer of parts in the flower, petals are often colorful and play an important role in attracting pollinators.

3. Stamens. Stamens are located next to the petals, or may even be basally fused to the petals. The stamens are the "male" reproductive parts of the flower; they produce the pollen. Pollen grains are fine, dustlike particles that pollinate the female portion of the flower. The tissue at the end of the stamen that holds pollen is called the anther.

4. Pistil. The innermost part of the flower holds the female reproductive apparatus for the plant. The stigma, located at the tip of the pistil, is often covered with a sticky substance and is the site where pollen is deposited. The stigma is held by a floral tube, called the style. At the base of the style, the ovary holds one to many ovules, which contain eggs that represent undeveloped seeds.

Pollination is the transfer of pollen from an anther to a stigma and is the first step in the production of seeds. Pollen can be transferred by an insect visiting the flower, by the wind, or even by the splashing of raindrops. After being deposited on a compatible stigma, the pollen grains grow into tubes that travel from the stigma down the floral tube into the ovary, depositing sperm cells to the ovules. If all goes well, sperm cells unite with the eggs inside the ovules, and fertilization takes place.

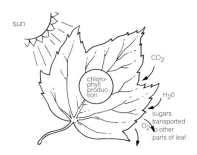

sun

CO_2

chlorophyll production

H_2O

sugars transported to other parts of leaf

O_2

After fertilization, the entire floral structure is transformed into a fruit. Fruit can be fleshy, like an apple, or dry like a pea pod. Within each fruit, fertilized eggs develop into seeds, complete with a cache of storage tissue and a seed coat.

BINOMIAL NOMENCLATURE

Scientific nomenclature of plants can be confusing and intimidating. However, once you are comfortable with the naming system, you'll appreciate its logic and simplicity, particularly in identifying plants correctly. Common names are often used to refer to plants. Unfortunately, several plants can have the same common name, adding to the confusion. To be absolutely certain of a plant's identity, use its scientific name. Every plant in the world has only one correct scientific name (usually in Latin or Greek) that is recognized throughout the world.

Binomial nomenclature means that each name has two parts. Almost all plants have at least a genus and species name. The genus name designates a group of plants that have more in common with each other than any other group. Examples of genus are Aloe, Hoya and Opuntia. The specific epithet is the second word in the name and is usually descriptive of the individual plant. For example, *Osmanthus fragrans,* sweetolive, is in the genus Osmanthus (common name for the genus is false holly). Its specific epithet, fragrans, is the Latin word for fragrant, descriptive of its flowers. The species name, consisting of the genus and specific epithet, for sweetolive is *Osmanthus fragrans.*

Some plants will have a variation found in nature which is indicated by the term "var." For example, *Opuntia microdasya* var. *pallida* is a variety of prickly pear cactus that has yellow pads instead of the usual green pads. Pallida is the Latin word for pale. Plants that are developed and cloned by humans are generally designated with a cultivar name (cultivar comes from "cultivated variety"). The cultivar name is sometimes descriptive and sometimes named for the person creating the cultivar. For example, *Saxifraga stolonifera* 'Tricolor' has three-colored leaves. Cultivars of unknown origin will not have a specific epithet -- for example, *Dieffenbachia* 'Bali Hai'.

If a plant is a hybrid, either occurring in nature or man-induced, the plant will usually have two names connected by an "x", indicating a hybrid. For example, *Coleus x hybridus* indicates that these coleus are hybrids.

ical support while extracting nutrients from water and pockets of soil collected by their roots. They require special growing conditions since their roots are different from those of plants that root firmly in soil. Desert plants are often grouped together because of their requirement for high light and arid conditions, even though they are a diverse group, including cactus, succulents, and woody plants. They all have some specialized method or structure for dealing with aridity. There is also a group of forest cactus that are technically cactus but grow as epiphytes in moist rain forests. Ferns are usually grouped together because of their primitive method of reproduction by spores rather than seed, although most ferns also require moist, humid conditions to grow optimally. For our purposes, we will group plants in this book according to their light requirements.

All discussions relating to plant care should begin with correct identity of the plant, including its scientific name. By having the name, you can locate specific information on origin as well as other helpful information that will enable you to properly care for the plant. Always label the pot in some way so that you have common name and scientific name. We often use common names to refer to a plant because for some the scientific name appears intimidating. The problem, however, is that several plants can have the same common name. By using the scientific or botanical name, you will always correctly identify the plant because every plant in the world has only one correct scientific name. And, since these names are in Latin or Greek, they are recognized throughout the world. The source for binomial nomenclature in this book is *Hortus III* from the Liberty Hyde Bailey Hortorium at Cornell University and the *Royal Horticultural Society Encyclopedia of Houseplants* by Kenneth A. Beckett. If changes have been made by taxonomists to individual plant nomenclature, we have made every attempt to use the most accepted names in the horticultural field.

THE AUTHORS Kate Jerome, Horticulturist and writer. Jerome came to the field of public horticulture to pursue a passion for plants and gardening and to educate gardeners by teaching and writing. After spending ten years in the private horticulture industry, she completed a graduate program in ornamental horticulture at the University of Wisconsin and came to the Chicago Botanic Garden as a horticulture information specialist. The Botanic Garden is a beautiful setting that gave Jerome the opportunity to educate the public about gardening through teaching, writing garden columns and informational brochures, speaking through various media outlets, and by directly answering gardeners' and professionals' questions through the Plant Information Service. Jerome has recently taken the next step by launching a career as a freelance writer and horticultural consultant.

Jerome has always been a strong proponent of gardening by the least invasive methods possible, particularly in insect and disease control. The Botanic Garden's Integrated Pest Management (IPM) philosophy has provided her a forum to speak to the public about maintaining stewardship of the Earth by reducing our chemical use and by using plants and cultural practices suited to particular garden sites rather than manipulating the site to fit the plant.

THE CHICAGO BOTANIC GARDEN
The Chicago Horticultural Society established the Chicago Botanic Garden in 1965. As a living museum, it is dedicated to stimulate and develop an interest in, an appreciation for, and an understanding of gardening, horticulture, botany, and conservation of natural resources by the development of a variety of gardens, plant collections, and education and research programs of excellence while recognizing a need to provide a continuing aesthetic landscape experience at the Chicago Botanic Garden.

Meegan McCarthy-Bilow, Horticulturist, Plant Information Supervisor. Plants and gardening have long been an integral part of McCarthy-Bilow's life, making a career in public horticulture a natural and rewarding choice. After receiving an associate's degree in horticulture from Joliet Junior College, she continued at the University of Illinois for a Bachelor's degree in horticultural education. The combination of these two degrees provided the background needed to supervise the Chicago Botanic Garden Plant Information Service, where she develops horticultural information. The service fields gardening questions and diagnoses plant disorders for homeowners and professionals.

Facilitating the responses to thousands of gardening questions each year since 1985 has given McCarthy-Bilow a special perspective on gardeners' concerns, common problems, and misconceptions, helping her form views on what sort of material should be included in this book. With houseplants or any type of gardening, she promotes a well-informed, common-sense approach that is in harmony with the environment. As an educator, she teaches, lectures, and writes to promote a greater understanding and appreciation for the plant world and our delicate and essential people/plant relationship.

Wanda Supanich, Education Greenhouse Supervisor. A bachelor of fine arts degree provided an unusual springboard to understanding the plant world and its curiosities. Years of growing plants in production and retail situations provided her with the practical knowledge necessary to successfully grow plants. Since 1982, the Chicago Botanic Garden greenhouses have been Supanich's easel, the plants the rich colors of her palette.

As supervisor, Supanich oversees the operation of three public-education conservatories which feature varied environments for plants from cactus and succulents across the spectrum to ferns and orchids. Plant selection, design, plant maintenance, and pest management are her primary responsibilities. Supanich feels that sharing her knowledge and experiences about plants with others, such as docents and interns, gives added value to the plants they see. It gives the collection a depth that is lacking for those who observe the collections from a purely visual perspective. The collections at this institution continue to teach her things about plants even after years of observation and interaction.

In 1987 Supanich began testing an IPM approach in the education greenhouses. She enjoys well-grown plants, but is not particularly interested in the traditional methods of insect control (plastic spray suits on 90 degree days in greenhouses with little air movement, and chemicals that she doesn't totally understand). She says, "Bugs were never high on my list of favorite things to deal with, let alone observe at a microscopic level. But, as I soon discovered, they are works of art in their own right. Using alternative pest control methods such as predatory insects, horticultural oils, and insecticidal soaps is a more reasonable alternative to standard chemical controls. Our public appreciates it—and I believe my children will be better off for it."

NOTES

Plants in this chapter are listed by their scientific names. For information on scientific names, see page 17; for a list of all the plants in this section, with their scientific and some common names listed, see table of contents; for a list of all common and scientific names, see index of plants. Here are scientific names for some well-known plants:

African violet: Saintpaulia
Areca palm: Chrysalidocarpus
Arrowhead plant: Syngonium
Croton: Codiaeum
Ivy: Hedera
Geranium: Pelargonium
Purple passion plant: Gynura
Spider plant: Chlorphytum
Staghorn fern: Platycerium
Venus flytrap: Dionaea
Wandering jew: Tradescantia

Some plants need to be placed or handled with caution because they have toxic sap or sharp spines or thorns. See page 65 for more information about plants that need special handling. Some (but not all) plants in this category:
Adromischus
Aechmea
Agave
Asparagus
Cephalocereus
Cleistocactus
Codiaeum
Dyckia
Cryptanthus
Dieffenbachia
Echinocactus
Euphorbia
Laelia
Nerium
Opuntia
Pedilanthus
Notocactus
Parodia
Trevesia
Never ingest any part of a plant or place it where children or pets may ingest it unless you are certain it is safe.

Gardeners don't always enjoy every part of the gardening process—but finding a great new plant is pure pleasure for just about everyone. Since thousands of different varieties and cultivars are currently being sold, and nurseries, botanists, and private gardeners all over the world are busy finding and creating more, there will never be a shortage of new plants to discover. Moreover, new methods of transportation and communication are making it easier for us to find and use houseplants that are common in other parts of the world. The key is finding out which ones are right for you.

This plant selector chapter is designed to give you basic information about plants to grow indoors. For information on techniques like how to repot or propagate, see Chapter 4; for information on how to design an indoor garden, see Chapter 3. In this chapter, you will find portraits of individual plants. Our gardening experts have selected about 200 varieties that work well for them; they mixed some common, easy-to-find selections with others that you might not know about, but should. Gardeners from other botanic gardens around the country added varieties that do well for them.

The following lists will help you find plants that will thrive in specific conditions or will meet specific needs. Choosing the right plant for the right location is the first—and probably most important—step to success.

PLANTS FOR SMALL SPACES
Adromiscus (all listed) 24
Dwarf agaves 27
Aloe haworthioides 29
Chamaedorea metallica 142
Cryptanthus 40
Euphorbia obesa, E. platyclada 52
Euphorbia pulcherrima (poinsettia) 156
Ficus pumila 100
Fittonia 100
Dyckia fosteriana 47
Gasteria 54
Haworthia 104
Saintpaulia 127
Saxifraga 129
Scirpus 130
Selaginella 132
Spathiphyllum wallisii 152

PLANTS FOR LARGE SPACES
Agave ferdinandi-regis 28
Agave victoriae-reginae 28
Brassaia 80
Carloduvica 83
Caryota 83
Cereus 33
Chamaedorea 85
Chrysalidocarpus 87
Citrus 35
Coccoloba 36
Curculigo 93
Cycas 42
Dicksonia 94
Dieffenbachia 94
Dizygothea 96

Dracaena 142
Ficus 97, 144
Hibiscus 56
Howea 109
Monstera 146
Nolina 65
Philodendron 118
Platycerium 70
Podocarpus 122
Polyscias 123
Rhapis 148
Spathiphyllum 150
Tanthsoma 152
Trevesia 136

PLANTS THAT REQUIRE A LOT OF CARE
(These plants frequently have insect problems, require frequent watering, changes in temperature, or high humidity, or are messy.)
Aphelandra 76
Asplenium 77
Cattleya 85
Cyclamen 154
Cymbidium 42
Cyperus 49
Dionaea 45
Drosera 47
Gardenia 102
Hibiscus 56
Hippeastrum 107
Homalomena 107
Laelia 60
Muhlenbeckia 112
Myrtus 112
Nephrolepis 114

Paphiopedilum 115
Pellaea 115
Polyscias 123
Pteris 124
Scirpus 130
Veltheimia 72

PLANTS THAT REQUIRE LITTLE CARE
Aechmea 27
Agave 27
Aglaonema 138
Aloe 28
Ardisia 76
Asparagus 76
Aspidistra 138
Brassaia 80
Campelia 83
Caryota 83
Cephalocereus 33
Chamaeodorea 85, 142
Chlorophytum 88
Cleistocactus 36
Cordyline 91
Curculigo 93
Cyanotis 93
Cyrtomium 93
Dracaena 142
Echinocactus 48
Epipremnum 143
Euonymous 50
Fatsia 144
Ficus 97
Gasteria 54
Graptopetalum 54
Gymnocalycium 55
Gynura 102
Haworthia 104
Hedera 104
Hemigraphis 107
Hoya 109
Mimosa 110
Monstera 146
Nolina 65
Notocactus 66
Parodia 69
Peperomia 116
Philodendron 118
Pilea 121
Plectranthus 122
Podocarpus 122
Psilotum 124
Rhapis 148
Rhipsalis 126
Sansevieria 150
Selaginella 132
Streptocarpus 133
Syngonium 135
Tradescantia 136

PLANTS THAT REFLOWER
Abutilon 24
Anthurium 74

Ardisia 76
Cattleya 85
Citrus 35
Cleistocactus 36
Columnea 90
Cuphea 41
Cymbidium 42
Epiphyllum 48
Eucharis 96
Fuschia 52
Gardenia 102
Haemanthus 55
Hippeastrum 107
Hoya 109
Ixora 59
Laelia 60
Mammillaria 62
Mimosa 110
Nerium 62
Ochna 66
Paphiopedilum 115
Pelargonium 69
Pilea 121
Punica 72
Rhipsalis 126
Rhoeo 127
Saintpaulia 127
Schlumbergera 130
Serissa 132
Spathiophyllum 150
Streptocarpus 133
Veltheimia 72

PLANTS WITH COLORFUL FOLIAGE
Aechmea 'Foster's Favorite Favorite' 27
Begonia 32
Billbergia 32
Calathea 140
Campelia 83
Codiaeum 90
Coleus 32
Cryptanthus 40
Gynura 102
Hemigraphis 107
Homalomena 107
Hypoestes 58
Ligularia 110
Maranta 144
Oscularia 68
Pedilanthus 69
Peperomia 116
Sansevieria 150
Saxifraga 129
Syngonium 135

PLANTS THAT TOLERATE COLD LOCATIONS
Agave 27
Aporocactus 29
Aucuba 77
Chrysanthemum 154
Citrus 35
Cyclamen 154

Cymbidium 42
Fatsia 144
Fuschia 52
Laurus 60
Nerium 62
Pittosporum 70
Primula 158
Pyrrosia 148
Rhododendron/Azalea 160
Saxifraga 129
Serissa 132
Spathyiphyllum 150

PLANTS THAT TOLERATE HOT LOCATIONS
Agaves 27
Astrophytum 29
Cephalocereus 33
Cleistocactus 36
Cotyledon 38
Dyckia 47
Echinocactus 48
Euphorbia 50
Kalanchoe 59
Mammillaria 62
Notocactus 66
Psilotum 124
Rhipsalis 126
Sanevieria 150

PLANTS THAT TOLERATE WINDY/DRAFTY LOCATIONS
Agave 27
Aucuba 77
Pittosporum 70
Rhipsalis 126
Saxifraga 129
Serissa 132

PLANTS FOR HANGING BASKETS
Abutilon 24
Aporocactus 29
Asparagus 76
Chlorphytum 88
Cissus 88
Cyanotis 93
Epiphyllum 48
Epipremnum 143
Ficus pumila 100
Fuschia 52
Gynura 102
Hedera 104
Hemigraphis 107
Hoya 109
Oscularia 68
Peperomia pereskiifolia 116
Pilea depressa 121
Plectranthus 122
Rhipsalis 126
Rhoeo 127
Saxifraga 129
Schlumbergera 130
Syngonium 133
Tradescantia 135

HIGH LIGHT
South or west exposure
A plant needing light at the high
end of the high-light category
can be placed in an area receiving direct sun for much of the
day. To decrease the amount of
light, place plants in a combined
exposure, such as a southeast
window, or place up to two feet
from the light source.

**PLANTS IN MEDIUM-LIGHT SECTION
(PAGES 74-137) THAT ARE SUITABLE FOR
HIGH-LIGHT SITUATIONS**
Aucuba
Araucaria
Caryota
Chrysalidocarpus lutescens
Codiaeum
Ficus
Gardenia
Haworthia
Ligularia
Muhlenbeckia platyclada
Myrtus
Podocarpus
Psilotum
Rhipsalis
Schlumbergera
Scirpus
Serissa
Syzygium
Trevisia

**PLANTS IN LOW-LIGHT SECTION
(PAGES 138-52) THAT ARE SUITABLE FOR
HIGH-LIGHT SITUATIONS**
Sansevieria

HIGH LIGHT

ABUTILON FLOWERING MAPLE *Malvaceae*

Native to tropical and warm temperate regions worldwide, this genus contains 150 species. These old-fashioned houseplants were extremely popular
during the Victorian era and are available with decorative foliage and flowers in many colors. They are upright and shrubby or weak-stemmed, suitable for hanging baskets. They flower spring through summer with pendant, bell-shaped flowers. The foliage is frequently variegated.

Abutilon prefers high light and average temperatures during summer.
Winter temperatures should be lower. Keep the soil evenly moist–leaves
will yellow and drop if the plant is allowed to wilt. If plant cannot be
watered as necessary, medium light is better for it. Fertilize three times in
summer or with dilute fertilizer at every watering during the growing period. Avoid drying winds and low humidity. Repot annually in spring or
when watering becomes difficult. Use an average, well-drained potting
soil. Prune after flowering to shape. Propagate by stem cuttings or seed.
Most flowering maples will suffer from whiteflies at some point; scale may
also be a problem.

SELECTIONS *A.* x *hybridum* **'Souvenir de Bonn'** Large pink flowers on a vigorous
shrubby plant.

A. **megapotamicum** Delicate pendulous shrub with green leaves. Flowers have
a large dull red calyx and bright yellow petals.

A. **striatum 'Thompsonii'** Vivid small leaves mottled with yellow (their color
overshadows flowers); makes an excellent hanging basket.

A. **'Moonchimes'** Compact upright grower with dark green leaves. Bright yellow flowers contrast nicely with foliage. Virtually always in flower. Slow
growing compared to other abutilons.

ADROMISCHUS *Crassulaceae*

Adromischus is a small plant from South Africa that rarely grows over four
inches tall. It grows very slowly, is a beautiful addition to a succulent dish garden, and has the character to stand on its own in a clay pot.

Adromischus is particularly suited to a sunny window that gets chilled in
the winter since it is tolerant of hot to cool temperatures. Allow the soil to dry
between waterings and hold back on watering in winter. Fertilize infrequently
and avoid using in areas where it might get bumped since the leaves are easily
scarred. Repot annually to prevent root mealybug and use a coarse, fast-draining potting mix. Propagate by leaf cuttings or by seed.

SELECTIONS *A. cristatus* (Crinkle Leaf, Pie Plant) The wavy edge, similar to a
piecrust ruffle, is much broader than the cylinderlike part of the leaf that
attaches to the stem. Pie plant is dark green and easy to grow. The stems may
become covered with red "hairs" that are actually roots.

A. **festivus** Similar to *A. maculata* in coloration and to *A. cristatus* in shape.

A. **maculata** (Calico Hearts) stems are thick and whitish. Leaves are gray-green

ABUTILON X HYBRIDUM CV. (FLOWERING MAPLE) Can be kept to five feet with frequent pruning; average summer and cool winter temperatures; evenly moist; fertilize three times in summer; average rate of growth.

ADROMISCHUS MACULATA (CALICO HEARTS) Only four inches tall; bright light and cool to hot temperatures; water and fertilize infrequently; repot annually; very slow growing.

AECHMEA X 'FOSTER'S FAVORITE FAVORITE' (LACQUERED WINE CUP) Up to fifteen inches tall; high to medium light and hot to average temperatures; easy to grow; moderate growth rate.

AGAVE PATONI (CENTURY PLANT) Compact (to twelve inches); high to medium light; medium or high temperatures; dry between waterings; water only once a month in winter; fertilize only three times in summer; slow growing.

AGAVE FERDINANDI-REGIS (CENTURY PLANT) Up to fifteen inches across; high to medium light; medium to high temperatures; fertilize and water infrequently; slow growing.

ALOE BARBADENSIS (MEDICINE ALOE, ALOE VERA) Ten to twelve inches high; high to medium light; cool, average or hot; dry between soakings; thrives on neglect; rarely flowers in the home; slow growing.

ALOE PLICATILIS Two feet tall in container; high to medium light; cool, average or hot; dry between soakings; rarely flowers in the home; very slow growing.

ALOE VARIEGATA (PARTRIDGE BREAST ALOE) To twelve inches high; high to medium light; cool, average or hot; dry between soakings; rarely flowers in the home; slow growing.

speckled with reddish brown blotches and are notched at the center of the margin, giving the common name.

AECHMEA LACQUERED WINE CUP *Bromeliaceae*

Aechmeas are epiphytic vase-shaped plants that are easily grown by beginners interested in getting started with bromeliads.

Give aechmeas high light and average to hot temperatures. Allow the potting mix to dry between waterings, but keep the vase filled with water. Fertilize three times in summer only. Prune after flowering and then only selectively as needed for grooming and to remove vases that have finished flowering. Keep away from cold drafts and high-traffic areas. Repot when the coarse, bark-type potting mix becomes mushy or when new plants form in spots that make the pot tip over easily. Scale can occasionally become a problem. After the plant has flowered, watch for side shoots from the base of the flowered vase. When the new shoots are six inches tall, remove the original flowered vase at the stem. You can further propagate by separating offsets. At the University of California Botanical Gardens, aechmeas that don't flower are put into a bag with an apple cut in half for a few days; the apple gives off ethylene gas, which will induce a reluctant plant to flower.

SELECTIONS *A. fasciata* (Silver Vase Plant) Large vases banded with silver and white and bearing large pink clublike flowers–common and easily grown.

A. fulgens (Coralberry) Narrow vases of deep, shiny burgundy color with colorful flowers that become long-lasting red berries.

A. pineliana A gray-green plant forming clusters with distinct conelike flowers and bright red bracts. Sharp blackish spines line the leaf margins.

A. x 'Foster's Favorite Favorite' grows to fifteen inches or more with two and one-half-inch-wide leaves at their broadest point. Broad bands of cream edge the stiff, toothed leaves, and the center is medium green. The plant has a distinct overall bright red color that intensifies in high light. This is a good choice if you want color year-round. It will flower eventually, but with foliage colors like this, who needs flowers?

AGAVE CENTURY PLANT *Agavaceae*

Native from southern North America to northern South America, these succulent plants offer something for everyone. They vary in size from two inches to fifteen feet or more across. The flower stems vary in height from six inches to thirty feet. Large specimens are best left in a conservatory, given the need for space. The leaves are frequently armed with curved teeth along the margins and a spearlike point at the apex. Many species exhibit raised, persistent impressions of the previous leaves on new leaves. Colors and textures vary considerably throughout the genus. They also contain an irritating sap–to be avoided unless extracting it for tequila or pulque. Sisal hemp is also harvested from agave leaves. Most are easy to grow and readily available.

Provide agaves with high light and low, medium, or high temperatures. They will benefit from a marked difference between day and night tempera-

Agave victoriae-reginae **has attractive white markings.**

CACTUS AND SUCCULENTS

All cactus are succulents but not all succulents are cactus. Cactus are differentiated from other succulents by their areoles, the "spots" on cactus from which hairs or spines arise; most gardeners know to handle with care. Other succulents such as agave and euphorbia also have prickles, thorns, or spines, some of which keep the succulent from being eaten.

Succulents and cactus resemble sponges on the inside. They have large cells that easily expand when filled with water and collapse when empty only to be refilled at the next rain. A cactus can be 90 to 95 percent water when fully engorged. They also have a unique respiration system that opens the stomates at night and closes them during day, keeping moisture inside the plant (the opposite of other plants). They collect carbon dioxide through stomata at night and their unique system stores it for use in photosynthesis during the day. A cactus or succulent that has reduced leaf surface by evolution or stress often has green stems that carry on photosynthesis to keep the plant alive.

Cactus and succulents vary in their care requirements, but in general, they require infrequent watering. The most common cause of death for this group is overwatering. Because of their nativity, most perform best in hot, dry situations (with the exception of the forest cactus). Many also need a cool, very dry winter to produce flowers.

tures. Allow the soil to dry between waterings and water only once a month in winter. If feasible, place outdoors in summer. Agaves can easily break clay or plastic pots if left in the same pot for years. Watering becomes difficult as lower leaves block access to the pot. Larger pots encourage large plants–use small pots to inhibit growth. It is also possible to control growth by holding back on fertilizer and water; fertilize only three times in summer. Use a coarse, fast-draining potting mix. Prune only selectively and avoid placing plants in high-traffic areas–the daggerlike leaf tips can be dangerous.

Propagate by seed or by separating offsets.

SELECTIONS *A. ferdinandi-regis* Native to New Mexico. Grows up to fifteen inches across with dark green, thick tapering leaves with white margins. Leaves terminate in a sharp, dark spine. Tidy in appearance, in time it will produce side shoots that may be removed to keep the plant in check. They are reluctant to flower in pots. This plant is heavier than it looks. Take care in transporting as it easily scars itself and the person carrying it.

A. patoni can be kept small for many years; leaves are broad bluish green with a distinct red-brown terminal point. The margins are toothless, and the leaves reflex slightly, tightly hugging the soil. Offsets are formed infrequently in large pots, so use small pots to control growth and encourage offset production.

A. patoni **'Nana'** is only four inches across–otherwise identical to *A. patoni.*

A. victoriae-reginae is similar to *A. ferdinandi-regis* but with more leaves and more white markings.

ALOE *Liliaceae*

The familiar aloes are native to Africa, Madagascar, and Arabia. This is a large genus of succulent evergreen, herb, tree, or shrub forms. Many aloes are popular for growing indoors or outside in areas where the temperature does not drop below freezing. There is a wide range of color and texture in foliage and flowers, and many are armed with teeth along the margins of the leaves–demanding respect. Also, the sap of many aloes will stain clothing. Many dwarf or windowsill selections are available. Aloes need high light, and the soil should be allowed to dry between soakings. They are not fussy about temperature–cool, average, or hot will suit just fine. Aloes can remain in the same pot for years or until the pot is broken from root expansion. Regular repotting encourages flowering, as does a cool period in winter. Pot in a mix that is coarse and fast draining. Fertilize three times in the summer and allow the plant to rest in winter. Aloes are virtually pest-free although there may be an occasional bout with mealybugs or scale. Aloes tolerate pruning fairly well but generally need only selective pruning when grooming. High-traffic areas are not conducive to attractive plants, although some of them do have built-in armor.

Propagate by stem cuttings, division, or seed.

SELECTIONS *A. barbadensis [Aloe vera]* (Medicine Aloe, Aloe Vera) Native to the Mediterranean region of northeast Africa or Arabia. The pale green leaves are flecked with white and are armed with relatively soft whitish teeth along the margins. The thick, gelatinous sap has been used for years as a soothing treatment for burns, and it is a fashionable addition to lotions and creams in the cosmetic industry. This is a plant of easy culture that tolerates high to medium light, although it is shy to flower in the home. It is a tolerant plant that thrives on neglect. It divides easily–plant offsets just deep enough to cover obvious roots.

A. plicatilis Native to South Africa, this aloe is without teeth on its leaves. It is an unusual-looking plant that is great for the collector of the curious. Long straplike leaves overlap at the stem as they grow opposite each other along the newest part of the stem. The leaves are shed with age. It grows to a small tree in nature, but stays small (to two feet) in cultivation. The leaves are soft gray-green with contrasting dark stems. It requires high to medium light.

A. variegata (Partridge Breast Aloe) Native to South Africa, this is a coarse but interesting aloe. Partridge breast aloe has thick triangularly shaped leaves with a distinct pebbly white cuticle along the margins. Irregular white markings form transverse bands on the leaves. It clusters with age and flowers relatively easily. Unfortunately, its leaves are susceptible to breakage so the plant should be handled with care. Unscarred specimens are to be prized. It is susceptible to leaf spots if watered too frequently and if the water chills on the leaves.

A. haworthioides A tiny hairy species that looks similar to haworthia.

APOROCACTUS *Cactaceae*

This is a group of six epiphytes found growing in trees or over rocks in Mexico. Their stems are produced in large numbers and are armed with many fine spines. Roots may form anywhere along the stem.

Provide high light and allow the soil to dry between soakings. Give cool, dry period in winter to get flowers in spring. If given the same temperatures year-round, it will not flower. It will, however, tolerate cold to hot temperatures. Fertilize plants infrequently and avoid high humidity, which scars the stems. Plants will do well in the same pot for years–we have had one at Chicago Botanic Garden in an eight-inch hanging basket for ten years.

Pot in a coarse, fast-draining potting mix. Propagate by stem cuttings and watch for occasional mites and mealybug.

SELECTIONS A. flagelliformis (Rat's Tail Cactus) Round pendant stems can grow to six feet, are about as big around as a finger, and are covered with light brown sharp spines. It does well in a hanging basket. It will flower profusely in spring if given a cold (not freezing), dry winter. Flowers are three inches long and bright reddish to pink. Easy to grow.

ASTROPHYTUM STAR CACTUS *Cactaceae*

These attractive plants from Mexico are grown as individual specimens since they don't produce offsets. Covered with white scales or felt in decorative patterns, these cactus are easy to grow.

CACTUS DISH GARDEN

Small cactus can be beautifully displayed in a dish garden. This is an excellent way to grow plants with similar cultural needs and enhance a table or windowsill in bright light.

Select an attractive container such as a terracotta bowl or rustic box, making sure that it does not leak or that it sits on a saucer to catch any runoff. Put gravel or coarse charcoal in the bottom half of the container and fill the rest of the container with a suitable cactus potting mix. Choose plants that will remain small and that will thrive under the same conditions, such as jade, chin cactus, beavertail cactus, aloe, and haworthia. Even small specimens of cactus that grow large can be used with the intention of moving them out of the dish garden as they grow too large. When placing the plants, use design principles of mixing textures, shapes, and sizes to achieve an attractive combination. Plants can be put close together for an instant impact or spread farther apart to accommodate their growth. Situate the roots so the plant is firmly planted and will easily support itself. Add design elements desired, such as decorative stones or driftwood. Finally, topdress the soil with attractive gravel and water the plants lightly. After moving the dish garden to its display spot, watch carefully for a few days to make sure the plants are settling in.

CACTUS FLOWERS

The cactus that flower best in the home are the forest types, like the Christmas cactus, *Schlumbergera* x *buckleyi,* and rhipsalis. To promote flowering, give plants the right conditions: proper light, correct humidity and temperature, and shorter days (fourteen hours of darkness) and cooler temperatures (60-70° F.) for about two months. Drafts cause bud drop and inconsistent temperatures, and should be avoided.
FRANCISCA PLANCHARD-COEHLO
THE NEW YORK BOTANICAL GARDEN

I grow succulents and cactus for their leaves, foliage color, and structure rather than for flowers–some need a drop in temperature or long/short days to set buds, but since most flower for short times, I haven't worried about whether or not they bloom. The exception may be the succulent, kalanchoe; various species have striking flowers that persist for several weeks, especially *K. feldschekdae.* They need short days to sets buds.
JULIE MORRIS
BLITHEWOLD MANSION AND GARDENS

Most cactus need good, bright light and lower night temperatures to flower well. A winter rest is also a must to get good flowering. Most mammillaria species flower easily in the home.
JERRY PARSONS
UNIVERSITY OF CALIFORNIA BOTANICAL GARDEN, BERKELEY

The variety of color and texture offered in the everyday growth of cactus give yearround interest. If treated properly, cactus flowers are the icing on a luscious cake. Intensely colored, these reproductive structures do their job well–they can't help being seen by their pollinators in nature. This incredible beauty is extremely costly in the moisture department, so flowers generally last only one or two days.
WANDA SUPANICH
CHICAGO BOTANIC GARDEN

Overwatering in fall can inhibit flowering; among the easiest to flower is the Thanksgiving cactus.
DEBORAH LALUMONDIER
MISSOURI BOTANICAL GARDEN

Provide high light and low humidity. Cool temperatures are required for flowering. Pot in coarse, fast-draining potting mix and allow the soil to dry between waterings. Hold off on water in winter. No pruning is needed. Fertilize three times in summer. Propagate by seed.

Aporocactus flagelliformis in flower

APOROCACTUS FLAGELLIFORMIS (RAT'S TAIL CACTUS) Stems up to six feet long; flowers three inches wide; high light; dry between waterings; provide cool dry period in winter; fertilize infrequently; slow growing.

ASTROPHYTUM ASTERIAS (SAND DOLLAR CACTUS) Five inches; high light and low humidity; dry between waterings; reduce watering in winter; fertilize three times in summer; slow growing.

ASTROPHYTUM ORNATUM (STAR CACTUS) Ten inches; high light and low humidity; dry between waterings; reduce watering in winter; fertilize three times in summer; slow growing.

BEGONIA X 'LOOKING GLASS' Three feet; high light; average temperatures; evenly moist; fertilize three times in summer; average rate of growth.

Astrophytum myriostigma in flower.

SELECTIONS *A. asterias* (Sand Dollar Cactus, Sea Urchin Cactus) A highly patterned round cactus with eight ribs that are not as distinct as in other species. White areoles appear as buttons running between and parallel to the ribs. Small white scales cover the surface in another decorative pattern over the bluish olive-green surface. Summer flowers are yellow with red centers and are borne in the center of the top of the plant. This plant is so decorative it doesn't look real. Mealybugs can be a problem and are almost impossible to detect because of the plant's white markings.

A. myriostigma (Bishop's Cap) can grow larger than other species; decorative.

A. nudum A more angularly stemmed, leathery-looking species similar to *A. ornatum,* but with no white markings or spines, hence *nudum,* as in "nude."

A. ornatum (Star Cactus, Ornamental Monkshood) Eight ribs are distinctly edged with whitish areoles bearing five to eleven sharp yellow to brown spines. Deep fissures between the ribs are marked with irregular white scales sometimes forming bands. Mature plants produce yellow flowers. Purchase unmarred plants because the scars will last for the life of the plant. Keep them in a spot away from traffic, such as a wide windowsill.

BEAUCARNEA *See Nolina*

BEGONIA *See page 78 for main* Begonia *entry*

B. x 'Looking Glass' A large fibrous begonia with large silvery-white leaves with olive green veins; the undersides of the leaves are bright red. Needs higher light than most other begonias.

B. x 'Venetian Red' A rex hybrid with rich but not flashy red color. The plant grows in dense tufts, and the leaves are medium sized, standing out in a collection. It is fairly easy to propagate from rhizome or leaf cuttings. This is an excellent candidate for a large mixed dish garden, although it needs high light. Powdery mildew may be an occasional problem, but can be controlled by removing infected leaves, improving air circulation at first indication, reducing humidity, and keeping water off the leaves. This begonia is slow to establish and wilts easily if too wet. Keep it warm and allow it to dry between waterings.

BILLBERGIA VASE PLANT *Bromeliaceae*

This group of "vase plants" is native to tropical and subtropical America and is well suited for home culture. The decorative flowers are usually accompanied by large colorful bracts that explode from vases on an annual basis. Once flowered, the vase dies but replaces itself with a new vase. The foliage is plain or variegated, narrow, straplike, and usually spiny.

Easy to grow and readily available, billbergias require high to medium light, average temperatures, and must dry out between waterings. The vase should be kept filled with water. They need repotting only when the stems fill the pot or the potting mix begins to break down. The mix should be coarse and fast-draining with a high component of bark, osmunda fiber, or tree fern fiber. Fertilize billbergias three times in the summer. Prune only after flowering by removing the vase that has flowered as soon as it begins to yellow. Also, avoid placing them in high-traffic areas because the spiny leaves are easily damaged and can also hurt passersby. The only pest problems with billbergias are occasional scale and mealybugs. Propagate by division or offsets.

SELECTIONS *B. saundersii* A parent of *B.* x 'Fantasia'; this plant grows taller and has longer, more arching flower stems. It grows relatively quickly to be a large cluster of vases. The flowers are extremely showy.

B. vittata A Brazilian native with silvery gray cross bands on the underside of the leaves. The flower petals are blue, violet, and green and curly; the sepals are violet, and the bracts are brilliant red.

B. x 'Fantasia' (*B. saundersii* x *B. pyramidalis*) A colorful vase of coppery green and pink spotted with white and pink. The most intense coloration appears in high light. The blue flowers appear to jump out of pink bracts. Slow growing, this billbergia tends to stay smaller and does not form dense clumps, as do others in the genus. Pots of three to five vases are spectacular in flower. Plants will tolerate poor conditions without exhibiting their true colors and are slow to recover from neglect.

CEPHALOCEREUS *Cactaceae*

This genus is in a constant state of taxonomic flux. Some say there are fifty in the genus, others feel there is only one. Found from the southern United States to Brazil, the columnar cactus are reluctant to flower until they become quite large.

As a general rule, plants that have white hairs or a white waxy coating require high light. This is an adaptation to natural situations with intense light–the white coating reflects light and keeps the plant cool enough to survive. Cephalocereus needs to be in full sun. Allow it to sit dry and reduce water even further in winter. It is often watered too frequently, causing the plant to grow abnormally conical at the top. The result is that the plant dies yet remains in a state of suspended animation until an unsuspecting gardener bumps, it and it falls over because it is hollow inside. Give it average to hot temperatures, never less than 55° F., and fertilize infrequently (never in winter). Pot in coarse, fast-draining potting mix and repot annually if needed to avoid root mealybugs. Propagate by seed.

SELECTIONS *C. senilis* (Oldman Cactus) Native to Mexico, this species is the only one in the genus that is worthwhile to grow as an indoor plant. Its native sites are foggy hillsides where it never rains. It is a popular columnar cactus that is distinctly recognizable by long, stiff white hairs covering the entire surface of the plant. These hairs conceal sharp yellow spines in groups of one to five. The nocturnal flowers are rarely seen on potted specimens. In nature, this cactus grows to thirty feet or more, but it is an extremely slow grower.

CEREUS *Cactaceae*

This is a group of vigorous, columnar cactus from South America and the West Indies. Given sufficient water, these are fast growers that branch and

C. peruvianus 'Monstrosus' displays the gnarled form called "monstrose." It grows more slowly than *C. peruvianus.*

BILLBERGIA X 'FANTASIA' (VASE PLANT) To sixteen inches high; medium to high light and average temperatures; must dry out between waterings; the vase should be kept filled with water; fertilize three times in summer; slow growing.

CEPHALOCEREUS SENILIS (OLDMAN CACTUS) Three inches to four feet; high light and average to hot temperatures (never less than 55° F.); infrequent watering–prefer misting; slow growing.

CEREUS PERUVIANUS (PERUVIAN APPLE) Up to twelve feet; medium to high light and average to cool temperatures; dry out between soakings; will tolerate higher humidity than most cactus; fertilize three times in summer and not in winter; fast growing.

X CITROFORTUNELLA MITIS (CALAMONDIN ORANGE) Keep small by pruning; high light; evenly moist soil; fertilize three times in summer or with dilute fertilizer at every watering; heavy feeder, medium growth rate.

become treelike with age. Night-blooming, large white trumpet flowers are followed by red fruits that are seedy but usually edible. Cereus are commonly available in grocery stores or at tropical tent sales (not that these are the best places to buy them).

Cereus require medium to high light, average to hot temperatures and drying out between soakings. These plants are semitropical and will tolerate higher humidity than most cactus. High-traffic areas should be avoided since they may pose a hazard. Repotting is generally not neccessary–these are very large plants that are quite heavy, making them difficult to handle. They will tolerate the same pot for many years and need to be repotted only if the plant becomes unstable in the existing pot. Pot in a coarse, fast-draining potting mix. Fertilize three times in summer and not in winter. Do not prune except to reduce the size or encourage branching early in the growing season–pruning produces unsightly scars. Propagate by stem cuttings or the easily germinated seeds. Keep watch for mealybugs and cactus scale.

SELECTIONS *C. peruvianus* (Peruvian Apple) In the trade, this plant is frequently (and incorrectly) called night-blooming cereus. It has large, white fragrant nocturnal flowers that are bat-pollinated. New growth is bluish-green changing to dull green with age. It will tolerate low-light conditions if water and fertilizer are withheld for long periods of time. The growth in low light will be slow, spindly, and abnormal. Frequently available with three stems per pot, they are particularly popular as part of the "Great Southwest" style of interior design. If grown in high light, this cactus is more forgiving of the common problem of overwatering by growers unfamiliar with cactus requirements. It infrequently flowers in the home. This cereus requires average to cool temperatures. The stems may be cut off and rooted. If the original plant is in sufficient sunlight and is cut in spring or summer, a new branch should appear at the cut.

C. peruvianus '**Monstrosus**' is a slower-growing, curious form that stays much smaller than the species and can be more difficult to grow.

CITRUS LEMON, ORANGE, LIME *Rutaceae*

Citrus, native to southeast Asia, make good houseplants for a sunny, cool spot. The foliage is dark, shiny green, and the bark is light brown. The flowers are waxy white and fragrant.

Provide high light and keep the soil evenly moist. Fertilize at least three times in summer or with dilute fertilizer at every watering during the growing period–citrus are heavy feeders. Also provide average to cool temperatures, but avoid cold drafts. Citrus like fresh air and sunshine, so placement outside in summer is beneficial. Repot infrequently in average, well-drained potting mix. Propagate by stem cuttings or seed. Insect problems may occur–mainly scale, thrips, mites, and whitefly. Citrus may have thorns, so be careful of placement.

SELECTIONS *C. limon* '**Meyer**' (Meyer's Lemon) Can be kept small easily by selective pruning after fruiting. It tends to be in flower or fruit almost continuously. Sometimes the fruit set is so heavy that selective removal is required to

I need hardly describe the scent of citrus hanging heavily in the air. Once perceived, the aroma remains captured in your sensory memory. It classifies as one of the world's favorite smells. . . Despite their finicky disposition, citrus trees have been grown indoors since the fourteenth century. In fact, their savory fruit provided the impetus to construct the first glass-sided houses. . . called orangeries in their honor. . . From the moment they laid eyes on these edible subtropicals, the gardening public lusted after their previously forbidden fruit. Where there is a will, there is a way, and citrus became one of the first plants to be grown on the windowsill.
TOVAH MARTIN, FROM *THE ESSENCE OF FRAGRANCE: FRAGRANT PLANTS FOR INDOOR GARDENS.*

THE NATURE OF PLANTS GROWN IN POTS

Cactus are good examples of the growth differences of plants grown in pots and plants grown in their natural settings in the ground. Cactus send out shallow but far-reaching roots to capture as much scarce rainfall as possible. These far-reaching "rain roots" shrivel as the soil dries, and the main roots seal themselves in preparation for drought. Cactus in containers do not have the opportunity to send out shallow roots, so the gardener should treat them as if they were constantly in the drought conditions of the desert. In other words, they can't take up any excess water, so let them dry thoroughly between waterings, but don't force them to go without water forever. Container-grown plants will usually look very different from the same plant grown in natural light. Growth will be softer and often dwarfed, and many characteristics will be less pronounced. For example, cactus spines will be soft and less dense than if grown outside.

keep the branches from breaking. The fruits lack the pinched or nipple end that other types of lemon have.

C. limon 'Ponderosa' (Ponderosa Lemon) Produces huge fruits even on small four-foot plants; very reliable.

C. medica 'Buddha's Hand' (Citron) Abnormally fingered fruit with yellow skin; for the grower interested in curiosities.

C. sinensis 'Washington Navel' (Washington Navel Orange) Dwarf seedless orange.

C. x paradisii 'Star Ruby' (Star Ruby Grapefruit) Pink grapefruit, easy and rewarding.

X Citrofortunella mitis (Calamondin Orange) Shrubby plant up to four feet tall with tiny, very tart fruit that make superb marmalade. Easy to grow and flower.

CLEISTOCACTUS *Cactaceae*

This genus holds thirty South American cactus that have narrow creeping or erect stems. The stems are covered with closely set areoles and fine spines. Tubular flowers are showy but anticlimactic since the narrow tubes open only slightly at the tip.

Cleistocactus should be grown in high light in almost any temperature (although not below 50° F.). Allow to dry between soakings and sit dry, particularly in winter. It thrives on neglect as long as full sun is provided. Too frequent watering causes abnormal narrowing of growth points. No pruning is required. Root mealybug may be an occasional problem–pull potbound plants out of the pot to check. Repot infrequently unless root mealybugs are present; to prevent, repot annually. Propagate by stem cuttings or seed.

SELECTIONS *C. smaragdiflorus* Stems grow long and begin to creep with age. Brown-green with red flowers that are tipped in yellow and green. Keep moist when in flower.

C. strausii (Silver Torch Cactus) Branching from the base, this cactus from Bolivia forms a delightful group of erect stems covered with short silver-white hairs that originate from obvious areoles. It grows to three feet or more and produces tubular reddish flowers at the tops of the stems.

COCCOLOBA SEA GRAPE *Polygonaceae*

This genus contains over 150 species of trees, shrubs, and woody vines. They originate in tropical and subtropical America and are specifically found along warm seacoasts.

Provide bright light–a south window is preferable–and average temperatures. Sea grape must be kept evenly moist and should be potted in a well-drained potting soil (remember that it is native to sandy beaches). Fertilize three times in summer. Sea grape is slow-growing so should seldom need pruning. Propagate by cuttings in spring. Watch for soft brown scale.

SELECTIONS *C. uvifera* (Sea Grape) Shrubby plant with large, round, light green leathery leaves; very coarse plant that is grown as a six-foot tree. The young leaves have bright red veins. (MISSOURI BOTANIC GARDEN)

CLEISTOCACTUS STRAUSII (SILVER TORCH CACTUS) To three feet or more; high light; almost any temperature; dry between soakings; rarely flowers in house; slow growing.

COCCOLOBA UVIFERA (SEA GRAPE) Up to six feet; bright light and average temperatures; evenly moist; fertilize three times in summer; slow growing.

COLEUS X HYBRIDUM CV. (FLAME NETTLE) One foot high; high light; average temperatures and high humidity; evenly moist in growing season; dilute fertilizer at every feeding; fast growing.

COTYLEDON UNDULATA (SILVER RUFFLES) Up to twenty inches tall; high light and cool to hot temperatures; dry between soakings; easily marked by touching; fertilize infrequently; slow growing.

Less is actually more! Removing the newest leaf or leaves with a small piece of the stem encourages a plant to become fuller. Growth points down the stem become activated by "pinching," causing more branches to be formed along the main stem. Some plants that benefit from regular pinching: wandering jew, jade plants, pink polka dot plant, ivy, Swedish ivy, coleus (shown above, ready to be pinched), peperomias, myrtle, Tahitian bridal veil, hibiscus.

COLEUS FLAME NETTLE, PAINTED LEAVES *Lamiaceae*

These herbaceous plants originate in the Old World tropics and are commonly cultivated as outdoor bedding plants. Many grow them indoors for their colorful leaves and easy culture. They have square stems, as do other members of the mint family, and some are used for culinary purposes. Coleus generally grows to a maximum of a foot high in the home. It has spikes of pale purple flowers, often removed since they tend to detract from its appearance.

Coleus is easy to grow providing you give it high light and fairly high humidity. Low light causes the plant to become leggy and the colors to fade. Keep the soil evenly moist during growing season; barely moist in winter. Lack of water will cause leaf drop. It will thrive in average temperatures. Fertilize with dilute solution every two weeks during growing season. Cut back and repot into average potting soil in spring. Pinch stems regularly to keep plant bushy and full. Propagate by stem cuttings in spring and summer or by seed. Spider mites may be a problem in warm conditions.

SELECTIONS *C. x hybridus* There are hundreds of cultivars to choose from, with leaf colors ranging from variegated red, green, maroon, yellow, brown, and white; leaves take all forms from smooth edges to deeply incised to ruffly.

COTYLEDON *Crassulaceae*

Native to South Africa, these are succulent plants that are either evergreen and shrubby with thick leaves or deciduous with thickened short stems and alternate leaves. The foliage on most species is poisonous. They are easy to grow and desirable because of the variety of leaf size, color, and texture.

Provide high light and allow the soil to dry between soakings. These are winter growers so be attentive to increased water requirements when the plants are actively growing. Cotyledons will tolerate cool to hot temperatures but should be kept away from cold drafts and high-traffic areas. Fertilize infrequently and not at all during the heat of summer. Repot infrequently in coarse, fast-draining soil. Propagate by stem cuttings or seed. Cotyledons have few insect or disease problems.

SELECTIONS *C. ladysmithensis* A fuzzy, bushy plant that grows to about one foot. The leaves are thick, pawlike and marked with white and green. The edge of the leaf is toothed with two to four teeth. Stems become tough and brittle with age. It makes a nice four-inch pot for a sunny windowsill. Propagate every couple of years to avoid woody, unproductive growth.

C. orbiculata* var. *oophylla Compact plant with fat elongate leaves edged with dark red.

C. undulata (Silver Ruffles) A real eye-catcher; this plant grows to twenty inches, usually unbranched. Multiple stems in a single pot are particularly effective. The leaves are covered with a dense, waxy white "bloom" and have thick ruffled or tightly wavy edges. The leaves overlap in a parallel plane down the thick round stem. The white coating on the leaves is easily marred so avoid handling them. Plants should be started over every couple of years; they are brittle and break easily.

COTYLEDON LADYSMITHENSIS Up to one foot; high light and cool to hot temperatures; dry between soakings; fertilize infrequently and not at all during the heat of summer; slow growing.

CRASSULA ARGENTEA (JADE) To four feet; high light and cool to hot temperatures; dry between soakings; fertilize three times in summer only; benefits from summer outside; slow growing.

CRASSULA PERFORATA 'VARIEGATA' (NECKLACE VINE) Eight- to ten-inch hanging basket; high light and cool to hot temperatures; dry between soakings; fertilize three times in summer only; slow growing.

CRYPTANTHUS BIVITATTUS 'PINK STARLIGHT' (EARTH STAR) Individual plants six inches across; forming clumps of overlapping plants; high to medium light and hot to average temperatures; dry between soakings; fertilize three times in summer; moderate growth rate.

Crassula falcata.

CRASSULA *Crassulaceae*

This large group of plants from South Africa is easy to grow and runs the gamut of physical characteristics. Readily available, you will be sure to find one that you like and that will fit your growing conditions.

Provide high light and cool to hot temperatures. Allow the plant to dry between soakings and fertilize three times in summer (not at all in winter). Pot in an average, well-drained potting mix and repot infrequently. Prune, if necessary, after flowering and propagate by stem or leaf cuttings or seed. There may be problems with mealybugs, thrips, scale, or stem rot.

SELECTIONS *C. argentea {C. portulacea}* (Jade) Given good cultural conditions, this plant will grow into a large, stately specimen. Although shy to bloom in the home, the flowers are pale pink stars held in clusters at the tips of the branches. The leaves are thick and shiny, and the branches or leaves that come into contact with the soil may root and form new plants. Prune as needed—it branches readily. Many people grow this species and lovingly call it "weeping jade," a nice name for a poorly grown plant that has been given too much water and not enough light.

C. falcata (Airplane Plant, Scarlet Paintbrush) Sickle-shaped leaves of gray-blue lay in tight layers along a thick stem. Pink flowers.

C. perforata 'Variegata' (Necklace Vine, String of Buttons) Opposite green leaves with speckled tops sometimes edged with red in good light seem to be threaded on a round, wiry stem. Makes a nice full pot if pinched early. Does well in a small hanging basket. Start the plant over from terminal stem cuttings every year and pinch regularly to keep the center productive.

C. rupestis Thicker leaves arranged similarly to *C. perforata.*

CRYPTANTHUS EARTH STAR *Bromeliaceae*

Native to Brazil, these are colorful terrestrial bromeliads. The offsets are easily removed from the parent, most of the time without any roots. The stiff, usually toothed leaves radiate around the center of the plant from which flowers appear. Flowers are small, held close to the plant, and not particularly showy on most. Leaf colors and markings vary greatly, as does the size of the plant.

Earth stars are easily grown if given high to medium light and hot to average temperatures. They should be kept out of high-traffic areas to avoid damaging the leaves. Typically, earth stars have many fine roots; repotting into a coarse mix is necessary only after flowering and offshoot production or if the bark mix becomes mushy. Usually the flowering part of the plant dies and should be removed. Fertilize three times in summer and allow the soil to dry between soakings.

SELECTIONS *C. acaulis* (Starfish Plant) Flattened rosette of medium green leaves covered with grayish scales. The flowers are small and white and borne at the center of the plant.

C. bivitattus 'Pink Starlight' Small, bright pink, whitish and green leaves make this small plant stand out in a crowd. It produces many offsets. It stays small and is well-suited to a dish garden or terrarium in good light. The root system is small, shallow, and delicate. Root problems and leaf spotting may occur in low light with too much water. Easy for the the first-time grower.

C. zonatus (Zebra Plant) A large plant, potentially reaching twenty inches across. The leaves are wavy-edged and finely toothed, tapering to fine points. The light greenish-brown leaves are cross banded with silvery-buff, and the undersides of the leaves are visibly scaly and white. The colors are intensified with high light, and the flowers are not nearly as spectacular as the foliage. Many cultivars are available.

CUPHEA *Lythraceae*

This is a much underused genus of tropical and subtropical plants native to the Americas. Cupheas may be herbaceous or woody–some are used as annuals in colder climates. Small flowers are produced in profusion, making many cupheas perfect candidates for bedding plants as well as for flowering pots indoors.

Provide high light and average to cool house temperatures. Keep the soil evenly moist and fertilize with a dilute solution at every watering. This plant is not forgiving if watering is neglected. The plant tolerates pruning well when performed after a season of flowering. Pot in a peaty, moisture-retentive mix and root prune annually after flowering. It benefits from starting over every couple of years and can be easily propagated by stem cutting or seed. Watch for problems with root mealybugs, mealybugs, thrips, and whitefly.

SELECTIONS **C. hyssopifolia** (False Heather) Purplish-pink flowers on plant with larger leaves.

C. hyssopifolia 'Compacta' A small form with darker purple flowers; flowers are difficult to see from a distance.

C. hyssopifolia 'Linda Downer' (False Heather) A delicate plant forming a mound wider than tall. The leaves are small, elongated, and bright green. Huge quantities of pure white flowers are formed over the entire plant in summer and fall. The tubular flowers are small and six-petalled. It tends to be a bit messy as it loses old leaves and flowers.

CUSSONIA *Araliaceae*

These members of the Aralia family are native to tropical and southern Africa and nearby islands. Cussonias tend to be somewhat succulent in nature. Leaves are held in tufts at the ends of the branches.

Give cussonia high light to control its growth somewhat and average to cool temperatures. Keep the soil evenly moist and fertilize three times in summer. Pot in an average, well-drained potting mix and repot infrequently. There is no need to prune since cutting the stem will only produce another single stem. Propagate if desired by stem cuttings or seed. Mites can be a serious problem; avoid by keeping the plant moist. If treatment is required, first strip off heavily infested leaves. When leaves look old and yellow, cut back on water until more growth is noticed. Then resume regular watering.

SELECTIONS **C. paniculata** (Cabbage Tree) This native to South Africa grows as a solitary stem, unbranched to six feet in a container and sixteen feet if planted outdoors in a mild climate. The leaves are tufted at the growth point and are

BROMELIADS

Bromeliads are unusual indoor plants that are grown for their beautiful foliage and their spectacular flowers. They generally have straplike leaves in a rosette that form a cup. The flower head emerges from this cup, which is also a receptacle to hold water. In its native habitat, the plant and its cup of water are home to wildlife, such as salamanders, spiders, and frogs, which use the plant for support and reproduction.

The flowers are usually quite showy because of colorful bracts and can last several months. The actual flowers are small and short-lived.

As part of the natural cycle, after flowering the leaves begin to die. At this time, the plant produces offshoots from the sides which can be separated from the mother plant and potted. Bromeliads are quite slow growing and may take several years to flower–a plant that definitely takes patience.

They are generally easy to care for, however, with the only caution to avoid overwatering. They have very small root systems and will rot if left sitting in moist soil. Keep the cup filled with water and empty and change this water every couple of months. Water the soil only when it dries out. Remember–these epiphytes are used to obtaining their moisture and nutrients from the air and tiny pockets of soil. Air around the roots is crucial. Use a well-drained potting mix such as bark chips.

If a plant is already in flower, medium temperatures will suffice. You can encourage a bromeliad to flower by sealing it in a plastic bag with half an apple for three days to two weeks; remove from bag and wait six months for flower.

PALMS

True palms make a large group of plants, many of which are favored for indoor use. They are tropical in nature and conjure up images of Caribbean islands and hot climates. Most palms have large pinnate or palmate fronds and varying types of stems. Some grow tall, sturdy trunks in the wild but remain short and succulent when grown indoors. Some, such as howea, produce only leafstalks until very mature. Palms have only one growing point on each stem and generally produce only one or two fronds a year. Mature palms will produce clusters of flowers, but this is seldom seen in the home (except on chamaedorea).

There are indoor plants referred to as palms that are actually members of other families. The tendency is to call anything that looks palmlike a palm, when in actuality, these plants may need very different cultural conditions to thrive. Cycas, the bread palm, and nolina, ponytail palm, are in different families than the palms and are quite a bit more tolerant of low light and cool conditions than true palms.

Most palms need an abundance of water and filtered bright light when they are young (mature specimens can tolerate full sun). Palm seeds can take from one month to two years to germinate.

shed with age, leaving interesting scars. The roots are coarse and twisted and may be partially exposed. It is often used by creative bonsai growers for this reason. The leaves are broad, toothed, and have seven to twelve leaflets. It is a curious plant for the grower who has everything.

CYCAS BREAD PALM *Cycadaceae*

These primitive plants are native to the Old World tropics: *cycas* is the ancient Greek name for "palm." The cycads are more tolerant of interior environments than many true palms.

Give bread palms high light and average to cool temperatures. Allow the soil to dry briefly between waterings; hold back on water in the winter. Fertilize three times in summer only. Pot in an average, well-drained potting mix and repot infrequently. Lift the plant and add soil as needed over time since it seems to sink in the pot. Pruning is necessary only as part of selective grooming. These can be propagated only by seed. Keep a close watch for scale and mealybugs and grow the plants out of high-traffic areas.

SELECTIONS *C. circinalis* (Crozier Cycad) Longer, softer fronds than *C. revoluta*. The young leaves unfurl like fern fronds and are bright green and shiny, darkening with age. Can reach fifteen feet or more in a greenhouse.

C. revoluta (Sago Palm) This is a slow-growing cycad from Japan and the Ryukyu Islands that is suitable only for a wide location. Small plants are tradiionally used for bonsai. It normally grows to five feet in a pot with many years of little attention to its meager needs, but will stay significantly smaller in the home. Sago palm performs well outside in summer and is frequently grown with three plants in a pot. One set of leaves is produced annually. The leaves all radiate from the center, which is covered with thick brown wool. The leaflets are sharply pointed black-green and arranged opposite one another along a medium to light green midrib.

CYMBIDIUM *Orchidaceae*

Native to tropical Asia and Australia, these plants are a good place to start for the orchid fancier. Long grasslike foliage is generated from elongated pseudobulbs. Long-lasting flowers are carried on long arching racemes. Thousands of cultivars are available in colors ranging from white, green, and yellow to pink and burgundy. Flower size varies and dwarf cultivars are especially suitable for the home. The hardest thing about cymbidium orchids is choosing the flower color!

Cymbidium orchids perform best in high light but will tolerate medium light. Keep evenly moist except during their fall cool period when watering should be cut back. Keep them relatively cool all the time (45-50° F. to induce flowering), but cut the temperature back to just above freezing in fall. Also, be sure to maintain adequate humidity and keep them away from drying winds. Pot in coarse, fast-draining orchid potting mix and don't repot unless absolutely necessary. It is best to leave these plants crowded. Fertilize with dilute solution at every watering during the cymbidium's growing peri-

CUPHEA HYSSOPIFOLIA 'ALBA' (FALSE HEATHER) High light and cool temperatures; evenly moist; fertilize with dilute solution at every watering; fast growing.

CUSSONIA PANICULATA (CABBAGE TREE) To six feet or more; high light; average to cool temperatures; evenly moist; fertilize three times in summer; average growth rate.

CYCAS REVOLUTA (SAGO PALM) Grows to five feet in a pot; high light and average to cool temperatures; evenly moist, reduce watering in winter; fertilize three times in summer; slow growing.

CYMBIDIUM CV. (ORCHID) Twenty inches to three feet depending on cultivar; high or medium light; evenly moist except during their fall cool period when watering should be cut back; keep at 45-50° F. to induce flowering; fertilize with dilute solution at every watering during growing period; slow growing.

This orchid collection includes cattleya, paphiopedilum, and vanda orchids.

od. (There are fertilizers formulated especially for cymbidium orchids for the addicted grower.) Pruning is necessary only as part of grooming. Propagate by separating the pseudobulbs from each other, but be aware that the plants will not flower for a year or longer after division. Potting to a larger-size pot is preferred to division in order to keep the plants blooming, depending on the original size of your plant and the cultivar. Miniature cymbidiums are favored for the house or where space is limited. These may also tolerate more heat in the summer.

SELECTIONS *C.* **Golden Elf 'Sundust'** One of the "new" warm-growing hybrids that do not require a cool period to initiate bud set. Uniform golden yellow fragrant flowers. Has potential to bloom all year.

C. **Clenet 'Chariot'** Rich orange with red band on lip. Compact and easily brought into bloom.

C. **Summer Nights 'Geyserland'** is a large, white variety with reddish speckled lip and light blush on the dorsal sepal.

C. **Mimi 'Sandlewood'** Very floriferous; small dark reddish flowers, many to a spike.

CYPERUS UMBRELLA SEDGE *Cyperaceae*

Umbrella sedges are semiaquatic herbs from the tropics and subtropics and have been grown for centuries, some for their fibrous qualities. They are generally found along rivers or streams or in areas that are frequently flooded. The leaves are generated from underground tubers.

Give umbrella sedges high light and keep the soil moist. They will tolerate cool to hot temperatures, but avoid drying winds. Fertilize infrequently and prune only as part of regular grooming. Pot in a loamy, moisture-retentive potting mix. Avoid peaty mixtures because they rot and smell bad when kept constantly moist. Repot before the plant begins to creep out of the pot. Propagate, if desired, by leaf cuttings, rhizome division, or seed. An interesting way to propagate is to put a leaf cutting upside down in a tall glass of water. Change water frequently. New plants will form in the center of the old leaves.

SELECTIONS *C. alternifolius* (Umbrella Plant) A clump-forming sedge with stiffly vertical leaf stems to three feet. Leaves are reduced to sheaths only. What appear to be leaves are actually long, narrow, recurving bracts. The flowers appear above the bracts as stars on the tip of fine filaments. This is a fun plant to propagate–bend a nonflowering stem over and pin to wet sand in a new pot. Or cut a leaf stem from the plant, cut the bracts back two-thirds, and invert in a glass of water. New shoots will form where the stem and bracts meet. Pot this plant in a container without drainage or stand it in water at all times. Avoid cold water, though, since it causes rotting.

C. alternifolius **'Gracilis'** Stiff dwarf variety; sensitive to chlorine, so before watering plants allow water to stand a couple of days to dissipate chlorine.

C. isocladus (Dwarf Papyrus) Delicate form–just like *C. papyrus*, but only one to one and one-half feet tall.

C. papyrus (Papyrus, Paper Plant) Native to tropical Africa; tall (seven feet in container), triangular leaf stems are airy in cross section. Pith was sliced from the length of the leaf stems and pressed together while wet to form the paper of ancient Egypt. The bracts of this species are reduced to thin threads that fork at the ends. The bracts form an airy terminal "ball" on the end of tall, thick stems—a unique sight. Cold water causes stem rot, and the plants are chlorine-sensitive. At the Chicago Botanic Garden, after cleaning the tank that papyrus overwintered in, the tank was refilled with potable city water. Within hours after replacing the papyrus, its healthy white roots turned black. Some of the plants survived, but many died.

DIONAEA VENUS FLYTRAP *Droseraceae*

This genus has a solitary species that is an herbaceous perennial. It has curious insectivorous habits that make it one of the most active members of the plant kingdom.

Provide high to medium light and keep the soil evenly moist. *Use distilled water or rain water only.* Keep one inch of standing water in a small terrarium. The water should be at least two inches below the surface of the moss it is planted in. Three to four inches of moss is sufficient as potting medium. New Zealand sphagnum moss lasts the longest but is expensive and hard to find (check with orchid growers for a source). Canadian long-fibered sphagnum is an acceptable substitute. Mix it with 25 percent coarse silica sand (not builders' or masons' sand–too alkaline). Repot only as the moss deteriorates every other year. Avoid situations with low humidity and drying winds. A terrarium works best for keeping dionaea healthy. Fertilize infrequently–it does quite well without feeding. The plant needs average to cool temperatures, but it must have a cool, dormant period (38-45° F.) from November 1 to March 1. Put the plant in a refrigerator and reduce the watering, but don't let it dry out. No light is required during this time. Dionaea will not survive more than two years without this dormancy period.

NOTE Flytrap is on the endangered species list. Plants available to the home grower are mass-produced in greenhouses from seed and are approved for sale. Never purchase plants that look like they have been dug out of the wild–you would be breaking federal law.

SELECTIONS *D. muscipula* (Venus Flytrap) This action-packed plant is native to North and South Carolina. An unsuspecting fly lands on the edge of a red-colored leaf. The doomed insect walks across the broad surface of the "trap." It trips two of the three trigger hairs in a row, and as quickly as you can blink, the trap snaps shut, ensnaring the fly. Rarely do they escape.

The traplike leaf adaptation secretes digestive juices, allowing the plant to consume the insect. Each trap can open and close about nine times before it turns black and is replaced by a new one. If proper conditions are met, this plant is easy to grow. If any steps are skipped, you'll be purchasing another one soon. Flowers appear in early summer. Venus flytraps summer well outside in bright light.

CYPERUS ALTERNIFOLIUS (UMBRELLA PLANT) Grows to three feet; high light and cool to hot temperatures; evenly moist—may stand in water, avoid drying winds; fertilize infrequently; fun to propagate; fast growing.

CYPERUS PAPYRUS (PAPYRUS) Grows to seven feet; high light and cool to hot temperatures; evenly moist–may stand in water, avoid drying winds; fertilize infrequently; fast growing.

DIONAEA MUSCIPULA (VENUS FLYTRAP) Three inches tall; medium to high light; evenly moist, high humidity; does well without feeding; slow growing.

DROSERA BINATA VAR. MULTIFIDA (ELKHORN SUNDEW) High light and cool to average temperatures; evenly moist (water with distilled water); flowers best with cool winter temperatures; fertilize infrequently; slow growing.

DROSERA SUNDEW *Droseraceae*

Native to the tropics and temperate regions, some are good companion plants for Venus flytraps. Some require a similar dormancy and others require none. These carnivorous plants attract insects with bright red coloration and sticky sweet honeydew that glistens off tips of filaments on leaf adaptations. All benefit from terrarium culture to maintain humidity levels.

Give sundews high light and cool to average temperatures. Keep the soil evenly moist and use distilled or rain water. Avoid drying winds, cold drafts, and low humidity. Fertilize infrequently. Pot in a 75:25 mix of sphagnum moss and sand (see *Dionaea* entry). Repot only as moss deteriorates (about every two years). Prune only after flowering and propagate by division or seed. Watch for aphids on the leaves (although most will be consumed by the plant).

SELECTIONS *D. binata* var. *multifida* (Elkhorn Sundew) Native to New Zealand and Australia, this is an easy-to-grow large, clump-forming sundew. The tips of the leaves are forked into two to four segments. The entire leaf is covered with fine hairs tipped with sticky mucuslike honeydew. The leaf curls over victims, which stick to the honeydew. Its leaves are fourteen inches long, and it has white flowers in spring. This is a good plant for a tall terrarium; it becomes invasive over time. A showy plant that may be given a dormant period, but it is not necessary.

D. capensis Leaves are short and spatulate; very red in good light.

D. rotundifolia Solitary rosettes to two inches across; narrow linear leaves end in round sticky traps.

D. spathulata Spoon-shaped leaves radiate from a central stem. Rounded ends of the leaves are covered with threadlike appendages that are tipped with sticky honeydew. White flowers in summer. Does not require cold dormancy, although cooler winter temperatures will ensure good flowering (70-95° F. in summer, 60-70° F. in winter).

DYCKIA *Bromeliaceae*

Unlike most bromeliads, dyckias are soil or rock dwellers that are tolerant of dry conditions (xerophytes). Dyckias are tough plants that protect themselves with spines along the leaf margins. Plants are rigid and seem to sit unchanged for long periods of time. The beauty of dyckias is in the detailed markings and patterns that are created on and under the leaves. The undersides of the leaves are scaly white and decorative. A formidable plant at first glance, a closer look reveals incredible color and texture. This is a much-overlooked genus that is good for sunny windows and the grower who is prone to neglecting plants.

Give dyckias high light and cool to hot temperatures. Allow the soil to dry between soakings and fertilize infrequently. Pot in a coarse, fast-draining potting mix and repot infrequently. Prune only selectively and avoid high-traffic areas since this plant can be painful. Propagate by division or seed. Dyckias have few insect or disease problems.

SELECTIONS *D. brevifolia* (Pineapple Dyckia) Native to Brazil; short compact leaves to twelve inches ending in a sharp point with sharp marginal spines.

CARNIVOROUS PLANTS

Insect-eating plants are naturally suited to terrarium culture. They grow on nutrient-poor soils in their native habitats, and grow best with high humidity, damp soil, and sunlight. Their unique features of trapping and digesting insects make them an amusing addition to a terrarium. Sundews (Drosera), pitcher plants (Sarracenia), and the traditional Venus flytrap (Dionaea) all perform fairly well if given the proper conditions (and it's not necessary to feed them insects–or anything for that matter!).

Echinocactus grusonii usually does not exceed twelve inches in the home; it grows to many times that outside in its native environment.

D. fosteriana To five inches across—a dwarf species with recurved silvery leaves; one of the most ornamental of the genus.

ECHINOCACTUS *Cactaceae*

This genus contains ten to sixteen species of strongly ribbed barrel- to cylindrical-shaped cactus native to the southwestern United States and Mexico. They do not flower or produce offsets as easily as other types of cactus.

As with most cactus, provide high light and allow to dry between soakings. Hold back on water in the winter. Fertilize three times in summer. It will tolerate cool to hot temperatures, but should be kept out of high-traffic areas. Pot in a coarse, fast-draining mix and repot only when the stem reaches the edge of the pot. Repot by carefully wrapping a piece of carpeting around the barrel. Hold the ends of carpet and carefully remove from the pot. Have the new pot prepared and once the plant is in the new pot, use a dowel or stick to gently tamp soil around the roots. Propagate by seed if available.

SELECTIONS E. grusonii (Golden Barrel Cactus) This solitary cactus from Central Mexico used to be more commonly available than it is today. Easy to grow and slow growing, this plant will reach twelve inches across or more in the home. It has a round habit with twenty or more distinct ribs sporting broad yellow spines to two inches long. The covering of yellow spines gives the common name. The center top seems to be covered with yellowish thick wool that supports elusive yellow flowers. Perfectly grown specimens are so appealing that you might have to have two or three. A white form is available but costly.

EPIPHYLLUM ORCHID CACTUS *Cactaceae*

Epiphyllums are epiphytes native to tropical South America to Mexico. They hardly remind one of a typical cactus, but they are. Grown for enormous, brightly colored and irridescent flowers, the broad arching stems suit hanging baskets. The foliage is as untidy as the flowers are beautiful. Many species have spines at the areoles, and their stiff stems scar and break easily.

Epiphyllums require culture similar to orchids and bromeliads rather than that for dry-climate cactus. If kept cool and dry in late fall and winter, they will reward with many flowers in late winter or early spring. Provide high light if possible, although they will tolerate medium light. They will also tolerate high temperatures in summer. Allow the soil to dry briefly between soakings and hold back on watering in winter. Fertilize three times in summer or with a dilute solution at every watering during growth periods. Repot in coarse, fast-draining potting mix (bark mix is appropriate) when the plants become top-heavy or watering becomes too demanding. Propagate by stem cuttings. Aphids often attack flower buds, and epiphyllums are prone to root rot if kept too wet. Watch for scale. Sterilize your pruning tools to avoid spreading virus.

SELECTIONS *E. ackermannii* Hybrids are produced using *E. ackermannii, E. crenatum, Heliocereus,* and *Selenicereus.* There are hundreds of spectacular hybrids available, all requiring the same culture. Flowers are five to nine inches across and stems grow to two feet. Flowers range from solid white to multicolored purple. These can easily be put outside in summer—under a shrub or hanging

DROSERA SPATHULATA (SUNDEW) To eight inches high; high light; cool to average temperatures; evenly moist; fertilize three times in summer; slow growing.

DYCKIA FOSTERIANA To five inches across; high light and cool to hot temperatures; dry between soakings; fertilize infrequently; slow growing.

ECHINOCACTUS GRUSONII (GOLDEN BARREL CACTUS) Up to twelve inches across; high light and cool to hot temperatures; dry between soakings; fertilize infrequently; slow growing.

EPIPHYLLUM ACKERMANNII HYBRID (ORCHID CACTUS) Two-foot stems; high light if possible, will tolerate medium; will tolerate high temperatures in summer; keep cool and dry in late fall and winter to bring into bloom; dry briefly between soakings; fertilize three times in summer; moderate growth rate.

Above: Euphorbia (right), with a braided coffee tree and an aloe plant.

in a tree (with frequent watering). This is a plant of great contrasts—the foliage is untidy and considered ugly by some, but the flower size and numbers make this a rewarding plant to put up with while in its vegetative state.
E. '**Reward**' Yellow.
E. '**Roger Williams**' Dark orange-red, iridescent.

EUONYMUS SPINDLE TREE *Celastraceae*

Cosmopolitan in its origin, Euonymus is a genus of woody, evergreen plants, many of which are hardy outdoors in the Midwest and other temperate climates. Nonhardy types are well-suited to a cold porch or entryway. All have opposite, simple leaves which vary in size and color, and inconspicuous flowers. These tough, reliable plants have four-angled stems and are easy to grow.

Euonymus performs best in high to medium light and cool temperatures, although it will tolerate average temperatures as well. Keep the soil evenly moist at all times and fertilize three times in summer. Pot in an average, well-drained potting mix and repot every couple of years to keep the roots active. They tolerate pruning well and can be propagated by stem cuttings. Scale can be a serious problem, and aphids are occasional pests, as are mealybugs.
E. japonicus '**Albomarginatus**' (Silver Queen Euonymus) Waxy, broad oval leaves are irregularly shaped, and rich green with a white border and irregular white mottling throughout. They can grow to six feet or more, but can easily be kept to one foot or less with regular pruning. Occasionally branches will grow that are solid green—just prune these out to keep the overall variegated appearance.
E. japonicus '**Microphyllus**' Small, dark green leaves, delicately toothed, are neatly arranged in strict columns along the stem. Slow to establish and slow growing, this plant can be kept small with infrequent pruning. It makes a good hedge and is a good candidate for bonsai or miniature landscaping (dollhouse accessory).
E. japonicus '**Microphyllus Variegatus**' Very slow growing—a ten-year-old plant at the Chicago Botanic Garden is seven inches tall and six inches wide.

EUPHORBIA *Euphorbiaceae*

Physically, this genus has every type of shape, habit, color, and texture known to the plant kingdom, ranging from the common Christmas poinsettia to succulent trees weighing many tons. The characteristic that ties them together is their flowering habit. All have a cyathium—a whorl of bracts that are fused together. The bracts surround seven stamens and one three-lobed ovary. Most euphorbias are succulent and scar easily. All euphorbias also contain an irritating sap. The sap of some is highly toxic. Try to avoid skin contact and wash thoroughly after handling any euphorbia.

Provide high light, cool to hot temperatures, and fertilize three times in summer. Keep the plants evenly moist when in flower, but otherwise allow to dry between waterings. Euphorbias tolerate pruning well, but generally require it only as part of grooming. Avoid high humidity and high-traffic areas. Pot in average, well-drained or coarse, fast-draining potting mix,

EUONYMUS JAPONICUS 'MICROPHYLLUS' Can grow to six feet or more, but can easily be kept to one foot or less; high to medium light and cool temperatures (will tolerate average temperatures); evenly moist at all times; fertilize three times in summer; moderate growth rate.

EUPHORBIA MILII 'SONORA' (CROWN-OF-THORNS) One to four feet; high light and cool to hot temperatures; evenly moist while flowering; dry between soakings during rest of year; fertilize three times in summer–starvation inhibits flowering; slow growing.

EUPHORBIA PLATYCLADA Prostrate growing, usually eight inches across; high light and cool to hot temperatures; evenly moist while flowering; dry between soakings during rest of year; fertilize three times in summer; slow growing.

EUPHORBIA TRIGONA (AFRICAN MILK TREE) Four to eight feet tall; high light and cool to hot temperatures; dry slightly between soakings; fertilize three times in summer; fast growing.

depending on the species. Repot infrequently. Propagate if desired by stem cutting, division, or seed.

SELECTIONS *E. milii* (Crown-of-Thorns) A good plant for the person who must have flowers–this plant is virtually always in bloom. Shrubby in habit, the stems are covered with long spines. Some are more upright with large spatulate leaves. Showy bracts vary from dark red to pinkish to salmon. A yellow variety is also available. Many cultivars have been developed and all are easy to grow.

E. milii **'Georgusis 1'** is a compact shrubby small-leaved variety with red flowers.

E. obesa (Living Baseball, Gingham Golf Ball) This small (six inches) round succulent from South Africa is dioecious. The male plants tend to be more conical or taller than the distinctly round, ball-like female plants. Both have five ribs that are elegantly marked with gray-green checkering and reddish-purple lines. The flowers are confined to the growth point in the center of the top of the plant. It sets seeds easily, and the seed pods shoot the seeds quite a distance when ripe. The markings vary from one plant to another. Their character also changes from tiny seedling to adult–you'll want several.

E. platyclada A flat-stemmed plant that stays close to the surface of the pot. The stems are pink overall and mottled with gray.

E. trigona (African Milk Tree) A commonly available plant offered as a cactus–which it is not. Clusters of vertical stems grow practically on top of one another and are easily scarred by their own spines, which are grouped in pairs along ridges running the length of the stems. Leaves appear and disappear at top sections of the stems as the plant is kept moist or is allowed to dry out for extended periods of time. The plant becomes top-heavy quickly so repot frequently and keep out of traffic. It tolerates pruning and will branch but has a tendency to scar. This is an outstanding indoor plant in a variety of situations.

FUCHSIA LADY'S EARDROPS *Onagraceae*

Fuchsia consists of about 100 species of trees and shrubs native to tropical climates in New Zealand, Central America, Mexico, and the Polynesian Islands. Their forms range from upright tree-type forms to low-growing shrubs to trailing woody vines that are used in hanging baskets. Their showpieces are the vivid, unusual flowers.

Grow fuschias in a sunny window in winter and light shade in the summer. They will tolerate cool night temperatures, moderate day temperatures, and the soil should be kept somewhat moist. Fertilize regularly January through October. Fuchsias benefit from summering outdoors in a shady spot where they will bloom vigorously. When bringing in for winter, cut back the stems severely. As new growth starts, keep pinched well to promote bushiness. Propagate by cuttings in late spring and early summer. Watch for whitefly.

SELECTIONS *F. triphylla* **'Gartenmeister Bohnstedt'** (Honeysuckle Fuchsia) Dark green, purplish leaves with reddish stems. Lovely pendant coral-red tubular flow-

Euphorbias come in all shapes and size, from the pencil cactus to the poinsettia. They all have the same milky sap and similar flowers; although the poinsettia's bracts are large and showy compared to the crown of thorns, if you look closely enough, you will see that the flower structures are identical. *Above: Euphorbia milii* flower. *Top: Euphorbia obesa.*

FUCHSIA TRIPHYLLA 'GARTENMEISTER BOHNSTEDT' (HONEYSUCKLE FUCHSIA) One to two feet; sunny window in winter and light shade in the summer; cool night temperatures, moderate day temperatures; kept somewhat moist; fertilize regularly January through October; moderate growth rate.

GASTERIA LILIPUTIANA (LAWYER'S TONGUE) Four inches across; high light; cool to hot temperatures; dry between waterings, especially in winter; fertilize infrequently; slow growing.

GRAPTOPETALUM AMETHYSTINUM (JEWEL-LEAF PLANT) Stems to fourteen inches across; high light, cool to average temperatures; allow to dry between soakings; fertilize three times in summer. Slow growing.

GYMNOCALYCIUM MIHANOVICHII (PLAID CACTUS) Two inches wide; high light; cool to hot temperatures; allow to dry between soakings; fertilize three times in summer; slow growing.

Fuchsia's pendant flowers are perfect in hanging baskets. This lovely mature specimen is a far cry from the immature plant on the previous page, which, with special training, can be expected to reach this stage in about five years.

ers–very floriferous. This is an exception to summer blooming–it blooms well indoors year-round. Can be trained as a standard. (BLITHEWOLD)

GASTERIA COW TONGUE *Liliaceae*

This is an unusual group of succulents from South Africa that is favored by collectors. The tough, fleshy leaves are frequently arranged opposite one another along one plane or in spiral rosettes. Textured physically or visually, the markings vary by species. Some form great clumps of seemingly inseparable plants; others are solitary. The many flowers are pleasantly colored and small on tall vertical stems.

Gasterias do well in a south or west window with little attention. They tolerate cool to hot temperatures and should be allowed to dry between waterings, especially in winter. They need infrequent fertilization and no pruning except to remove damaged leaves (leaves are succulent and snap easily). The clump-forming varieties benefit from division once the pot becomes filled with plants. The smaller varieties usually need soil added to replace that which is washed away more frequently than they need repotting. They have coarse, shallow roots, so pot in a coarse, fast-draining soil. Gasterias are virtually pest-free, although leaf spots may be a problem.

SELECTIONS *G. armstrongii* is a great little plant for a sunny window–no one can resist the urge to touch it to see if it is actually alive. It grows to about four inches across, and the leaves are one half as wide as long. The tips tend to grow toward the soil tightly compressed to the previous row of leaves. The center of the leaves seems to be cut into a deep "V." Dark green leaves are occasionally softened with green or white tubercles (warts) and eventually form a rosette.

G. batesiana is a medium-textured, rough-leaved plant with white tubercles that grow in a spiral.

G. liliputana (Lawyer's Tongue) has narrow leaves spotted white and arranged in a spiral from an invisible stem. The top sides of the leaves are concave, and the undersides are convex and keeled. The leaves are shiny and waxy and tipped with a surprisingly sharp point. It forms a dense, overlapping clump that fills a pot quickly. Excellent plants for small pots; they add interesting texture to dish gardens.

G. maculata Larger than the others mentioned; leaves are thick and up to eight inches long, white-spotted, dark green, and shiny.

GRAPTOPETALUM JEWEL-LEAF PLANT *Crassulaceae*

These evergreen, coarse succulent perennials are native to the southwestern United States and Mexico. They are handsome plants closely related to echeverias. Most have leaves of gray-blue. Flowers seem to be elusive–Chicago Botanic Garden's plant (*G. paraguayense*) has not flowered in thirteen years.

Give jewel-leaf plant high light, cool to average temperatures, and allow it to dry between soakings. Fertilize three times in summer and prune only to groom. Pot in average, well-drained to coarse, fast-draining potting mix. Repot infrequently because it is difficult to do without damaging the plant. Start over from stem or leaf cuttings before repotting. It may have a problem

with mealybugs and stem rot is possible if it is watered too frequently.
SELECTIONS *G. amethystinum* Native to Mexico, heavy robust stems support thick leaves that are two and one-half inches long and blue-gray with a lavender hue. The unusual coloration attracts attention to this succulent. The waxy leaf surface is easily marred, and the stems are brittle, so handle with care and avoid high-traffic areas. The stems become pendant with age, creeping over the edges of the pot. This is a whimsical, cartoonish plant, and the fat, rounded lavender leaves make it irresistible to the touch.

GYMNOCALYCIUM CHIN CACTUS *Cactaceae*
These are round, usually solitary cactus from South America that have ribs with bumps or chins between each areole. The spines are usually recurved, so they seem more friendly than many cactus. Flowers vary in color even within species from whitish to dark red.

Provide high light (but protect from direct sun), cool to hot temperatures, and allow to dry between soakings. Hold back on watering in winter. It will flower easily if given a cool, dry rest in winter. Fertilize three times in summer and avoid high humidity. Plant in coarse, fast-draining potting mix and repot only as the plant reaches the sides of the pot. Propagate by offsets or seed.
SELECTIONS *G. baldianum* Solitary, dark green cactus with lovely wine-red flowers.
G. denudatum (Spider Cactus) Native to southern Brazil and northern Argentina, the rich dark green stem is divided by five to eight broad ribs with woolly areoles. The light-colored curving spines seem to be pressed against the dark green stem, giving them a spidery look. Flowers are white to pale pink. The plant grows to six inches in diameter. Although it requires high light, protect it from direct, burning sun. This is an easy-to-grow plant for beginning cactus growers. Repotting annually helps avoid problems with root mealybugs.
G. mihanovichii (Plaid Cactus) A small (two-inch) round, reddish-green cactus with distinctly pointed ribs and whitish banding that runs from the areole toward the center in a zigzag pattern around the plant. Flowers are two inches long and yellow-green to bright pink. Mutants of this species are frequently grafted onto hylocereus stems since the mutants themselves lack chlorophyll and cannot survive on their own. They are the pink and yellow balls available as novelty items. Watch for mealybugs and thrips on flowers and protect from direct sunlight in summer.
G. saglionis A large species (to twelve inches) that is somewhat flat on top with pale pink flowers.

HAEMANTHUS AFRICAN BLOOD LILY *Amaryllidaceae*
This is a group of bulbous plants from tropical South Africa and Arabia known for their red or white flowers. Plants should be given a dry winter rest with a night temperature of 50-55° F. They are easily managed as indoor plants or outdoor plants in summer.

Provide high light and cool to average temperatures. Keep evenly moist and fertilize three times in summer, but hold back on water in winter. (At The

SCARRED FOR LIFE
Succulent plants are filled with water—so full and tender that they are easily injured by physical contact. An innocent act such as tipping over the pot may result in broken stems or leaves or even a bruise that turns into a scar weeks after the incident is forgotten. Injuries usually heal and the plant survives, but is forever changed visually. Depending on the growth habit, scars may eventually be covered by new growth. Plants like *Gasteria armstrongii* (above), however, will have obvious scars forever. This plant grows slowly and in such a way that the broken tips and calloused creases in the leaves will always be visible. When a plant becomes unsightly, it should probably be replaced.

Hibiscus is grown for its spectacular flowers; it requires specialized care and patience.

New York Botanical Garden, gardeners begin fertilizing as new growth appears in spring.) Pot in average, well-drained potting mix and prune only selectively when grooming. Propagate by bulb separation and seed. There are few insect or disease problems, although there may be an occasional mealybug when foliage is present.

SELECTIONS *H. albiflos* (Blood Lily, Paintbrush) Broad bright green tongue-shaped leaves are edged with white hairs. The leaves recurve toward the pot and are soft and easily damaged. Flowers are held on thick, hollow stems above the plant. Yellow anthers are held in a boat-shaped appendage and may be followed by red berries. Give this plant an early summer rest and it will flower in early winter.

H. katherinae (Blood Flower, Katherine-Wheel) Large bulbs produce tubelike new growth that uncurls into large, broad, bright green crinkly leaves. Fertilize while foliage is present. As the foliage fades in summer, large flower buds emerge from the bulb to produce spectacular pink, salmon, orange, and reddish flowers to nine inches across. Truly a showstopper in flower.

HIBISCUS *Malvaceae*

This is a large group of plants found throughout the tropics and subtropics. Most have alternate leaves, and the five-petaled flowers come in a wide range of colors. Some hybrids are exceedingly showy.

It is essential to provide high light and to keep the soil evenly moist. They will tolerate cool to average temperatures and should be fertilized with dilute fertilizer in every watering during the growing period. Avoid drying winds, cold drafts, and low humidity. Repot infrequently in average, well-drained potting mix. Hibiscus flowers on new growth so take care to prune selectively. Watch for scale, whitefly, mealybugs, and aphids, which are always a problem; these plants can attract aphids in the dead of winter.

SELECTIONS *H. rosa-sinensis* (Rose of China, Chinese Hibiscus) Growing to six and a half feet in a container, this plant from tropical Asia has as many problems as it does flowers. Dark green foliage with leaves that vary in shape from cultivar to cultivar make a nice backdrop for the large, intensely colored flowers that appear at the ends of the stems. Unfortunately, aphids and whitefly appear more frequently than the flowers. Flowers last only one day (excepting some newer cultivars) but appear over a long period of time. Leaf drop is common if conditions are changed, but leaves will reappear on old wood in time. If you are easily frustrated, try another plant. The straight species is rarely available; cultivars are available in single and double flowers and variegated foliage.

H. rosa-sinensis **'Amour'** Clear dark pink with darker center; single flower.

H. rosa-sinensis **'Hula Girl'** Dark yellow with red eye; single flower.

H. schizopetalus (Japanese Lantern) Bushy plant with drooping branches and toothed leaves–slightly smaller than *H. rosa-sinensis*. Flowers are red with fringed petals and prominent stamens. They hang down, reminiscent of a

HAEMANTHUS ALBIFLOS (BLOOD LILY, PAINTBRUSH) Up to twenty inches high; high to medium light, cool to average temperatures; give dry, cool early summer rest for bloom in winter; keep evenly moist in growing season; fertilize three times in summer; slow growing.

HIBISCUS ROSA-SINENSIS CV. (ROSE OF CHINA) To six-and-one-half feet in container; high light, cool to average temperatures; fertilize at every watering; keep evenly moist; avoid low humidity; grows moderately if fertilized; otherwise, grows slowly.

HYPOESTES PHYLLOSTACHYA (POLKA DOT PLANT) Will grow to two feet; medium to high light and average temperatures; evenly moist soil; fertilize three times in summer; fast growing.

IXORA COCCINEA (JUNGLE GERANIUM, FLAME-OF-THE-WOODS) To three feet; medium to high light and warm temperatures; high humidity; evenly moist; hold back on watering in winter in cool conditions; use dilute fertilizer at every watering during growing period; slow growing.

DISH GARDENS

Dish gardens are composed of several plants in one container. They have many of the same design features as described in the design section, but careful planning is needed to select plants with similar needs. All the plants will be maintained the same way since they share one container. As these mixed planters mature and fill in, plants need to be pruned, divided, removed, or replaced so the dish garden does not become overcrowded.

Below: Syngonium, chrysanthemum, buttonfern. *Bottom:* Polka dot plant, dragon tree, arrowhead vine, nerve plant, ti plant. *Below right:* Syngonium, Chinese evergreen, ivy, bird's nest fern.

Japanese lantern. Can be trained to grow in a hanging basket. Blooms on new growth.

NOTE Many hibiscus sold as potted plants covered in flowers have been chemically dwarfed. They will outgrow the dwarfing effect and will return to a more open, graceful habit.

HYPOESTES POLKA DOT PLANT *Acanthaceae*

These festive plants from tropical Africa, Asia, and Madagascar usually have spotted leaves. They grow quickly and take time and attention to keep them in bounds and under control. The colors intensify in high light and the plants go dormant after flowering. If allowed to flower, purple flowers form one after another on long stems.

They require high to medium light, evenly moist soil, and average temperatures. They are quite tolerant of pruning. The plants become leggy and floppy and should be cut back to the ground after flowering. New growth appears at the soil level, producing compact, full plants. Fertilize three times in summer and avoid spots where drying winds will strike the leaves. They need repotting annually and can also be started over annually from cuttings taken from nonflowering stems or from seed. Watch for mealybugs and whitefly.

SELECTIONS *H. phyllostachya* will grow to two feet if left unattended. The leaves are busily marked with pink dots that overlap, forming large areas of color. It holds its color well in medium to low light, although it tends to stretch in lower light.

H. phyllostachya **'Splash'** A bright pink-freckled plant.

H. phyllostachya **'Wine Red'** Dark red spots.

IXORA *Rubiaceae*

This is a large genus of about 400 species of shrubs or trees, native to tropical Asia and Africa and pantropical Australia, Pacific Islands, and America. Handsome foliage and long-blooming periods of intensely colored flowers make this a genus to consider. Some flowers are fragrant. The four-petaled flowers are borne in terminal clusters and paired leaves are opposite. Most of these are difficult to grow in the home and are not for the dilettante.

Ixora demands warm temperatures and high humidity and will tolerate medium light, although it performs best in high light. Keep the soil evenly moist and hold back on watering in winter in cool conditions. Occasionally the leaves are chlorotic, a pH problem or nutrient deficiency. To avoid, use dilute fertilizer at every watering during growing period. Ixora needs repotting infrequently—use an average, well-drained potting mix and repot with care given to its sensitive roots. Ixoras are prone to mealybugs, especially when in flower. Thrips can also be a problem. Pruning is rarely needed because of its slow growth. It can be propagated by seed in spring and by stem cuttings in summer.

SELECTIONS *I. coccinea* (Jungle Geranium, Flame-of-the-Woods) This slow-growing evergreen shrub that is native to India blooms heaviest in summer, but is virtually always in flower. It grows slowly to four feet. It is infrequently offered in the trade in the Midwest, but is frequently used in tropical areas as hedging. The stiff green foliage makes a fine foundation for the explosion of color when in bloom.

I. coccinea **'Jay Gee Yellow'** Yellow-flowering type (pink and orange-yellow types are also available).

I. javanica Orange-red flowers; its tolerance of semishady conditions makes it a good choice for indoors.

KALANCHOE *Crassulaceae*

These natives of Africa and southern Asia are grown for their interesting foliage and some for brightly colored flowers. There is great variety in leaf size, color, and texture, ranging from small succulent leaves on wiry vines to broad leaves on upright stems that produce plantlets along leaf margins. Flowering pot varieties are not always easy to make flower again, so they are often considered "disposable" plants. Many indoor gardeners grow the flowering pot varieties as foliage plants.

Provide kalanchoe with high light and cool to hot temperatures. Keep succulent types dry between waterings and hold back on water in winter. Keep flowering types evenly moist. Fertilize three times in summer. Pot in average, well-drained soil and repot infrequently. They tolerate pruning well, but prune flowering types only after flowering and the succulent types only as part of selective grooming. Propagate by stem cuttings, leaf cuttings, or seed.

SELECTIONS *K. pumila* A shrubby plant to one foot tall. Leaves are delicately scalloped and covered with a thick white waxy bloom, giving the plant an overall silvery appearance. The shimmering rose-pink flowers appear in clusters at the

Kalanchoe produces tiny plantlets along the leaf margins. When mature enough to grow on their own, they drop from the mother plant and take root wherever they fall. *Above: Kalanchoe daigremontiana* (devil's backbone).

ends of the stems. Shy to flower indoors, but makes a nice hanging basket. ***K. tomentosa*** (Panda Plant) A bluish-gray shrub to twenty inches tall. Fuzzy leaves are succulent with indistinct teeth toward the tip. The teeth and edge of the leaves are tinted brown. The flowers are small and yellowish to purplish, but are seldom produced in the home. Has a potential problem with mealybugs. This is a textural plant with unusual coloration–kids love it.

LAELIA *Orchidaceae*

These epiphytic orchids are native to the high altitudes of Mexico and tropical South America. They generally have small flowers with quite attractive coloration. Their flower structures are similar enough to cattleya orchids that they are used in hybridization with cattleya. One of the hybrids is x *Laeliocattleya*.

Provide bright light, plenty of fresh air, and medium temperatures. Water liberally in summer allowing it to dry out between soakings. After its flowering period, let it rest somewhat drier. Fertilize three times in summer or use a dilute solution at every watering. Withhold fertilizer in winter. Pot in fir bark (large pieces for large species, small for small species)–these plants must have perfect drainage. Repot only as they become overcrowded or the bark deteriorates. Propagate by division or seed.

SELECTIONS *L. anceps* Mexican species that flowers in midwinter; the flowers last two months or more. Flowering stems arch and reach three feet with three flowers per stem. The flowers are large (four inches) in rosy lavender. The "lip" is colored with red stripes, purple and yellow.

L. crispa Large ruffled fragrant white flowers with a yellow and purple lip. Summer flowering with five to six flowers per stem; plants up to seventeen inches tall.

L. rubescens Flat pseudobulbs bear one leaf and an eighteen-inch wiry flower stem. The stem holds a cluster of muted lavender flowers with a light yellow lip and purple throat; flowers fall and winter.

L. tenebrosa Spring flowering with coppery bronze to citron yellow flowers; flowers have purple and white lip with dark veins. Parent of many hybrids.

LAURUS BAY *Lauraceae*

The two species of these evergreen trees are native to the Mediterranean region and Micronesia. One is grown for its decorative and culinary characteristics. Simple alternate leaves are stiff and fragrant. Flowers are small.

Provide high to medium light and keep the soil evenly moist during its active growing season. Fertilize infrequently, particularly to control size. Bay will tolerate average to cold temperatures and tolerates pruning quite well. Pot in an average, well-drained potting mix. Repot when watering becomes overwhelming and keep in mind that large pots produce large plants. It is possible to prune the roots to keep plants smaller, but you must also cut back the same percentage of foliage when you root prune. Bay is difficult to propagate. Early summer is the best time of year to try cuttings–it may take up to two months for the cuttings to root, and the percentage that actually take is

KALANCHOE TOMENTOSA (PANDA PLANT) Up to twenty inches tall; high light, cool to hot temperatures; keep dry between waterings and hold back on water in winter; slow growth rate.

KALANCHOE BEHARENSIS 'FANG' Up to twenty inches tall; high light, cool to hot temperatures; keep dry between waterings and hold back on water in winter; slow growth rate.

KALANCHOE BLOSSFELDIANA (FLAMING KATY, POT KALANCHOE) Twelve to fifteen inches high; high light, cool to hot temperatures; evenly moist when flowering, dry between waterings when not in flower and hold back on water in winter; slow growing.

LAELIA PURPURATA VAR. WERKHAUSERI 'TREASURE OF CARPENTE-RIA' One to two feet tall; bright light, plenty of fresh air; medium temperatures. Water liberally in summer allowing it to dry out between soakings. After flowering, let rest somewhat drier. Fertilize three times in summer. Moderate growth rate.

low. When available, seeds are a more reliable means for propagating laurus. Bay may have a problem with thrips and scale.

L. nobilis (Sweet Bay) A forty- to sixty-foot tree in the wild, this useful plant may be kept to four feet or less in a pot. Glossy green leaves are fragrant when crushed and are used in cooking. The plant suckers from the base–older stems may be removed to keep the plant in check. Sweet bay grows dense and tough when placed outside for the summer. It is a good plant for drafty, cool areas in the home during winter. One plant produces enough leaves to supply all the cooks in the neighborhood with a winter supply.

MAMMILLARIA PINCUSHION CACTUS, STRAWBERRY CACTUS
Cactaceae

This is a large genus, native from southwestern North America to northern South America, that offers great variety in color, shape, and texture. They may occur as solitary plants or in clumps of many heads. Many are easy to grow and readily available. Small in stature, they do well on a sunny windowsill. Flowers appear in rings around the top of the plant and are usually followed by red fruits that contain many seeds. The stems are not divided by ribs, but are covered with tubercles, protruding structures that are arranged systematically around the stem. The delicate spines of this genus are deceiving–though fine in texture, many have barbed or hooked ends that are not easily removed from one's flesh.

Give pincushion cactus high light, average to hot temperatures in summer, and cool (50- 60° F.) in winter. Allow the plant to dry between soakings and even sit dry, particularly in winter–overwatering causes stem rot. Fertilize three times in summer only and avoid situations with high humidity. Pot in coarse, fast-draining soil and repot annually. Propagate by division or seed. No pruning is needed. Watch for root mealybugs and scale.

SELECTIONS ***M. elongata*** (Lace Cactus) This plant comes in several shades of gold. The long fingerlike stems form a tight clump, first erect and then creeping and filling a small pot in a short period of time. The yellow to white flowers are small and appear only in the brightest conditions. With little attention, these plants will live a long time. Easy to propagate.

M. geminispina Appears white because it is covered with long, stiff, white spines. Solitary stems eventually form dense clumps. Flowers appear only in very high-light situations. They are red to carmine and are followed by half-inch fruits.

M. prolifera (Silver Cluster Cactus, Little Candles) Many small heads growing close together gradually form a large mound. Spines are silvery white over dull green stems. Flowers are yellow with reddish orange stripes and are produced in profusion. Red fruits are frequently produced and are held until next season's flowers appear.

NERIUM OLEANDER, ROSE-BAY *Apocynaceae*
Native to the Mediterranean region and Japan, all parts of nerium are poiso-

Oleander can grow to seven feet (with similar spread) or more in a container.

LAURUS NOBILIS (SWEET BAY) May be kept to four feet or less in a pot; high to medium light and average to cold temperatures; evenly moist; fertilize infrequently, particularly to control size; slow growing.

MAMMILLARIA ELONGATA (LACE CACTUS) Six inches tall; bright light and average to hot temperatures; allow to dry between soakings and sit dry in winter; fertilize only three times in summer; medium growth rate. NOTE: THIS ILLUSTRATION SHOWS A VARIANT FORM OF THE SPECIES.

MAMMILLARIA GEMINISPINA Up to six inches; bright light and average to hot temperatures; allow to dry between soakings and sit dry in winter; fertilize only three times in summer; slow growth rate.

NERIUM OLEANDER 'COMPACTA' (OLEANDER, ROSE-BAY) Three feet high and spread; bright light and cool to medium temperatures; dry between soakings; poisonous; fast growing.

NOLINA RECURVATA (PONYTAIL PALM) Usually not over five feet in the home; high light and warm temperatures; if in low light and low temperatures, keep very dry; otherwise, allow soil to dry between soakings; slow growing.

NOTOCACTUS LENINGHAUSII Three feet tall; high light and average to hot temperatures; allow to dry between soakings; keep cool and dry in winter; high humidity will scar stem; fertilize three times in summer; very slow growing.

NOTOCACTUS MAGNIFICUS Clustering to fourteen inches; allow to dry between soakings; keep cool and dry in winter; high humidity will scar stem; fertilize three times in summer; slow growing.

OCHNA SERRULATA (MICKEY MOUSE PLANT) Fifteen to eighteen inches high or three feet as a standard; high light and fairly cool temperatures; dry out briefly between waterings; fertilize once a month; slow growing.

nous, so it is not an appropriate plant for homes with small children or animals who might chew on plants. The sap of this genus is not milky like other members of the dogbane family.

Maintain high light and allow the plant to dry between soakings. Fertilize infrequently; frequent fertilization may cause the plant to grow too large for an interior space. Provide cool to hot temperatures. It performs best if kept quite cool and dry in winter. Pot in an average, well-drained potting mix. Repot every few years and root prune to increase vigor. Oleander tolerates pruning, but flowers on new wood, so prune in winter after flowering. Watch for mealybugs, thrips, and scale. Aphids often appear on flower buds. Propagate by stem cuttings or seed.

SELECTIONS *N. oleander* (Oleander) Oleander grows to seven feet (with similar spread) or more in a container and trains easily as a shrubby form or tree form. One of its positive aspects is drought tolerance, which is the reason it is such a popular landscape plant in California and Texas. If allowed to wilt severely, it will survive, shedding some leaves. Flowers are single or double and come in a variety of shades, from white to pink to red-purple. The medium green leaves are narrow with a distinct midrib.

NOLINA [BEAUCARNEA] *Agavaceae*

These succulent plants are native to the hot, dry regions of the southern United States and Mexico. The swollen stem stores moisture, and the older leaves are shed as the plant grows. It will survive with surprisingly few roots for the size of the stem. They are undemanding plants; a beautiful specimen in Wanda Supanich's personal collection lives in a bright corner of a room that is only heated above 50° F. in winter on occasion; it gets watered five times a year, whether it needs it or not.

Nolinas do best in high light but will tolerate medium or low light as long as the temperature is high. They perform best in hot temperatures, will adapt to average temperatures and do not do well in temperatures below 65° F. if the soil remains moist. They do well in lower temperatures if they are watered infrequently. Allow the soil to dry between soakings. Grow nolina in a small pot–potting to a larger size will encourage it to grow larger. Use a coarse, fast-draining soil mix, fertilize infrequently, and prune leaves only selectively. Mealybugs may be a problem. Nolina can be propagated by stem cuttings or by seed although seed is the preferred method.

SELECTIONS *N. recurvata* (Ponytail Palm, Elephant Foot) Native to southeast Mexico, this is a delightfully, unusually shaped plant for indoors. Long gracefully arching ribbonlike leaves crown the slender stem, which spreads and anchors itself broadly at soil level, swelling into a thick woody caudex. It thrives in hot sunny spots that are hard to fill, but will also perform similarly in low light and medium temperatures. This species varies physically from one plant to the next. The size of the stem, single or multiple stems in a pot, branches off the main stem, curly or arching leaves are just a few of the many variations that make this a real "character" in any collection.

CAUTION, NOT FEAR

A small number of plants are harmful to humans or pets. It is therefore important to know the plants that you are growing in your living space and to be cautious of unfamiliar ones.

Young children (especially those under three or those who tend to put things in their mouths) and pets are at highest risk. Plants that are in a play area or within the reach of children should be correctly identified and cross-referenced with a poisonous plant book. Garden books, botanical gardens, and poison control hotlines can help identify poisonous plants. Chicago Botanic Garden uses the *American Medical Association Handbook of Poisonous and Injurious Plants,* by Dr. Kenneth F. Lampe and Mary Ann McCann as its primary source of information. If a plant is determined to be risky, it should be removed or placed where it cannot possibly be reached.

Plants can harm by causing or irritating allergies through wind-blown spores or pollen; by causing dermatitis or skin irritation through direct contact with a plant (or its sap); through internal poisoning caused by eating plant parts; or by injury from sharp prickles, spines, or thorns (called mechanical injury). A few plant families to be wary of:

- Euphorbiaceae: sap is often toxic and irritates skin.
- Araceae: All plant parts contain oxalates (crystals) that can cause dermatitis and internal irritation.
- Cactaceae: Many plants protect themselves with sharp spines that can harm people and pets.
- Solanaceae: Many plants in the nightshade family cause or irritate allergies.

Many toxic plants are beautiful and should be enjoyed–but from out of arms' reach!

Notocactus (above) exhibit a wide variety of coloration in their spines as well as flowers.

NOTOCACTUS BALL CACTUS *Cactaceae*

Noto means "southern" in Greek, a reference to its nativity in southern South America. Typically small, solitary or clustering roundish cactus, notocactus are closely allied to echinocactus. Most have prominent ribs edged with woolly areoles and spines that are fine and threadlike to stiff and sharply needlelike. Although the plant is decorative even when not in flower, the flowers are arranged on top of the stem like a crown and are usually yellow (some are red).

Give notocactus high light and average to hot temperatures in summer. Cool temperatures and a distinct dry period in winter are essential to trigger many cactus into flower. Placement on a windowsill where it is naturally cooler and withholding water in winter is usually sufficient. Avoid situations of high humidity because it causes scarring on the stem. Allow the soil to dry between soakings and fertilize three times in summer. Pot in a coarse, fast-draining potting mix and repot annually. Be aware of possible problems with scale, root mealybugs, and thrips on the flowers. Pruning is generally unnecessary. Propagate by division or seed.

SELECTIONS *N. leninghausii* (Golden Ball Cactus) The common name applies to this plant when young. Over the years, it becomes cylindrical and three feet tall–not very "ball"-like. As one stem grows tall, the other "balls" are held close to the base of the tall stem. Overall it is a rich golden color and looks soft. Flowers are yellow and ruffly in a dense cluster at the top of the plant. This cactus is slow-growing and scars easily from high humidity.

N. magnificus [Parodia magnifica] Initially a solitary globular cactus that elongates in time and sends up numerous side shoots. Dull gray-green in color, the stems are highlighted with ribs edged in cream-colored wool with gold spines. Stems become wrinkled during drought, but smooth out after watering. Yellow flowers are located at the center top of the plant–a quietly elegant plant.

N. scopa Mostly white-spined, but with reddish central spines arranged on spiraling areoles; yellow flowers.

OCHNA BIRD'S-EYE BUSH *Ochnaceae*

This genus contains about ninety species of tropical trees and shrubs that are native to Africa and Asia. They have large, showy yellow flowers and attractive fruits.

Grow in a southern or eastern window and in fairly cool temperatures. Let dry out briefly between waterings–don't allow to stay dry. Pot in standard potting mix and fertilize once a month with a balanced fertilizer. Propagate by stem cuttings in summer or by seed. Rarely bothered by pests.

SELECTIONS *O. serrulata* (Mickey Mouse Plant) Woody shrub with shiny leathery bright green leaves that have a delicately toothed margin that grows to about two and one-half inches. The shrub grows fifteen to eighteen inches high but can be trained as a three-foot or taller standard. In late winter, it blooms with long-lasting primrose-yellow fragrant flowers. After the petals fall, the sepals and calyx turn bright red. Shiny black fruits develop and persist for several months, giving it a dramatic appearance. Occasionally will bloom again while the fruit is still on it. (BLITHEWOLD)

OPUNTIA MICRODASYS (BUNNY EARS) One foot high; high light; cool to hot temperatures; dry between soakings, hold back on water in winter; fertilize three times in summer; slow growing.

OPUNTIA MICRODASYS VAR. PALLIDA (YELLOW BUNNY EARS) One foot high; high light; cool to hot temperatures; dry between soakings, hold back on water in winter; fertilize three times in summer; slow growing.

OSCULARIA DELTOIDES (TIGER JAW VINE) Performs well in eight-to ten-inch hanging basket; dry between soakings and fertilize three times in summer; hot to cool temperatures; moderate grower.

PARODIA MUTABILIS Six inches tall; direct sun; average temperatures; water sparingly, allowing soil to dry thoroughly between soakings, only once or twice in winter; fertilize three times in summer; slow growing.

VARIATION WITHIN A SPECIES

Although species are grouped together because of common characteristics, there are often variations of these characteristics, such as flower color or leaf shape. These plants, although they may look different from each other, may still be of the same species. This is designated in scientific nomenclature as a var. or variety. An example of this is the bunny ears cactus. The white, yellow, and cinnamon bunny ears are all of the species *Opuntia microdasys,* but they are each a different naturally occurring variety. White bunny ears is *O. microdasys* var. *albispina;* yellow bunny ears is *O. microdasys* var. *pallida;* and cinnamon bunny ears is *O. microdasys* var. *rufida.*

OPUNTIA PRICKLY PEAR *Cactaceae*

A common and aggressively spiny group of cactus native to North and South America, these are the reason many people dislike cactus. One bad encounter with an opuntia will be remembered forever, and frequently the bad attitude is applied to the entire cactus family. Broad padlike segmented stems often look harmless, but quickly prove opposite. Tiny irritating spines called glochids become embedded in any material (skin or trousers!) they come in contact with. The larger, more obvious spines are no less painful. Easy to grow, easy to propagate, these cactus offer large, mostly yellow flowers (sometimes pink or orange-red) that are followed by fruits, many edible.

Opuntias perform best in high light and cool to hot temperatures. Allow the soil to dry between soakings and hold back on watering in winter. Fertilize three times in summer. Avoid high humidity and high-traffic areas. Pot in a coarse, fast-draining potting mix and repot infrequently. This is one of the few cactus that may be pruned. If done in spring or summer, new growth will appear where the cactus is cut. Watch for scale and mealybugs on the stems and aphids on the flowers. Propagate by stem cuttings or seed.

SELECTIONS O. basilaris (Beavertail Cactus) Blue-gray to purplish thick, padlike stems four to eight inches long grow slowly. The areoles sport reddish-brown glochids and sometimes one short spine. Flowers are reddish purple and are about three inches across. This plant may be kept small for quite some time.

O. microdasys var. albispina (White Bunny Ears) This plant looks velvety soft, but tiny white glochids in large numbers are clustered at the closely set areoles. The plant in the Chicago Botanic Garden was rubbed to death by visitors who learned the hard way to look with their eyes, not their hands! Easy to grow and propagate, relatively fast-growing.

O. microdasys var. pallida (Yellow Bunny Ears) Yellow polka dot-like areoles.

O. microdasys var. rufida (Cinnamon Bunny Ears) Brown polka dot-like areoles.

OSCULARIA *Aizoaceae*

Oscularia comes from the Latin for "little mouth," which describes the pairs of leaves arranged like little toothed mouths. These five shrubby species have great flowering potential. Masses of pinkish flowers appear in spring, masking the blue-gray or green succulent foliage–a treat any time of the year!

Allow the soil to dry between soakings and fertilize three times in summer. Oscularia tolerates hot to cool temperatures and should be potted in an average, well-drained potting mix. Instead of repotting, start the plant over from cuttings every two years. It benefits from selective pinching to keep the top of the pot full. Oscularia can also be propagated by seed and has relatively few insect or disease problems.

SELECTIONS O. deltoides (Tiger Jaw Vine) This succulent makes a great hanging basket for a sunny location. The plant becomes heavy as it grows because of its leaf succulence. The wiry stems become intensely pink in strong light and the blue-gray leaves become blue and grow close together. It grows leggy in less light and loses its color. The flowers are pink.

PARODIA *Cactaceae*

Parodias are desert cactus from South American that have small, globelike stems when young and then become broad cylinders with age. Cup-shaped yellow to red flowers appear at the stem tops in late spring.

Provide direct sun for parodias along with average temperatures. Water sparingly, allowing soil to thoroughly dry out between soakings. In winter, keep cool; water lightly only once or twice during winter. Fertilize only three times in summer. Pot in coarse, well-drained potting mix and repot only if the stems are against the pot sides. Propagate by removing offsets or from seed.
SELECTIONS *P. nivosa* Blood-red flowers on six-inch stems crowned in dense white wool.
P. mutabilis White fuzz caps area from which golden-yellow hooked spines emerge; yellow flowers.

PEDILANTHUS *Euphorbiaceae*

An odd group of succulent plants native from Florida and Mexico to South America and the West Indies. These shrubs have the milky sap common to all members of the Euphorbia family and should be handled with respect as some people may be sensitive to the sap.

Allow the soil to dry between soakings and fertilize three times in summer. Provide average to hot temperatures. Pot in an average, well-drained potting mix and repot infrequently. Prune as needed for shaping. There are relatively few insect or disease problems with which to be concerned. The plant can be propagated by stem cutting or seed.
SELECTIONS *P. tithymaloides* 'Variegatus' (Slipper Cactus, Devil's Backbone) Thick, waxy stems start out erect and then bend as new growth appears. Stems zigzag in an obvious manner, making it look almost artificial. Pointed, somewhat triangular leaves are keeled and medium green with cream variegation and pinkish-red edges. The color is much intensified in high light. Flowers are pointed and red, appearing in terminal clusters. It grows to three feet but may be kept shorter in small pots. A winter rest, with cold but not freezing temperatures and soil kept quite dry, is needed to initiate flowering.

PELARGONIUM GERANIUM *Geraniaceae*

Geraniums are common bedding plants that are sometimes grown indoors as well. They are native to South Africa, indicating the type of conditions they need to thrive. There is an almost endless selection of species and cultivars to suit every taste, including lacy and variegated foliage and such fragrances as orange, chocolate mint, coconut, ginger, and pine.

Geraniums must face a sunny south or west window to bloom well indoors, especially during the winter. Provide good air circulation and allow the plants to dry out only briefly between waterings. Provide a heavy, well-drained soil and fertilize regularly during the growing season with a fertilizer formulated for flowering plants. Geraniums are traditionally grown outdoors in summer and brought indoors when the weather cools. They take up a good

VIEWPOINT

GERANIUMS AS HOUSEPLANTS

Geraniums have long been grown in and around the home. They are easy to grow and reward the gardener with strong color and the scent of summer. Some people make the effort to bring their faithful flowerers in for the winter to protect them from sure death at the first frost. I say: let them freeze. Yes, it is possible to force them into dormancy in a cool dark corner of a basement, or nurture them along on a sunny windowsill and get a flower or two over winter . . . but I feel there are much more interesting and rewarding plants available to the contemporary gardener for winter color. It is hoped that the geranium lovers of the world will find something appealing within these pages from which to choose a substi-tute–and support their local growers by buying a new geranium in May!
WANDA SUPANICH
CHICAGO BOTANIC GARDEN

I don't grow geraniums for their flowers as much as for their scent. I have an apple-blossom geranium that's been thriving for years; brushing up against it and releasing its scent is always a delight. My grandmother grew geraniums that lasted for a long time as well. If a lot of sunlight can be provided, geraniums make great houseplants.
JULIE MORRIS
BLITHEWOLD MANSION AND GARDENS

Geraniums are fine houseplants, but they are not long-lived, and they must have a lot of sunlight. Many people bring their outdoor geraniums in for winter color; they should not be expected to make it through the season.
FRANCISCA PLANCHARD-COELHO
THE NEW YORK BOTANICAL GARDEN

Geraniums do better in dry rooms in winter than many other plants. They need a lot of sun and a cool room–sometimes hard to provide at the same time. Given those conditions, they do well for a long time.
JERRY PARSONS
UNIVERSITY OF CALIFORNIA BOTANICAL GARDENS, BERKELEY

V I E W P O I N T

PLANTS WITH UNDESERVED BAD REPUTATIONS

Citrus species are not as difficult to grow as people think. Pests seem more of a problem than cultural conditions–a cool, sunny window works just fine. Gardenia is also usually successful under the right conditions: 60° F. night temperature, good light. And platycerium species are thought of as hard to grow–I put mine in the sink and spray thoroughly twice a week and never have had problems.
JULIE MORRIS
BLITHEWOLD MANSION AND GARDENS

Plants with undeserved bad reputations? Orchids! especially phalenopsis and vandas
ROBERT BOWDEN
HARRY P, LEU BOTANICAL GARDEN

I think most orchids have gotten a "bum rap." As long as you know their needs and give them what they want, you will be rewarded with the fantastic flowers they provide. They really are very easy.
JERRY PARSONS
UNIVERSITY OF CALIFORNIA BOTANICAL GARDENS AT BERKELEY

I don't know why people think alocasias are difficult to grow. They have just about the same requirements as xanthosoma.
FRANCISCA PLANCHARD-COELHO
THE NEW YORK BOTANICAL GARDEN

bit of room, so the most convenient way to grow them indoors is to take cuttings in late summer to bring indoors in September. If you plan to overwinter them without trying to keep them blooming, give them cool temperatures, dry soil, and low light. Insect problems include whitefly, aphids, and mealybugs. At the first indication of black areas on the stems or if the leaves look unhealthy, discard the plant to avoid spreading fungal disease. Pinch stems regularly to encourage new growth and remove spent flowers and yellow leaves to promote healthy plants.

SELECTIONS *P. crispum* (Lemon Geranium) Strongly lemon-scented leaves.

P. domesticum (Martha Washington, Regal Geranium) Lovely large, single blossoms in clusters that resemble rhododendron flowers. Often best discarded after blooming since they are hard to bring back into flowers. Plants need several months of night temperatures below 60° F. to produce new flower buds. They will quit flowering altogether in hot weather. Provide partial shade if grown outdoors.

P. hortorum (Zonal Geranium) Available in white, pink, red, and salmon; fancy-leaved varieties available as well. (BLITHEWOLD)

PITTOSPORUM *Pittosporaceae*

This genus consists of 150 species of evergreen trees and shrubs found all over the world in warm temperate and tropical areas. They are used as landscape plants in the southern and western United States, particularly as hedge plants.

Pittosporums must have bright light (south window) and temperatures from 50-70° F. Allow the soil to dry out between waterings and use standard potting soil. Fertilize during the growing season with a balanced fertilizer. Prune to maintain size–nodes tend to produce one to three new stems. Propagate by cuttings of half-ripened wood in the spring. Watch for scale.

SELECTIONS *P. tobira* (Mock Orange) Leaves are one inch rounded, thick and leathery, and arranged in whorls at the ends of branches. These wide, shrub-type plants are best grown for a tabletop or the floor where they have room to spread. The flowers are small, white, and fragrant. Good candidate for bonsai.

P. tobira 'Variegatum' Beautiful pale green leaves with creamy margins–more common than the green variety.

PLATYCERIUM BIFURCATUM STAGHORN FERN *Polypodiaceae*

This fern, native to Australia, Africa, South America, and Polynesia, is epiphytic. It grows by producing young plants from its roots and is propagated by separating these suckers. The sterile kidney-shaped basal leaves form a plate or vase from which the fertile fronds protrude. They are thick, grayish green, and forked, resembling antlers with brown spores at their tips. As the sterile fronds age, they decompose, forming rich humus that feeds the plant. They are fairly easy to grow in the home, although they may be awkward because of their size.

Grow staghorn fern in bright light with no direct sun. If grown in a hanging basket, use a mixture of equal parts peat moss and sphagnum moss. They may are also be mounted on slabs of bark to which they eventually root. The

PEDILANTHUS TITHYMALOIDES 'VARIEGATUS' (SLIPPER CACTUS, DEVIL'S BACKBONE) Grows to three feet but may be kept shorter in small pots; dry between soakings; fertilize three times in summer; average to hot temperatures and winter rest with cold; moderate growth rate.

PELARGONIUM 'FIREFLY' (GERANIUM) Ten to twelve inches; sunny south or west window; dry out only briefly between waterings; fertilize regularly during the growing season; take cuttings in late summer to bring indoors; to overwinter them without bloom, give them cool temperatures, dry soil and low light.

PELARGONIUM 'PRINCE RUPERT' (SCENTED GERANIUM) Ten to twelve inches; sunny south or west window; dry out only briefly between waterings; fertilize regularly during the growing season; to overwinter without bloom, give them cool temperatures, dry soil, low light; moderate growth.

PELARGONIUM DOMESTICUM (MARTHA WASHINGTON, REGAL GERANIUM) Ten to twelve inches; sunny south or west window; dry out only briefly between waterings; fertilize regularly during the growing season; take cuttings in late summer to bring indoors; partial shade if grown outdoors.

Who loves a garden loves a
  greenhouse too.
Unconscious of a less propi-
  tious clime,
There blooms exotic beauty
  warm and snug,
While the winds whistle and the
  snows descend.
WILLIAM COWPER, FROM "THE
TASK," 1785

slab can be hung on the wall so the fronds hang down normally. The young
fertile fronds are covered with downy hairs—do not handle or dust. They will
thrive in average temperatures but will languish if air does not circulate. Let
the plant dry briefly between soakings. Water in the shower or sink every
other day if in very strong light. Fertilize with dilute fertilizer during growing
season and withhold in winter. Reduce fertilizer to keep plant smaller.
Remove old leaves and watch for mealybugs and scale. Propagate by spores.
(THE NEW YORK BOTANICAL GARDEN)

PUNICA POMEGRANATE *Punicaceae*

Only two species make up this genus. One is a shrub and the other a tree that
is cultivated for its fruits in tropical climates. The leaves are oblong or rounded light green. Its beauty is in the orange flowers at the ends of the branches.
The flowers are sometimes followed by orange fruits. It is naturally a deciduous plant, but will retain its leaves indoors if given proper conditions.

    Pomegranate performs best in a cool, sunny window and is tolerant of a
wide range temperatures. It may be overwintered on a cool sunporch (above
freezing) where it will drop its leaves as part of its natural cycle. When over-
wintering this way, allow it to dry thoroughly. If keeping in a warm window
for the winter, water it well regularly—don't allow it to stay dry for any length
of time. Pot in standard potting mix and fertilize monthly to encourage flowering. If you have trouble getting it to flower, try giving it the cool, dry winter treatment. Prune only after flowering since flower buds are borne at the
tips of branches. Propagate from tip cuttings or from fresh seeds.
SELECTIONS *P. granatum* Grows to six feet in a pot; has four-inch fruits that are
edible; flowers are one-and-one-half inches.
***P. granatum* 'Nana'** (Dwarf Pomegranate) Lovely small indoor tree; can be
trained as bonsai. Grows fifteen to twenty-four inches in a pot; can be kept
smaller by pruning. (BLITHEWOLD)

VELTHEIMIA *Liliaceae*

This South African genus consists of five species of bulbous plants. The bulbs
are usually planted in early fall and about three to four months later the flowers arise. In late spring, the leaves begin to yellow and die at which time the
bulb should be allowed to rest.

    Provide veltheimias with a minium of three to four hours of direct sun daily.
Give them cool temperatures (about 55° F.), however, throughout the winter.
Water a newly planted bulb sparingly until growth begins. Gradually increase
the amount of water but let the top inch of soil dry out between waterings. As
the leaves begin to die, gradually decrease the water. When all the leaves have
died, store the bulb dry in its pot until new growth appears. Fertilize regularly
during active growth. Use well-drained potting mix and plant with half the
bulb out of the soil. Repot only when offsets begin to appear.
SELECTION *V. capensis* Wavy-edged leaves to a foot long and one inch wide;
around sixty bell-shaped stunning pink flowers with greenish tips on a one-
foot flower stalk.

PITTOSPORUM TOBIRA (MOCK ORANGE) To ten feet over many years; can be kept at about two feet; bright light (south window) and temperatures from 50-70° F.; dry out between waterings; fertilize regularly during the growing season; slow growing.

PLATYCERIUM BIFURCATUM (STAGHORN FERN) Leaves to one foot across and three feet long; bright light with no direct sun; average temperatures with good air circulation; dry briefly between soakings. Fertilize with dilute fertilizer during growing season and withhold in winter; slow growing.

PUNICA GRANATUM 'NANA' (DWARF POMEGRANATE) Grows fifteen to twenty-four inches in a pot; can be kept smaller by pruning; cool, sunny window; may be overwintered dry on a cool sunporch (above freezing); water well regularly—don't allow to stay dry for any length of time; slow growing.

VELTHEIMIA CAPENSIS Foot-long leaves, flower stalk one foot high; direct sun; cool temperatures in winter; dry out between waterings; decrease water as leaves begin to die; fertilize regularly during active growth; slow growing.

MEDIUM LIGHT
West or east exposure
A plant that grows best in medium light is one that receives
some direct light, is placed in a
brightly lighted spot, such as a
west or east window, or is placed
in filtered southern light.
Medium light is the ideal situations and many of the plants suggested in this book will accommodate it readily.

**PLANTS IN HIGH-LIGHT SECTION
(PAGES 24-73) THAT ARE SUITABLE FOR
MEDIUM-LIGHT SITUATIONS**
Abutilon
Aechmea x 'Foster's Favorite
　　Favorite'
Agave patoni
Agave ferdinandi-regis
Aloe barbadensis
Aloe plicatilis
Aloe variegata
Billbergia
Cereus
Cryptanthus
Cyperus
Cymbidium
Dionaea
Epiphyllum
Euonymus
Gymnocalycium
Haemanthus albiflos
Hypoestes phyllostacha
Ixora
Laurus
Nolina
Pittosporum
Platycerium

**MOST PLANTS THAT ARE RECOMMENDED
FOR LOW LIGHT WILL PERFORM JUST FINE
IN MEDIUM LIGHT.**

MEDIUM LIGHT

ANTHURIUM TAILFLOWER *Araceae*

Anthurium is a large genus of plants of varying beauty from tropical America and the West Indies. Most of them have, at the very least, stately leathery leaves incised with distinct deep veins. Others are strikingly marked with veins highly contrasting the rich, green background. Still others are known for their bright exotic flowers that are popular in the floral industry. Anthurium flowers are typical of the Arum family. The spadix, a fleshy spike with flowers embedded in it, is surrounded by a spathe, a brightly-colored leafy bract that protects the spadix.

Most are easy to grow if provided medium to low light and high humidity. One method to keep anthuriums flowering is to fill a saucer with gravel and place the plant on another smaller saucer inverted in the center as a pedestal. Keep the gravel covered with water to add humidity to the air surrounding the plant and allow the soil to dry between soakings. Anthurium will not tol-erate drying winds or cold drafts, and the foliage is easily scuffed by passersby. Anthurium does well in average temperatures but will tolerate hot conditions. Use a soil that is coarse and fast draining–70 percent bark is the best choice since good drainage is imperative. Repot when bark medium breaks down to a slow-draining muck-type soil or when the stems crowd the pot. Fertilize three times in summer and prune only when necessary as part of grooming. Aphids occasionally attack the new growth as it uncurls. Mites can be a prob-lem if the plant is stressed. Scale is an infrequent pest. Propagate by rhizome division, offsets, or seed.

SELECTIONS *A. andraeanum* (Flamingo Flower) The species most people associate with anthurium. Grown all over Hawaii, it comes in red, pink, white, and yel-low.

A. scherzerianum (Flamingo Flower) Rich, deep green eight-inch leaves stand on erect petioles off low stems. Coarse roots are frequently visible along the stem. Brilliant red flowers with a distinctively curled spadix. It will flower in the home if watered carefully and provided sufficient humidity–it is one of the easiest anthuriums to flower. The flowers last a long time when cut. Watch for scale insects and mist leaves frequently.

A. scherzerianum* var. *rothschildianum (Dotted Pink) Large, almost platelike flowers that are freckled red and white.

***A.* 'Lady Jane'** A reliable bloomer with bright pink flowers. The plant gets large with age. Long springy petioles support leathery dark green heart-shaped leaves. The flower consists of a dark pink spathe with a protruding lighter pink to white spadix. Occasional removal of older stems helps keep the plant vigorous and flowering year-round. If you have trouble getting 'Lady Jane' to flower, increase the humidity.

***A. plowmanii* 'Rancho Ruffles'** This is a large, fancy-leaved cultivar grown for its distinctive foliage rather than flowers and can reach a diameter of three feet. Striking ruffly leaves makes this anthurium stand out in a crowd. A tissue cul-

ANTHURIUM SCHERZERIANUM (FLAMINGO FLOWER) Up to one foot tall; eight-inch leaves; high humidity and low to medium light; average to hot temperatures; fertilize three times in summer; slow growing.

ANTHURIUM 'LADY JANE' (TAILFLOWER) High humidity and low to medium light; average to hot temperatures; fertilize three times in summer; slow growing.

APHELANDRA SQUARROSA 'LOUISAE' (ZEBRA PLANT) Two feet; bright light; average temperatures; evenly moist soil; high humidity; slow growing.

ARDISIA CRENATA (CORALBERRY) Three feet tall; medium light and average temperatures; evenly moist; fertilize three times in summer; slow growing.

... At once thickets of palms, latanias, dracaenas, and trades-cantias, asparagus, clivias, and begonias, in all their tropical beauty rise before his eyes, and among them, or course, a forced primula, and hyacinth, and cyclamen will flower; in the corridor we shall make an equatorial jungle, hanging tendrils will flow from the stairs, and in the windows we shall put plants that will flower like mad. Then he glances quickly round; no longer does he see the room in which he lives, but a forest of paradise which he will create here...

KARL CAPEK, FROM *THE GARDENER'S YEAR*, 1929

ture selection of *A. plowmanii* (native to the the rainforests of Peru) was developed by Rancho Tissue Technologies, a California breeder. This particular anthurium performs best in warm temperatures.

APHELANDRA *Acanthaceae*

This genus includes approximately eighty species from tropical America. They have large leaf blades and are grown for their showy spikes of red, yellow, orange, or white flowers. They are striking plants and have great appeal for purchase. Unfortunately, they are short-lived in the home.

Provide bright light, but protect from direct sun in summer; average temperatures and evenly moist soil. High humidity is essential. Cold temperatures or dry periods will cause defoliation. It is not uncommon for a newly acquired plant to totally drop its leaves within forty-eight hours. These plants are hard to keep looking good in the home and hard to bring back into bloom. Propagate by stem cuttings or seed.

SELECTION *A. squarrosa* 'Louisae' (Zebra Plant, Saffron-Spike) Leaves are dark green with silvery veins; grows two feet tall; red-tipped bracts.

ARDISIA *Myrsinaceae*

Native to the tropics and subtropics (Asia, America, and Australia), this is a large group of evergreen trees and shrubs of which few are cultivated as houseplants. All have alternate, simple leathery leaves.

Ardisias thrive best in medium light and average temperatures but are quite tolerant of many conditions. Keep the soil evenly moist and repot only occasionally. Use an average, well-drained soil mix and fertilize three times in summer. Although ardisia is tolerant of extensive pruning, it is usually only necessary to selectively groom the plant. Watch for scale and mealybugs. Ardisia is easily propagated by stem cuttings or by seed.

SELECTIONS *A. crenata (A. crispa)* (Coralberry) Native to southeast Asia, coralberry is an evergreen shrub that is slow-growing, tolerant of most conditions, and showy. Coralberry has ever-present bright red fruits of the previous year and bright green fruits of the current year. The plant can grow to six feet, but it usually tops out at three feet in the home. It has small pinkish-white fragrant flowers. The berries can be held longer by dropping the temperature into the fifties or by keeping it in good light with added humidity. Many seeds will germinate in the pot if left where they fall.

ASPARAGUS ASPARAGUS FERN *Liliaceae*

This group of plants, native to Europe, Africa, Asia, and Australia, is commonly linked by the true leaves having been reduced to scales. Small, narrow photosynthetic structures appear to be leaves but are not. The flowers are small, followed by round berries (which are toxic), irregularly produced in the home. Although the common names suggests a relationship to ferns, these are not true ferns.

Provide medium light and keep the soil evenly moist. Asparagus performs best in cool, but will tolerate average or hot temperatures. Repot in rich, organic, well-drained soil when the plant makes its pot bulge or break from the enlarging rootball. When daily watering becomes necessary, it's time to repot. Fertilize with dilute solution every time plant is watered during its growing period unless you desire to inhibit its growth. Prune only selectively when grooming the plants–some species have prickles or thorns at the nodes and must be handled with care. Watch for aphids on the new asparagus spearlike growth. Spider mites can be a problem in dry conditions. Propagate new plants by dividing rhizomes or by seed.

SELECTIONS *A. densiflorus* **'Meyers'** (Foxtail Fern) Unusual in habit, this plant is irresistible to the touch. The tapering taillike stems jut out from the center of the plant in various directions. Bright green in color, the leaflike structures cover the stems in a starry pattern. Even though not a true fern, the plant is very demanding of water and space. Once established, it seems to use water as fast as you can supply it. Unfortunately, this race for water allows the root system, with many large obvious reservoirs, to expand to the point of breaking its container. Restrained watering and good light cultivates tougher, more robust growth.

A. densiflorus **'Sprengeri'** Commonly used indoors or outdoors in summer as a hanging basket or container plant.

ASPLENIUM SPLEENWORT *Polypodiaceae*

Spleenworts are distributed worldwide–most are tropical, but there are a few hardy species that occur in temperate regions. They are fairly easy to grow if you understand their peculiar needs for watering. Some form plantlets along the edges of the leaves, and some are epiphytes requiring coarse soil with lots of air around the roots.

Provide asplenium with medium light and, in general, keep the soil evenly moist. They will thrive in average temperatures, but avoid drying winds, cold drafts, and high-traffic areas. They must have better than average humidity to look really good. Epiphytic types require coarse, fast-draining soil and frequent watering; others require a peaty mix that is moisture-retentive. Aspleniums require infrequent fertilizing and pruning only as necessary for grooming. Scale may be an occasional problem; leaf spots may appear if the plant is in an improper soil mix. Propagate asplenium by separating plantlets from the mother plant or by spores.

SELECTIONS *A. daucifolium* (Mother Fern) Fronds are graceful, lacy, and arch to a point. Easily propagated by plantlets formed on the edge of the fronds.

A. nidus (Bird's Nest Fern) is native to tropical Asia and Australia. This is a popular fern that gets large with age. Spores form patterned lines on the underside of the leaves. An epiphyte in its native land, this plant requires a coarse, open soil mix to grow normally. It may perform in average soil for a while, but leaf spots, stunted growth or no growth are good indicators of the need for a soil change. Haphazard watering results in misshapen new fronds.

AUCUBA *Aucubaceae*

This is a small group of evergreen shrubs native to eastern and central Asia. The foliage is bright and glossy, frequently with flecks of color throughout.

Tolerant of cool temperatures, these plants are perfect inside building entrances in cold climates.

They perform quite well in low light where they should dry slightly between soakings, or place in full sun where they should be kept evenly moist. However, avoid full sun in summer. Aucuba is particularly sensitive to drying winds, so avoid this situation if possible. They will need annual repotting in an average, well-drained mix due to vigorous growth. Fertilize infrequently and prune when necessary to keep the plant attractive. Watch for mealybug infestation; dry conditions will attract spider mites. Propagate by stem cuttings in late summer or by seed.

SELECTIONS _A. japonica_ 'Variegata' (Japanese Spotted Laurel) If kept pruned to four feet, will be full and robust. The broad, thick leaves are covered with irregular golden flecks. Pruning aids in shaping and promoting new growth. Cool temperatures promote flowering and decorative fruiting. Neither is seen often in the home. This is a good plant for extending your patio container season–put it out early in spring and bring it in before fall frost.

A. japonica **'Crotonifolia'** and **'Speckles'** are males; **'Gold Dust'** and **'Variegata'** are females. In order to get fruit in cool conditions, a male must be grafted onto a female plant or vice versa. At University of California Botanical Garden at Berkeley, male plants are planted in close proximity to female plants and bear fruit.

ARAUCARIA _Araucariaceae_

The fifteen species of this coniferous genus are native to South America, Australia, and the Pacific Islands. Several are grown for timber and one is grown for edible seed. In the home, juvenile plants make attractive small trees.

Provide medium light and warm to cool temperatures. Keep the soil evenly moist but never allow it stand in water. Fertilize with a dilute solution every two weeks during the growing season for fast growth or three times in summer for more controlled growth. Repot only every two to three years or when the roots appear on top of the soil or out the bottom of the pot. Do not prune–it causes unnatural-looking growth. Commercial propagation is done by cuttings but is not usually successful for the home gardener.

SELECTION _A. heterophyllya_ (Norfolk Island Pine) Branches in tiers with prickly needles. Four to six feet high, grows moderately. New needles are light green, and turn dark green with age. Commonly used as a Christmas tree. Will drop branches that fall below window level–best grown where entire plant receives light.

BEGONIA _Begoniaceae_

This is a large genus of plants from the subtropics and tropics that is commonly cultivated for decorative foliage and flowers. The leaves are mostly asymmetrical and may be extreme in color. Hybrids are particularly fancy and desirable. Begonias can be fibrous-rooted, such as wax begonias, rhizomatous, as rex begonias, or tuberous, as the group grown for their large glowing summer flowers.

ASPARAGUS DENSIFLORUS 'SPRENGERI' Stems to thirty inches long; medium light and cool, average or hot temperatures; evenly moist; very demanding of water and space; medium growth rate.

ASPLENIUM NIDUS (BIRD'S NEST FERN) Leaves to three feet long; medium light and average temperatures; keep evenly moist; must have better than average humidity; slow growing.

AUCUBA JAPONICA 'VARIEGATA' (JAPANESE SPOTTED LAUREL) Four feet tall; low light; tolerant of cool temperatures; dry slightly between soakings or evenly moist in full sun; moderate growth rate.

ARAUCARIA HETEROPHYLLA (NORFOLK ISLAND PINE) Four to six feet high; medium light; warm to cool temperatures; evenly moist; fertilize with a dilute solution every two weeks during the growing season; grows moderately.

Begonia 'Edinburgh brevimosa'.

Begonias should be given medium light and average house temperatures and kept evenly moist at all times. They will not tolerate drying winds, cold drafts, or high-traffic areas. Annual repotting in an average well-drained mix and pruning after flowering keeps them vigorous. Use dilute fertilizer at every watering during active growth. Many begonias are susceptible to leaf spotting. This can be avoided by allowing the soil to dry somewhat between soakings, avoiding water on the leaves, and allowing for good air circulation by placement and pruning. Propagation, depending on the root type, can be done from stem cutting, rhizome division, leaf cutting, tuber division, or seed. New plants should be started regularly because many types go into decline after a year or so.

SELECTIONS *B. dregei* (Grape Leaf Begonia) A soft green-bronze begonia of medium size; tolerant of cool temperatures. Parent plant of many hybrids.

B. x erythrophylla (Beefsteak Begonia) Commonly grown in the home for many years. Waxy green leaves with red undersides.

B. floccifera An Indian species with velvety leaves and low mounding form.

B. foliosa (Fernleaf Begonia) Long arched branches with small toothed leaves. Tolerant of cool temperatures (55-65° F.)

B. heracleifolia (Starleaf Begonia) Six- to ten-inch green leaves in a star shape, arranged high above the stem; striking plant with attractive pink flowers.

B. x rex Many cultivars; treasured for beautifully colored leaves.

B. schmidtiana A tidy, dense grower from Brazil with olive green leaves with dusty red undersides. Delicately toothed leaf margins enhance the flowers that are present most of the time. It benefits from occasional pinching of a third or more of the stems to keep it productive. This rewarding small begonia is perfect for the windowsill. It will creep out of its pot with time, so starting the plant over from the escaping stems is a good way to keep the plant youthfully vigorous.

B. 'Black Richmondensis' An easy-to-grow, fibrous rooted basket-type begonia. Virtually always in flower, this plant has small, wavy-edged glossy dark burgundy leaves with rich red undersides. The flowers are pale pink to white and bloom over a long period. Old leaves and flowers drop periodically, making a bit of a mess. Start new plants from cuttings annually since older plants become woody and don't flower well.

B. x 'Stained Glass' A large hybrid begonia with palmate, distinctly marked leaves that is suitable for large pots and spaces. This is a rhizomatous type that sends up straight tall stems with silver and green marked leaves. It may go dormant in some situations. The leaves are easily damaged so provide it with ample space. Leaf spots can be a serious problem but can be avoided with good air circulation and dry foliage. Divide annually to keep it active.

BRASSAIA [SCHEFFLERA] UMBRELLA PLANT *Araliaceae*

Brassaias are large, handsome plants native to tropical Asia, Australasia and the Pacific Islands. They have palmate compound leaves–the leaflets are arranged in whorls at the tip of the petiole. Shiny and bright green, the leaves are held perpendicular to the long leaf stems.

B. maculata var. *wightii* (angel wing begonia)

B. 'Jean Pernet'

B. 'Tom Ment'

B. 'Deliciosa'

B. 'El Partita'

B. *rex* 'Mardi Gras'

BEGONIA SCHMIDTIANA Under twelve inches high; medium light and average temperatures; evenly moist at all times; use dilute fertilizer at every watering during active growth; pinch stems to keep it productive; fast growing.

BEGONIA X 'STAINED GLASS' Medium light and average temperatures; evenly moist soil; dilute fertilizer at every watering during active growth; fast growing; avoid moisture on leaves.

BRASSAIA ACTINOPHYLLA 'AMATE' (UMBRELLA PLANT) To ten feet; medium light and average temperatures, although will tolerate heat; evenly moist but cut back on watering in winter; fertilize three times in summer; fast growing.

CAMPELIA ZANONIA 'MEXICAN FLAG' (MEXICAN FLAG) To four feet; medium light and warm temperatures (up to 85° F. during day); dry briefly between thorough soakings; high humidity; moderate growth rate.

Provide medium light and average temperatures, although brassaias will tolerate hot conditions. Avoid drying winds, cold drafts, and high-traffic areas. Keep the potting soil evenly moist but cut back on watering in winter. Fertilize three times in summer and then infrequently throughout the rest of the year. Repot in average, well-drained potting mix. Brassaias tolerate pruning well, but it is usually only necessary as part of grooming. Propagate by stem cuttings, seed and air layering. Watch for scale, mites, and mealybugs; aphids may be a problem on new growth.

SELECTIONS *B. actinophylla* '**Amate**' (Umbrella Plant) A vertical selection that is more resistant to spider mites than the species. The stems grow tall relatively quickly, but if removed, sprouts will form on the stumps. New stems are generated from below the soil level also. Keep this cultivar evenly moist and in good light to avoid spider mite infestation.

B. actinophylla '**Mauggi**' A small, bushy, cute cutleaf variety.

Campelia will grow tall and leggy; if that is not the look you want, prune to ground level and wait for it to regenerate.

CAMPELIA ZANONIA 'MEXICAN FLAG' MEXICAN FLAG

Commelinaceae

This genus has only one species which is native from Mexico to Brazil. It is a clump-forming plant with canelike stems to four feet tall. The leaves are thick and lance-shaped and are green with yellow-white stripes and red margins. Its purple and white flowers are small and inconspicuous.

Grow campelia in partial shade in warm temperatures (up to 85° F. during the day). It should be allowed to dry briefly between thorough soakings and needs ample humidity. Pot in an organic potting mix and fertilize with a dilute solution at every watering except during winter. Pruning is usually necessary only for grooming, but if the plant gets leggy, cut the stems at ground level where they will regenerate. Use cuttings from the underground stems to start new plants. Mealybugs can be a minor problem.

CARLUDOVICA *Cyclanthaceae*

These tall plants from Central America are nearly stemless with broad, palm-like leaves. They are cultivated as ornamentals and as a source for fiber and food (the young leaves are eaten).

Provide medium light and average house temperatures for best growth. They will tolerate hot temperatures. Carludovicas should be kept evenly moist and fertilized three times in summer. Avoid drying winds and cold drafts. Pruning is necessary only as part of selective grooming. Repot into coarse, fast-draining potting mix only when they split their pots. Propagate by rhizome division and seed. Mealybugs may be a problem.

SELECTIONS *C. palmata* (Panama Hat Palm) Long, round stiff leaf stems support broad leaves that are bleached and used to make Panama hats. Flowers are held like corndogs on heavy stems about fourteen to sixteen inches from soil level. Whitish filaments explode from the corndogs and fade quickly.

CARYOTA FISHTAIL PALM *Arecaceae*

Fishtail palms are a small group of large, elegant, and unusual palms from the Asiatic tropics. The leaflets are asymmetrically shaped, appearing as a fishtail.

CARLUDOVICA PALMATA (PANAMA HAT PLANT) To ten feet; medium light and average temperatures; will tolerate hot temperatures; evenly moist; fertilize three times in summer; moderate growth rate.

CARYOTA MITIS (FISHTAIL PALM) Up to eight feet tall; medium to high light and average temperatures; dry slightly between waterings; fertilize infrequently to keep the plant within bounds; fast growing.

CATTLEYA AURANTIACA 'LITTLE LADY' (CATTLEYA ORCHID) Ten inches to two feet; high light and average temperatures; high humidity; dry between waterings; dilute fertilizer every time the plant is watered during flowering; slow growing.

CHAMAEDOREA SEIFRIZII (BAMBOO PALM) Up to five feet, leaves two to three feet long; low to medium light and average temperatures; dry slightly between soakings; fertilize bamboo palms three times in the summer; slow growing.

Caryota urens is economically important in India for its fiber, sap, and timber. Caryotas are tapped in their native lands for sap that is distilled into wine. Others are valued as ornamental plants. These palms flower when mature and then die.

Fishtail palms require medium to high light, average temperatures, and should be allowed to dry slightly between waterings. Avoid drying winds. Fishtail Palms require repotting every two years or so in an average, well-drained potting mix. Fertilize infrequently to keep the plant within bounds. Removing suckers and older stems will also help keep it contained. Otherwise, prune only when needed for aesthetics. Propagate by seed.
SELECTIONS *C. mitis* Easy to grow, this palm is tolerant of a wide range of care; clumping habit. *C. mitis* makes a perfect specimen as a young plant. It suckers from the base and becomes full and graceful quickly. Large stems may be sawed out as the plant becomes too big for its space. Unusually shaped leaves and long, somewhat arching branches make this a showpiece.

CATTLEYA CATTLEYA ORCHID *Orchidaceae*
Native to South America, Mexico, and the West Indies, these epiphytes have leathery leaves that grow from roundish or flattened pseudobulbs. Flowers vary from the large, showy corsage type to those that are delicate and exquisitely colored. Many of the flowers have delightful fragrance.

Cattleyas do well in a sunny window or bright filtered light with average home temperatures if given a little extra humidity. A pebble tray with water standing in it and an inverted saucer to support the pot work well to increase the humidity in the immediate vicinity. A humidifier works even better. Protect them, however, from direct summer sun. Allow the potting mix to dry briefly between waterings and fertilize with a dilute fertilizer solution for flowering plants every time the plant is watered during its growing season. Repot every two to three years when the plant has outgrown its pot or the bark has decomposed. Use a coarse, fast-draining bark mix. Prune only selectively when grooming and sterilize tools between cuts to avoid spreading virus. Old pseudobulbs should be left on the plant to act as storage compartments for food. Avoid cold drafts and high-traffic areas. Propagate by separating the pseudobulbs (seed is possible, but not practical for the home grower). Watch for scale—many orchids are sensitive to repeated oil or soap sprays for insect control. Individual plants may be treated by wiping scale off by hand using a dilute solution of insecticidal soap or horticultural oil.
SELECTIONS *C. aurantiaca* Vigorous, tall, slender, cylindrical stems terminate in two thick broad leaves that recurve. Bright orange flowers apppear in clusters. Flowering time is usually winter to spring. Must have strong light.
C. mossiae (Easter Orchid) Free-blooming with fragrant flowers to five inches or more; often in clusters of three to five. Flowers are light rose with frilled lip of crimson and rose and golden yellow markings. Blooms March through June.

CHAMAEDOREA BAMBOO PALM, REED PALM *Arecaceae*
Bamboo palms are native from Mexico to Central America. They are elegant, small, solitary or clustering palms well-suited to interior use. They are rela-

PSEUDOBULBS
Many epiphytic orchids have special structures called pseudobulbs used for storage of moisture and food. These structures are thickened stems, usually light green, that vary in shape from globe to pear to spindle-shaped. They emerge from creeping ground stems or rhizomes and can be bare or leafy. Pseudobulbs left on the mother plant will often send up a flower shoot, but will flower only once. After flowering, pseudobulbs provide food for the rest of the plant, so should be left in place unless they are needed for propagation. Roots will grow from these pseudobulbs, so they are excellent structures for propagation.

Many houseplants are grown for their beautiful foliage to accent the home. Foliage plants come in a variety of sizes and shapes. Often, they need less light than flowering plants, making them adaptable to a wide variety of location. At right, bottom row: aucuba, dieffenbachia, calathea, dracaena; tall plant in second row: dracaena.

tively slow-growing and are commonly used in shopping malls and hotels.

Bamboo palms perform well in low to medium light and should be allowed to dry slightly between soakings. They need average temperatures of 65-80° F. and will not tolerate drying winds. They may be kept in the same pot for many years in an average potting mix that drains well, but should be potted up to a larger size when watering demands increase. Fertilize bamboo palms three times in the summer and prune only when needed for aesthetics. Mealybugs usually appear with the flowers and mites are a possibility in dry conditions with low humidity. Bamboo palms can be propagated by seed and by rhizome division. Gardeners at The New York Botanical Garden find that slow-release fertilizers (3-1-3) are very effective.

SELECTIONS *C. elegans* (Parlor Palm) Dwarf palm that is relatively fast growing. Stems are slender, to six feet tall, crowned with a cluster of leaves that are spirally arranged. Small yellow flowers are followed by black fruit. Flowering stem turns from green to bright red.

C. metallica (Miniature Fishtail Palm) This native of Mexico is an uncommon dwarf palm growing to three feet with dark bluish-green forked leaves. The leaves are broad and coarse compared with slender stems. It is commonly sold in groups of three stems per pot and is quite appropriate for small spaces. It is generally underused because of its scarcity. It may have a problem with mites and mealybugs, especially during flowering.

C. seifrizii (Bamboo Palm) These tall, narrow palms are often confused with bamboo because of the straight cylindrical stems that are generated below soil level. The narrow leaflets are also reminiscent of bamboo. Arching flower stalks appear from beneath papery covering at the nodes along the stems. They adapt well to a home environment because of their small stature. Remove the old and dry papery leaf sheaths to eliminate a hiding place for insects.

CHRYSALIDOCARPUS LUTESCENS ARECA PALM, YELLOW PALM

Arecaceae

The genus contains only one species that is ornamental and suited to interiorscape. This is a clump-forming palm with gracefully arching fronds of light green. Older stems become decoratively ringed with leaf scars. It reaches twenty feet in large tubs indoors but can be kept shorter by removing older, taller stems. Narrow leaflets and clumps of new growth around the base give this plant a light, airy texture. This plant changes its character as it matures. Young plants have an almost grassy appearance and are yellow, hence the common name. Given the proper care, the stems become stiff and palmlike as they mature.

Areca palms require medium to high light, average to hot temperatures, and evenly moist soil. They will not tolerate drying winds, cold drafts, or constant cool temperatures. They do well when potbound, so repot in an average, well-drained mix only when watering becomes a problem. Fertilize infrequently and prune selectively when grooming. Yellowing and tip burn occur when the palms are underwatered or overfertilized, and they may have prob-

PLANTS IN THE BEDROOM

Contrary to some old myths, sleeping with plants in the bedroom is good for your health. Plants use the byproduct of human respiration, carbon dioxide, to produce their own byproduct, oxygen, which we all use. Besides, research has shown that plants do a remarkable job of cleaning the air. NASA has studied plants for use in absorbing carcinogenic toxins such as benzene, formaldehyde, and trichloroethlyne from the air. According to the study, eight to fifteen plants will help improve the air substantially in an average home. Plants that filter the best include philodendron, spider plant, golden pothos, bamboo plant, corn plant, sansevieria, dracaena, spathiphyllum, English ivy, and chrysanthemum. So, bring your plants to bed with you and you'll wake up refreshed and cleansed!

lems with mealybugs, scale, and particularly mites. Fluoride toxicity also causes tip burn. Propagate by division or seed.

CHLOROPHYTUM SPIDER PLANT *Liliaceae*

Chlorophytum is a large genus from Africa, South America, Asia, and Australia of which only a few are cultivated. They are easily grown, easily propagated, and are rewarding houseplants that are popular because of the types of variegation available. These plants have been the topic of much publicity concerning clean air indoors. They are said to filter toxins from the air. The National Space Technology Lab has found that spider plants are superb plants for filtering nitrogen and formaldehyde from the air. The average home requires fifteen plants to filter all the formaldehyde emitted from synthetic products used in home construction.

Spider plants perform best in medium light and average to cool temperatures. The soil should be allowed to dry out briefly between waterings–spider plants have coarse roots that tend to fill the pot quickly. Repot in average potting mix when the pot fills with plantlets. Fertilize three times in summer and prune selectively when grooming. Propagate by seed or plantlets. They may be bothered by scale or mites, particularly if water stressed.

SELECTIONS *C. comosum* (Common Spider Plant) Light to medium green, same habit and texture as variegated types; easy to grow and can be weedy.

***C. comosum* 'Variegatum'** Yellow edged form favored by collectors.

***C. comosum* 'Vittatum'** (Variegated Spider Plant) Commonly seen in hanging baskets, this plant is so easy to propagate that it will fill a ten-inch basket in no time. The leaves are curved with a central white stripe. This plant is sensitive to overwatering and fluoride in public water systems, which can cause tip burn.

CISSUS GRAPE IVY *Vitaceae*

Cissus are mostly climbing or shrubby plants that usually have tendrils and small, inconspicuous flowers. They are natives of the tropics and subtropics and are grown for their lush foliage. Some species have hairy leaves. These commonly available and extremely popular plants have been in cultivation since houseplants became popular. Cissus require medium light, average to hot temperatures, and must dry out slightly between waterings. They will tolerate low light if kept on the dry side all the time. They will not tolerate drying winds. Repotting is rarely necessary since they will tolerate the same pot for a long time. Fertilize infrequently and remove leaves as they yellow; they tolerate pruning quite well, and regular pinching keeps them full. Propagate by stem cuttings or seed (some species can be difficult to propagate).

SELECTIONS *C. adenopoda* (Pink Cissus) has olive-green leaves, densely covered with rosy hairs; exceptional for hanging basket.

C. antarctica (Kangaroo Vine) has a stemmy, stiff habit. Fast-growing; ideal for a cool, bright location with lots of air space.

C. discolor (Rex Begonia Vine) Climbing plant with five-inch-long toothed, dark green and silvery white leaves. Petioles are wine red, and occasionally leaves have wine-colored blotches between the veins.

CHRYSALIDOCARPUS LUTESCENS (ARECA PALM) Two to ten feet; medium to high light and average to hot temperatures; evenly moist soil; will not tolerate drying winds; fertilize infrequently; average growing.

CHLOROPHYTUM COMOSUM 'VITTATUM' (VARIEGATED SPIDER PLANT) Two feet wide; filter nitrogen and formaldehyde from the air; medium light and average to cool temperatures; dry out briefly between waterings; fertilize three

CISSUS RHOMBIFOLIA (GRAPE IVY) Performs well in ten-inch hanging basket; medium light and average to hot temperatures; dry out slightly between waterings; will tolerate low light if kept on the dry side all the time; fertilize infrequently; fast growing.

CODIAEUM VARIEGATUM VAR. PICTUM 'CORKSCREW' (CORKSCREW CROTON) Four feet tall; high light and medium to warm temperatures; high humidity; medium growth rate.

Above: Croton foliage.
Opposite: Hawaiian ti plant.

C. quadrangula Odd, four-angled stems produce leaves only occasionally; some-what succulent; grown as a curiosity.

***C. rhombifolia* 'Ellen Danica'** (Oak Leaf Ivy) Similar to 'Manda Supreme' except leaf margins are deeply cut, resembling an oak leaf.

***C. rhombifolia* 'Manda Supreme'** (Manda Supreme Grape Ivy) has broader, more curved leaves than the species. It is dark green with reddish brown stems and tendrils. It makes a handsome pedestal or hanging-basket plant. It has a ten-dency to become woody and unproductive over time, so renew it regularly by starting cuttings or cutting back severely to regenerate growth.

C. striata (Dwarf Grape Ivy) Reddish stems with tiny five-fingered leaves; long-lived appealing small hanging plant.

CODIAEUM CROTON *Euphorbiaceae*

The *Codiaeum* genus is a group of six species of evergreen shrubs of which only one species is cultivated for ornamental use. Hundreds of cultivars are offered, most sold unlabeled. Variety in leaf shape and size adds to the visual interest.

Crotons require medium to warm temperatures, high humidity, and good light (from soil level to crown in order to remain full and keep its color varia-tions). Avoid cold drafts and high-traffic areas because the brittle leaves are easily damaged. The mark of excellent culture is a plant with leaves held intact from top to bottom. Place outside in summer in protected area if possi-ble. Repotting is needed infrequently because of its tolerance of a small pot in relation to its size. Use average, well-drained potting mix. Propagate by stem cuttings or air layering and prune when necessary to maintain attractive form (be careful not to get the staining sap on your clothes). Remove flowers imme-diately to avoid attracting mealybugs. Thrips, mealybugs, scale and mites can be a problem. Thrips, in particular, are difficult to detect because of the vivid leaf colors. Early detection is essential for control.

SELECTIONS *C. variegatum* var. *pictum* (Croton) has stiff leathery leaves in bright col-ors that are held on stems by knobby leaf petioles.

***C. variegatum* var. *pictum* 'Corkscrew'** (Corkscrew Croton) This lively-looking plant has long, narrow, twisted leaves of yellow and several shades of red with a lit-tle green peeking out here and there to assure you that it is not a fake. It can grow to four feet in the right spot–a curious plant that tends to look artificial in certain situations.

***C. variegatum* var. *pictum* 'Norma'** Grown exclusively for its wide range of color–broad, boldly marked leaves of yellow, red, and burgundy. Easily con-fused with ***C. variegatum* var. *pictum* 'Petra'**, a cultivar that is widely used.

COLUMNEA GOLDFISH PLANT *Gesneriaceae*

These relatives of the African violet are epiphytic shrubs or vine plants native to tropical America. Most species have neatly arranged pairs of leaves forming a distinctly patterned backdrop for highly contrasting vibrantly colored flow-ers. They are more difficult to bring into flower than African violets, but are immensely rewarding when they do flower.

Columnea require medium light and warmth. Elevated humidity encourages flowering. Keep evenly moist during active growing time and allow to dry between waterings in winter. Use tepid water to avoid unsightly leaf scarring. Columnea will not tolerate drying winds, cold drafts, or low humidity. They should be fertilized three times in summer and need repotting annually with an average, well-drained mix. They will occasionally have a problem with mealybugs and thrips when in flower. Columneas can be propagated by stem cuttings rooted in soil or water.

SELECTIONS *C. arguta* Native to Panama, the leaves are smaller and more sharply pointed than other species. The flowers are two inches long and orange-red with yellow markings in the throat.

C. gloriosa '**Superba**' This goldfish plant has blackish-maroon succulent leaves that literally glow with a covering of reddish-purple fuzz. The attractive, delicately small foliage gives no clue to the explosive three-inch red flowers that appear even on young plants. It is slow-growing but well worth the wait.

C. '**Volcano**' One of the easier cultivars to bring into bloom. It has large orange, red, and yellow hooded flowers that leap out from the foliage. The leaves are small with a distinct midrib. It does not branch well, so many cuttings should potted together for a full hanging basket. When not in flower, this plant, as with many columneas, does not attract more than a passing glance.

C. '**Yellow Dragon**' A well-branched plant with reddish leaves and bright yellow and red flowers.

Nemanthus gregarius This species is closely related to columnea. A dense-growing vine with small, rigid shiney leaves. Frequently exhibits small orange and yellow goldfishlike flowers.

CORDYLINE *Agavaceae (Liliaceae)*

Often confused with dracaenas, these plants are usually offered with multiple plants in a single pot. (Cordylines have creeping, knobby white roots; dracaena roots are non-creeping and bright orange-yellow.) The stems are heavily marked with decorative leaf scars. Easily grown from cuttings, this plant is commonly offered to tourists in tropical areas as small stem sections ("logs") of good luck or Hawaiian ti plant.

Cordylines require medium light and average temperatures. Leaf spotting or tip burn may occur from low humidity and cool temperatures. Leaf yellowing is caused by overwatering. Fertilize three times in summer and keep evenly moist. Allow soil to dry between waterings in winter. Repot infrequently because keeping the plant rootbound encourages shoots to appear from the roots. Propagate by stem cuttings, root cuttings, or seed. Prune when needed for grooming and be alert for mealybugs, mites, and scale.

SELECTIONS *C. indivisa* Lance-shaped leaves to six feet in length that are green above and bluish beneath.

C. terminalis (Hawaiian Ti, Good Luck Plant) Native to east Asia and Polynesia, the ti plant is useful as well as decorative. It is used for thatching, skirts, and cording in Hawaii in addition to being a product for the tourist trade. Broad leaves taper and wrap around straight gray stems. Older leaves are shed, leaving raised leaf scars on decorative stems, giving it a palmlike appearance.

C. terminalis '**Kiwi**' Brightly variegated with longitudinal stripes of various widths of pink-red, yellow, and light green.

COLORATION IN FOLIAGE

We often choose houseplants for attractive foliage, particularly if it offers a variety of colors. The standard foliage color is green, so any variation on this theme adds interest to the design scheme.

Foliage comes in all colors, from blue to gray to red to pink to white to yellow. Each color appears because of the chemical make-up of the plant. Pigments called anthocyanins are responsible for blues and reds, and carotenoids are responsible for yellows and oranges. Chlorophyll, which usually dominates, is responsible for the green color. If the other pigments are brilliant enough, they mask the chlorophyll and give the striking hues we see on such plants as ti plants and bromeliads. These pigments are often intensified by light, giving brighter colors as with the croton. In low light, not only does the color fade, but so does the variegation.

Pale blue, whitish, or gray foliage is often a product of very fine hairs or a waxy bloom that covers the leaves. Pure white areas on variegated leaves are devoid of pigments, including food-producing chlorophyll. White coloration, particularly on succulent plants, usually suggests the plant is native to areas that are extremely hot and bright.

CODIAEUM VARIEGATUM VAR. PICTUM 'NORMA' (NORMA CROTON)
Four feet tall; high light and medium to warm temperatures; high humidity; medium growth rate.

COLUMNEA GLORIOSA 'VOLCANO' (GOLDFISH PLANT) Stems may grow to ten feet long; medium light and warmth; elevated humidity encourages flowering; evenly moist during active growing time and dry between waterings in winter; fertilize three times in summer; slow growing.

NEMANTHUS GREGARIUS (GOLDFISH VINE) Wiry stems grow to two feet; medium light and warmth; keep evenly moist during active growth but dryer in winter. Fertilize three times in summer. Slow growing.

CORDYLINE TERMINALIS CV. (HAWAIIAN TI, GOOD LUCK PLANT)
May grow to five feet; medium light and average temperatures (will not tolerate low humidity or cool temperatures); fertilize three times in summer; keep evenly moist; slow growing.

CURCULIGO PALM GRASS *Hypoxidaceae*

These evergreen perennials from the tropics are grown mostly for their palm-like foliage. Thick rhizomes produce dense clusters of narrow, sometimes pleated leaves. Small, inconspicuous yellow flowers appear at the base of the plants.

Palm grass requires medium light and average to hot temperatures. (It also does fairly well in low light at The New York Botanical Garden.) It should be kept evenly moist and fertilized three times in summer. It does not tolerate drying winds or cold drafts. Tip browning may occur in low humidity. Low light and soil dryness will produce weak growth. Pot in an average, well-drained potting mix and prune only when necessary for grooming. Propagate by rhizome division or seed.

SELECTIONS *C. capitulata (C. recurvata)* Pleated leaves to three feet long are reminiscent of an immature palm. At the widest point, the leaves are six inches, tapering to a point at the outside edge, held on stiff petioles that arch to the ground–a decidedly tropical effect.

CYANOTIS *Commelinaceae*

This genus from the tropics and subtropics gets it name from terminal blue (*kyanos*) flowers (*anthos*). These creeping, trailing, weak-stemmed plants are similar to the more familiar tradescantia (Spiderwort). The leaves are small and alternate. Frequently the stem is totally concealed by the leaf bases.

Give cyanotis medium light, average temperatures, and keep the soil evenly moist at all times. Fertilize three times in summer and prune only selectively when grooming–these plants do not branch well. Also, the stems are succulent and snap easily, so keep them away from high-traffic areas. These plants need to be started over from fresh cuttings annually. The center tends to die out, many times from the weight of the stems as they elongate. Repot in average, well-drained potting mix. These plants are virtually pest-free although they may have occasional mealybugs. Propagate by stem cuttings in soil or water. At New York Botanical Garden, these plants are used for hanging baskets; they are pruned to the edge of pot or basket, and not restarted annually.

SELECTIONS *C. kewensis* (Teddy Bear Vine) Native to southern India, the fuzzy, overlapping leaves grow in two ranks along a fragile stem. These stems, large or small, break off easily. The leaves are olive green above and reddish below, giving an overall red-green appearance. Pinching helps keep the center of the plant attractive, but inevitably, the plant must be started over from cuttings.

C. somaliensis (Pussy Ears) Bright green leaves covered with longish white hairs; slightly more succulent than *C. kewensis*.

CYRTOMIUM *Polypodiaceae*

This genus consists of about ten species of ferns native to southeast Asia and Polynesia. They have scaly rhizomes and the sori are large, scattered or patterned, and generally decorative. The fronds are arching with distinct segments, quite asymmetrical in shape.

Provide medium light and average to cool temperatures if possible.

EPIPHYTES

Epiphytes are unique plants which use other plants or rocks for support instead of soil. They are often found high in the canopy of the rain forest where there is light. They obtain water and minerals from the humid air of the canopy and from debris that has settled and decayed in crevices where the plants are attached. They cling to their support with aerial roots and are not parasitic. This special group includes orchids, bromeliads, some cactus and ferns, among others.

Epiphytes are usually grown in the home on slabs of wood to which sphagnum moss has been attached or in pots of very loose bark. Roots of epiphytes must have air around them or the plant suffers noticeably. Therefore, coarse, well-draining soil is essential. These conditions resemble their natural habitats. Moisture is provided by wetting the bark or moss and by frequent misting of the leaves, again mimicking their native situations.

Cyanotis kewensis.

Cyrtomium ferns are quite tolerant of cold and warm interiors. Keep the soil evenly moist, provide adequate humidity, and avoid drying winds. Repot mature plants annually in order to maintain desired size. Use a peaty, moisture-retentive potting mix. Fertilize infrequently and prune only as a selective part of grooming. The plants are easily propagated from spores or rhizome division. Watch especially for thrips; mealybugs and scale may also be problems.
SELECTIONS *C. falcatum* (Holly Fern) A fern with stiffly arching, dark green fronds. Pinnae ("leaflets") are glossy, wavy-edged, and pointed—hence the common name. The stems are hairy and rich red-brown. This is a good fern for the home since it doesn't require high humidity and can survive dehydration now and them.
C. falcatum var. *rochfordianum* (Fringed Holly Fern) Similar to the species except leaves have closely fringed margins.
C. fortunei Smaller overall than holly fern and more cold-hardy.

DICKSONIA TREE FERN *Dicksoniaceae*
The tree ferns are native to the mountains of the tropics and the warm temperate regions of the southern hemisphere. They are generally single-trunked, several feet tall, and have very large fronds.

Grow tree ferns in partial shade in average temperatures (although they will tolerate warm temperatures). Direct sun may burn the foliage, especially if the air is dry. Keep the soil evenly moist—the fronds will be damaged if allowed to wilt. Tree ferns benefit from daily misting of the foliage, especially in winter when the home is dry. If feasible, place outside in the shade during the summer. Use a slow-release fertilizer in spring only. Pot in rich, organic potting soil with added peat moss and leaf mold. Remove old leaves as necessary. Propagate by spores—it will take many years to have a sizable plant. Watch for mealybugs and scale.
SELECTIONS *D. squarrosa* (Rough New Zealand Tree Fern) reaches about six feet indoors; the trunk is black and covered with old leaf bases. Has divided green fronds with blackish petioles.
D. antarctica (Tasmanian Tree Fern) grows to five feet or more.

DIEFFENBACHIA DUMB CANE *Araceae*
Dumb canes are tropical-looking plants from tropical America and the West Indies that are seen frequently in interior landscapes. Delightfully patterned foliage and a range of leaf and plant sizes offer a wide palette of color and texture. Stems and leaf midribs are brittle and snap easily. The sap is irritating and can be poisonous (it also smells bad). Dumb Canes lose their lower leaves in insufficient light and with maturity, giving ample opportunity to try propagating by air layering.

Dieffenbachia require medium light, average temperatures, medium to high humidity, and should be allowed to dry briefly between waterings. Fertilize three times in summer and keep out of drying winds and cold drafts. Repot annually while small in an average mix, but as plant matures, take cut-

CURCULIGO CAPITULATA [C. RECURVATA] (PALM GRASS) Leaves to three feet long; medium light and average to hot temperatures; evenly moist; fertilize three times in summer; tip browning may occur in low humidity; moderate growth rate.

CYANOTIS KEWENSIS (TEDDY BEAR VINE) Eight-inch hanging basket; medium light and average temperatures; evenly moist at all times; fertilize three times in summer; start over from cuttings regularly; fairly fast growing.

CYRTOMIUM FALCATUM (HOLLY FERN) Fronds up to two feet long; medium light; average to cool temperatures; evenly moist, high humidity; fertilize infrequently; moderately fast growing.

DICKSONIA SQUARROSA (ROUGH NEW ZEALAND TREE FERN) About six feet; medium light and average temperatures (will tolerate warm temperatures); direct sun may burn the foliage; evenly moist; benefit from daily misting; slow release fertilizer in spring only; slow growing.

Eucharis grandiflora.

tings and start new plants. Old canes may be removed in summer, and new shoots will appear at the cut. Prune as necessary for grooming and be on the lookout for mealybugs, scale, and mites, particularly when in flower or in lower humidity.

SELECTIONS *D. amoena* Large variety that is frequently available.

D. maculata A great clustering species, much used in interior landscaping.

D. 'Bali Hai' One of the toughest of the dieffenbachias. It stands up better to physical abuse than others of its size. The leaves tend to actively point upward and show off the distinctly bright white and green markings. The stems are also heavily marked with white. Interior landscapers are choosing this variety more often due to its tolerance for being sleeved and unsleeved without damage. Will grow to three feet with vertical, rigid, heavy stems. Older canes may be removed and side shoots allowed to fill the gaps.

D. 'Forest' Small cultivar that performs well in a small pot; it produces many side shoots.

D. 'Triumph' Small cultivar with lime green and cream centers of leaves edged in green. Similar in stature to *D.* 'Forest'.

D. 'Tropic Snow' Large variety with broad ivory splotches.

DIZYGOTHECA FALSE ARALIA *Araliaceae*

This group consists of about fifteen species of small shrubs or trees from Australasia. They all have compound leaves, and the species that is grown in the home is generally appreciated for its graceful juvenile foliage.

False aralia performs best in the medium light of an east or west window and in average home temperatures. The soil must be kept evenly moist–water just as the topsoil begins to dry out (too much dryness causes leaf drop). Overwatering may cause root rot. High humidity is beneficial. Pot in an average potting soil and fertilize during the growing season with standard houseplant fertilizer. As the tree grows and matures, the leaf pattern changes. The leaf "fingers" will become broad and flat and the notched edges more rounded. Pruning the plant back will produce new growth that is again juvenile in appearance. This pruning can be done any time the foliage starts to change. False aralia may have problems with soft brown scale, spider mites, and mealybugs. This is a good candidate for air layering or stem cuttings to propagate.

SELECTIONS *D. elegantissima* (False Aralia) grows from four to six feet indoors. Its palmately compound leaves are dark green, almost black, and heavily notched. They resemble a hand with long skinny fingers. Its multiple trunks add grace and elegance to the home setting. (Missouri)

EUCHARIS AMAZON LILY *Amaryllidaceae*

Daffodil-like fragrant flowers of pure white contrast with broad dark green leaves. This native of tropical South America is easy to grow and easy to bring into flower. It is bulbous by nature, and the group does not require the distinct lengthy dormancy of many members of this family. It has the potential to be used more in the interior landscape as long as its culture is understood.

Dry periods following new growth can trigger multiple flowering periods throughout the year. Give it medium light, average to warm temperatures (not below 60° F. at night, although a specimen at University of California Botanical Gardens at Berkeley has survived nights of 45-50° F.), and keep it away from drying winds and cold drafts. Fertilize it infrequently and repot every couple of years in average soil as the pot fills with roots and bulbs. Prune only as needed for grooming and propagate by dividing the bulbs. Keep a watch for mites and mealybugs.

SELECTIONS *E. grandiflora* Shiny rich green leaves are broad and arching. The plant does quite well in a six- to eight-inch pot. White fragrant flowers are held on upright hollow stems with multiple flowers per stem. The shape of the flower is similar to narcissus except that the filments are fused at the base, forming the cup part of the flower. It is an undemanding plant—elegant in foliage and flower.

FICUS FIG *Moraceae*

The figs, native to tropical and subtropical regions, are in a genus of great variety that has been used for many years in the home and conservatory. All members of the genus have a milky sap, or latex, and many also produce fruits, some of which are edible. (The sap is easily removed from hands with an industrial mechanics' hand cleaner, but will permanently stain clothing.) The flowers are interesting botanically, but are not much visually. Aerial roots may be produced along the stems of some of the large species, adding visual interest.

Most ficus will adapt to low, medium, or high light and have varying water

Several species of vining ficus, such as *Ficus repens* 'Variegata' (which is shown at left) are well-suited to topiary techniques. Unlike its cousin the weeping fig, this vining ficus is easily trained around a wire form and fills in quickly.

DIEFFENBACHIA MACULATA (DUMB CANE) Three feet; medium light and average temperatures; medium to high humidity; dry briefly between waterings; fertilize three times in summer; sap is irritating and can be poisonous; slower growing than other dieffenbachias.

DIZYGOTHECA ELEGANTISSIMA (FALSE ARALIA) Four to six feet; medium light; average temperatures; evenly moist, high humidity; fertilizer during growing season; slow growing.

EUCHARIS GRANDIFLORA (AMAZON LILY) To 20 inches high; medium light and average to warm temperatures (not below 60° F at night); dry periods following new growth can trigger multiple flowering periods throughout the year; fertilize infrequently; slow growing.

FICUS BENJAMINA (WEEPING FIG) Can grow to twenty feet if not pruned; medium to high light and average temperatures; milky sap or latex; dry between soakings; fertilize three times in the summer or less frequently if you are trying to control growth; fast growing.

requirements. The small-leaved vining species require evenly moist soil and are less tolerant of drying out between soakings than the tree forms. Average temperatures should keep most ficus in good condition. It is important to acquire plants that have been properly acclimated to interior use. If not, massive leaf drop will occur before subsequent regrowth. Careful watering is a must during this period of adjustment. Repotting into more moisture-retentive soil is often required once the plant leafs out. Pot size may be used to inhibit the growth of larger plants. Smaller types need frequent repotting into peaty, moisture-retentive soil to avoid dehydration. Most ficus species should be fertilized three times in the summer or less frequently if you are trying to control growth. Ficus species tolerate pruning well. Some only have to be groomed and selectively pruned while others may need annual pruning to control size and to allow light to penetrate to the center of the plant. Most ficus are susceptible to mealybugs, mites, and scale if not properly cultivated. See individual species for more information. Ficus can be propagated by stem cuttings or seed.

SELECTIONS *F. acaulis* (Clown Fig) Shrubby plant with eight-inch leaves that are mottled ivory white and sometimes in pink; the fruit is the same color.

F. benjamina (Weeping Fig) This tree form is native to tropical Asia and is one of the oldest plants used for commercial interior landscapes. Light green small leaves and beautiful light gray bark adorn this tree, which has a dramatic weeping form if pruned properly. It can grow to twenty feet if not pruned to keep it small. It requires medium to high light and can be maintained at six to seven feet with annual or biannual pruning (prune large branches instead of tip pruning to maintain proper shape). Root pruning should be done every third year to maintain pot size; take one-third off top and one-third off roots. Weeping fig has an attractive habit and is easy to grow but will shed leaves if moved from its established spot or the existing conditions are changed. It may fruit heavily under good conditions. The fruits are smaller than a marble, dry, and produced in great numbers, sometimes a litter problem.

F. deltoidea (Mistletoe Fig) Native to Malaysia, mistletoe fig is a slow-growing, continuously fruiting plant. The leaves of mistletoe fig are triangular in shape, which gives the plant a distinctive look. It grows to two feet as a shrub but may be trained to a slightly taller standard. The fruits are decorative and drop only when they are dry. This is a good candidate for use in bonsai and topiary standards.

F. elastica (Rubber Tree) gets quite large but tolerates pruning; available in several cultivars with attractive variegated leaves.

F. montana (Oak Leaf Fig) Native to the Malay Archipelago and southeast Asia. A coarse, horizontal, wiry vining ground cover with leaves like sandpaper that resemble those of white oak. Leaves are a rich, dark green. This ficus fruits easily and is best suited to in-ground planters or wide shallow pots. It tolerates low light and heavy pruning. It will be pest-free if properly cultivated. This is an unusual plant that is available through mail order-sources—it is difficult to imagine it as a ficus.

F. nitida **'Green Gem'** (Green Gem Fig) A tough, low-light tree that has good leaf-

LONGEVITY IN PLANTS

Plants, like all living things, have a finite life span—some longer, some shorter, but plants do die of old age. A philodendron passed from parent to child over generations will one day decline and die. The caretaker of this heirloom will feel guilty and wonder what went wrong. It very well may be that nothing was done to kill the plant, it just reached the end of its life span. Some plants (like marigolds or petunias) live only one year and die (these are called annuals and are not covered in this book); others give pleasure for many years. The most common cause of plant death is not old age, but lack of understanding of the specific needs of the plants.

Ficus lyrata.

holding power during extended periods of dim light. This is a broader-leaved tree than *F. benjamina* yet has the same beautiful light gray bark. It doesn't weep as dramatically as *F. benjamina* and has the potential of being a large tree, although it may be kept small with pruning. Mealybugs, scale, and thrips can appear, but none is a real threat.

F. petiolaris Native to Mexico, these plants have great potential for bonsai. As a young plant the trunk is quite swollen at the soil level and tapers to the point at which broad heart-shaped leaves appear. The leaf veins may be pink in full sun. It may be pruned to keep it around four feet tall in a container. These plants are fun for a caudiciform or arid plant collection and are occasionally seen in grocery store floral departments in bonsai pots.

F. pumila (Creeping Fig) Creeping figs are perfect for the topiary beginner. This creeping, small-leaved plant has medium to dark green leaves on trailing slender stems. These also make excellent groundcovers under large potted plants. Easy to care for if kept moist, they are tolerant of low light and do well when pruned frequently. Great variety in color and texture are available in the many cultivars and bring topiary animals alive. Restarting plants annually lowers potential for infestation.

F. pumila 'Minima' The leaves resemble the species except that they are much smaller and appear quilted.

F. pumila 'Quercifolia' This is a really smart-looking tiny three-lobed type.

F. pumila 'Snowflake' A border of white distinctly sets this apart from other creeping figs. The leaves are three-quarter-inch long on wiry stems.

F. repens 'Variegata' Leaves longer and larger than *F. pumila,* with white markings and similar habit.

F. triangularis 'Variegata' (Sweetheart Tree) has thick triangular variegated leaves, green to cream with whitish margins; fairly slow grower.

F. 'Jacqueline' Excellent variegated-leaf tree form for full-sun area. The form resembles *F. benjamina*, but the leaves are variegated green and white.

FITTONIA NERVE PLANT *Acanthaceae*

Fittonia is a group of evergreen perennial creeping plants from the rain forests of Peru, Brazil, and Colombia. Fittonias are exceptional foliage plants because of their intricate leaf markings. Their small size makes them good candidates for dish gardens and terrariums.

Grow fittonia in medium light in moderate to warm temperatures. Keep the soil evenly moist and avoid drying and sunny situations. Plant in a small pot in rich, organic potting soil. Fertilize once a month with a balanced fertilizer. Pinch regularly to keep the plant bushy and full. Propagate by seed, division, or cuttings. Although fittonia is resistant to most pests, watch for occasional mealybugs.

SELECTIONS F. verschaffeltii (Nerve Plant) Creeping plant that grows about six inches high. Has olive green leaves with reddish pink veins and long fuzzy stems. Small, yellow flowers add very little to the overall appearance.

F. verschaffeltii var. argyroneura 'Minima' (Silver Nerve, Net Plant) Grows only one-

FICUS DELTOIDEA (MISTLETOE FIG) Grows to three feet after many years; medium to high light and average temperatures; milky sap or latex; dry between soakings; fertilize three times in the summer or less frequently if you are trying to control growth; slow growing.

FICUS MONTANA (OAK LEAF FIG) Prostrate growth to eighteen inches wide; low light; and average temperatures; fertilize three times in the summer; slow-growing; sap may permanently stain clothing; slow growing.

FICUS NITIDA 'GREEN GEM' (GREEN GEM FIG) Four to twelve feet; low light and average temperatures; milky sap or latex; dry between soakings; fertilize three times in the summer or less frequently if you are trying to control growth; moderate to fast growing.

FICUS PETIOLARIS Four feet tall; medium to high light and average temperatures; milky sap or latex; dry between soakings; fertilize three times in the summer or less frequently if you are trying to control growth; slow to moderate growth rate.

The flowers of *Gardenia jasminoides* are beautiful and richly fragrant.

half-inch high; light green leaves with white veins grow to one-and-one-half inches long. It is mat-forming and will spread one to two feet across. (University of California Botanical Garden, Berkeley)

GARDENIA *Rubiaceae*

Native to Asia and Africa, there are more than 200 evergreen shrubs or trees in this genus. They all have opposite or whorled dark green leaves. Fragrant flowers appear singularly or in pairs and have dense petals of white or cream. Gardenias are seldom easy to grow in a home because of their intense need for humidity.

Gardenias require medium light and average temperatures although they will grow well in cool (50-55° F.), well-lighted situation. (Gardeners at Blithewold Gardens have found that they tend to become chlorotic if grown below 55-60°F.). They must be kept evenly moist at all times and should be fertilized frequently during the summer with an acid fertilizer. They can be moved outdoors for the summer, although they have a tendency to lose leaves when making the transition. They will generally leaf out again if sufficient light, fertilizer, and humidity are provided. Gardenias tolerate pruning well and should be regularly trimmed in late winter or early spring after blooming. When they are pruned, they may be root pruned and returned to the same-size pot in order to maintain a certain size. Pot in a peaty, moisture-retentive acid potting mix. Propagate when desired by stem cuttings. Watch for scale, mites, thrips, aphids, and mealybugs, particularly when flowering or in low humidity.

SELECTIONS *G. jasminoides* (Common Gardenia) from China, is grown for its heavily scented, large, many petaled flowers that bruise easily. The foliage is shiny and dense, making a rich stage for flower presentation. Can grow to six feet in a conservatory. Many large plants are grafted for more vigorous flower production.

G. jasminoides 'Prostrata', a small-leaved variety that grows more horizontally and has smaller, but no less handsome flowers. Sometimes offered as *G. radicans* and often cultivated for bonsai.

GYNURA *Asteraceae*

Gynuras are native from Africa to eastern Asia and Malaysia. These members of the aster family are grown in the home for their decorative foliage—the flowers are fairly insignificant. Gynuras are easy to grow and propagate. One species commonly grown is shrubby; the other is vining, making an attractive hanging basket.

Good, medium light intensifies the color in the foliage. Provide average to cool temperatures and keep the soil evenly moist except in winter when watering should be reduced. Fertilize three times in summer and pinch frequently to keep the center full and inhibit flowers. Start new plants every year or two from cuttings. Be sure to remove the flowers since they smell bad. Propagate by stem cuttings in soil or water. Watch for occasional mealybugs.

FICUS PUMILA 'SNOWFLAKE' (CREEPING FIG) Mat-forming, to two inches high; low light and average temperatures; keep moist; fast growing.

FICUS TRIANGULARIS 'VARIEGATA' To ten inches; medium light; broad temperature range (will drop leaves if conditions change drastically); evenly moist but will tolerate occasional dry periods; fertilize three times in summer; average growth rate.

FITTONIA VERSCHAFFELTII VAR. ARGYRONEURA (NERVE PLANT) Six inches high; medium light and moderate to warm temperatures; evenly moist; avoid drying and sunny situations; fertilize once a month; moderate growth rate.

GARDENIA JASMINOIDES (COMMON GARDENIA) Can grow to six feet but usually only eighteen inches in the home; medium light and average temperatures (tolerates cool, well-lighted situations); evenly moist; high humidity; fertilize frequently during the summer with an acid fertilizer; slow growing.

SPORTS

Sometimes plants will send off a shoot that looks different from the rest of the plant. This is called a sport, and is usually due to a genetic mutation in that area of the plant. Sports can have a different color, different leaf shape, different variegation or no variegation, or any number of other characteristics. Sports are often used to propagate new and unusual varieties of plants. Sometimes a plant that is propagated from a sport will revert to its natural characteristics at some point. For example, a variegated sport from a solid green plant may be used to produce more variegated plants. It is possible that at some point, one of those variegated plants will begin sending out solid green shoots, reverting to its natural form.

SELECTIONS *G.* **'Purple Passion'** (Purple Passion) This is the most commonly available gynura and is grown for its purple, fuzzy foliage. The leaves are toothed, intense red-purple below and dark green with purple fuzz on the upper side. Stems cascade over sides of pot; does well in hanging basket

HAWORTHIA WINDOW PLANT *Liliaceae*

Haworthias make up a large group of succulents from South Africa that displays a wide range of color, texture, and plant sizes. They are easily kept in small pots on the windowsill, or they may be allowed to clump as in their natural habitats into large mounds of many plantlets. Stiff, sometimes hard leathery leaves are succulent and may be marked with raised wartlike bumps or transparent areas ("windows"). These plants deserve more attention as curious small windowsill plants. Many different types are available through mail-order sources.

Haworthias need medium to high light and should be allowed to dry between soakings. They tolerate average to high temperatures and perform best in low humidity levels. They may be fertilized three times in summer; pruning is unnecessary. They are extremely undemanding. If allowed to remain in the same pot for several years, many types will cover the soil with small plants or mound up over the sides of the pot. Use a coarse, fast-draining soil mix and propagate by separating offsets. Watch for mealybugs and scale.

SELECTIONS *H. tessellata* (Star Window Plant) This colorfully marked haworthia is one of the smaller species. Coloration and markings vary slightly from plant to plant, but all exhibit an overall pink color in good sunlight. Green and white cross-hatching interrupts the translucent upper surface of the basically triangular leaves, which form small rosettes to two inches across. The plants are rigidly succulent. This plant does well in a succulent dish garden—it will act as a colorful groundcover, sprouting up in many open areas of the garden.

H. truncata This stemless succulent has six to eight or more neatly arranged leaves in two rows opposite one another. The leaves are long and curve dramatically together at the base, with the top edge flattened and translucent. Overall, the plant is waxy and dark green. In nature it is buried in the ground with only the translucent "window" edge of the leaves exposed. It will clump with age.

HEDERA IVY *Araliaceae*

A painter's palette of color and texture is available in this group of easy-to-grow plants from Europe, western Asia, and northern Africa. Hederas have been successfully used as pot plants since Victorian times. They perform particularly well in cool environments. They are easily propagated by stem cuttings. Put multiple plants in a pot and pinch to make a full, beautiful hanging basket. Many hundreds of varieties of *H. helix* are available, from tiny-leaved forms to large, fancy ruffled varieties. White or gold flecks or splotches add to the selection.

Hederas perform best in medium light and cool temperatures. Plants grown in a particularly cool or cold location show a reddish blush overall and

GYNURA 'PURPLE PASSION' Cascading stems to two feet; medium light; average to cool temperatures; evenly moist; fertilize three times in summer; average growth rate.

HAWORTHIA TESSELLATA (STAR WINDOW PLANT) Small rosettes to two inches across; medium to high light and average to high temperatures; dry between soakings; low humidity levels; fertilize three times in summer; slow growing.

HAWORTHIA TRUNCATA To two-and-one-half inches; medium to high light and average to high temperatures; dry between soakings; low humidity levels; fertilize three times in summer; slow growing.

HEDERA CANARIENSIS (ALGERIAN IVY, CANARY IVY) Ten-inch hanging basket, leaves to six inches; medium light and cool temperatures; keep evenly moist and fertilize with a dilute solution at every watering; slow growing.

Hederas come in a wide range of shades and colors.

are much tougher than plants grown in warm situations. Their soil should be kept evenly moist, and they should be fertilized with a dilute solution every time they are watered during their active growing period. They need an average, well-drained potting mix and will grow into woody old plants if kept in the same pot for many years. Start new plants every two to three years to keep the plants vigorous and productive. Mites are a continual threat to hedera, particularly if the humidity is low. Also watch for aphids and mealybugs on new growth and scale on woody plants.

SELECTIONS *H. canariensis* (Algerian Ivy, Canary Ivy) This large-leaved, vigorous species is considered a nuisance outdoors in warm climates. The rich green leaves have reddish stems and petioles. The leaves are mostly three-lobed, coarse, and have long internodes. They do quite well in large hanging baskets but do not branch well when pinched. These make a great substitute for curtains although they are so vigorous they are sometimes difficult to keep moist.

H. canariensis **'Gloire de Marengo'** A cultivar with highly contrasting white marked leaves. Very susceptible to mites.

H. helix **'Calico'** White mottled leaves; medium sized. Tips may brown in low humidity and heat. A "must have" if you like ivies. When planted in the display houses at the Chicago Botanic Garden, this ivy received more attention than any other we used.

H. helix **'California Fan'** A large-leaved variety with wavy lobes. The medium green color grays in low humidity or high temperatures. This variety branches fairly well when pinched, but gets woody quickly and must be propagated every two years. It is a nice variety where a coarse texture is required.

H. helix **'Little Diamond'** A small-leaved cultivar with long, narrow, irregularly shaped leaves that are boldly marked with bright white. Not aggressive, this plant can be controlled easily in six-inch pots. It is a nice bright variety that is a little more difficult to grow due to its slowness and inconsistent branching habit.

H. helix **'Needlepoint'** has tiny, three-lobed dark green leaves—good topiary candidate.

HEMIGRAPHIS *Acanthaceae*

These spreading plants are native to tropical southeast Asia and Australia and are closely allied to ruellia. Only two species are commonly cultivated. The leaves are opposite and quite colorful, and the flowers are small and white. The plants have a similar habit and texture as Swedish ivy (plectranthus).

Hemigraphis performs best in medium light and average to high temperatures. The soil should be kept evenly moist, and fertilizer may be applied three times in summer. Try to keep the plant away from drying winds and cold drafts. Pot in an average, well-drained soil and repot annually. Also, start new plants every other year from stem cuttings (roots as easily as Swedish ivy) to maintain vigorous, attractive plants. Hemigraphis tolerates pruning well, so pinch periodically to keep full.

SELECTIONS *H. colorata (H. alternata)* (Red Ivy, Flame Ivy) Truly a plant of a different color—puckered leaves are metallic blue-gray-purple above and dark red-purple below. The plant grows in a spreading mound similar to Swedish ivy. It makes a beautiful display in a hanging basket. This hemigraphis has a narrow light range–suffers from high and low light. The color, not often seen in tropical plants, makes it stand out from other houseplants.

H. 'Red Equator' Small pointed metallic green leaves with burgundy undersides. Similar habit to *H. colorata,* but more compact.

HIPPEASTRUM AMARYLLIS *Amaryllidaceae*

This group of bulbous plants is native to Central and South America and have straplike leaves that follow showy six-petal flowers that appear on tall hollow stem. The plants often seen around holiday time are cultivars of *H.* x *ackermanii.*

Grow amaryllis in bright light and average to cool temperatures. Direct sun will scorch its leaves. Allow the plant to dry out briefly between soakings. Plant in a loamy, rich potting mix and fertilize with a balanced fertilizer during the growing season as new foliage appears. Remove old leaves when necessary and propagate by seed or division. The plant takes a long time to mature from seed. This plant is usually pest-free.

SELECTIONS *H. reticulatum* var. *striatifolium* (Stripe-leaf Amaryllis) This particular amaryllis is a bulbous terrestrial plant with beautiful one-foot-long strap-shaped dark green leaves with a distinct white midrib. The flowers are fragrant, rose-pink miniature amaryllis blossoms. The plant blooms in the fall (occasionally in summer).

HOMALOMENA DROP TONGUE *Araceae*

A group of plants from the ever-popular Araceae family, these natives of tropical Asia and South America are becoming more available in the trade as they are "discovered." Many have leaves marked similarly to aglaonema although they are broader and softer in texture. Some are also slower-growing.

These plants require humidity levels similar to anthuriums. Provide medium to low light and keep the soil evenly moist–the plants suffer noticeably when allowed to dry out. Average to high temperatures will suffice, and avoid drying winds and cold drafts. Fertilize infrequently. Pot in a peaty, moisture-retentive mix and repot when the stems fill the pot or the plant dries out too frequently. Annual repotting is recommended. Prune only selectively when grooming and propagate by rhizome division. Watch for mealybugs and mites.

SELECTIONS *H. calyptrata* Neat, suckering habit; silver-green tapering bands along the midribs of the leaves.

H. picturata Broad, heart-shaped leaves with silver-green markings that are heaviest near the tip of the leaf.

H. pygmaea var. *purpurascens* Small clumping type with bronze-purple pointed leaves that are reddish beneath. The leaves grow to six inches. Makes a nice five-inch pot in time.

H. sulcata Broad leaf blades, up to eight inches long, are green with coppery undersides. The plant grows to one and a half feet. It is a handsome, large clump-forming type suited for a humid environment. Low humidity will

FORCING BULBS

Forcing bulbs into flower involves gently stimulating a bulb's natural cycle, causing the bulb to act as if it had been through the dormant cycle of winter. Some garden centers offer bulbs that have already been cooled and need only to be planted and watered (a common example is paperwhite narcissus). It is easy, however, to do the cooling process yourself and stagger your planting times to have a continuous display.

In fall, select top-quality bulbs and plant in clean, sterile pots and potting soil. Plant tulips, hyacinth, and narcissus with their tips just above the soil line. Plant small bulbs such as scilla, dwarf iris, crocus, and grape hyacinth about one half inch below the soil line. Water thoroughly and put into cold storage at about 40-45° F. (window well, covered trench, unheated garage, refrigerator). After twelve to sixteen weeks, depending on the bulb, the bulbs should begin to produce pale sprouts. At this time, bring them into a bright, cool (55-65° F.) room. As soon as the flower buds begin to show color, place them for display.

After they have finished blooming, either discard them or remove only the flower stalks and put them in a bright windowsill for the rest of the winter. Although bulbs cannot be saved to force again the following winter, occasionally it is successful to plant them in the garden at their proper depth as soon as the soil can be worked. It is essential to keep the foliage on the plant indoors and feed it regularly to allow the bulb to store as much food as possible. Bulbs that survive outdoors will bloom the following spring (a year later).

Other types of bulbs such as caladium can be forced for their foliage. They do not need a cooling period–simply plant them in a pot of soil, water them well, and put them in a warm spot. Soon you will have beautiful multicolored foliage that adds a bright focus to any room.

HEDERA HELIX 'CALICO' Eight- to ten-inch basket, leaves to two inches wide; medium light and cool temperatures; keep evenly moist and fertilize with a dilute solution at every watering; medium growing.

HEMIGRAPHIS 'RED EQUATOR' To one foot; medium light and average to high temperatures; evenly moist; fertilize three times in summer; keep away from drying winds and cold drafts; medium growth rate.

HIPPEASTRUM RETICULATUM VAR. STRIATIFOLIUM (STRIPE-LEAF AMARYLLIS) Leaves about one foot long; high light, average temperatures; allow to dry between waterings; fertilize regularly when foliage appears; fast growth rate; has dormant period.

HOMALOMENA SULCATA (DROP TONGUE) Up to eighteen inches long; medium to low light and average to high temperatures; high humidity; evenly moist; fertilize infrequently; moderate growth rate.

cause the leaves to curl or look limp.

H. wallisii (Speckled Drop Tongue) Native to Venezuela, this is a short, spreading plant with medium green leaves irregularly marked with gold-green splotches. The leaves are broad and eight inches long on short petioles. It is similar in appearance to aglaonema and tends to wander in an open bed in a conservatory.

H. wallisii '**Camouflage**' A darker plant overall, with a more compact habit.

HOWEA *Arecaceae*

This genus consists of two species of palms that are named for the Lord Howe Islands where they are found. These handsome plants grow as solitary specimens with long arching stems. Both grow to be large plants in pots. In nature they grow to ten times the size of container-grown plants.

Medium to low light is preferable, as are cool temperatures, although howeas will tolerate average temperatures as well. Keep the soil evenly moist and hold back on watering in winter. These palms should not sit wet or dry, so repot to a larger size container when watering pressure becomes unmanageable. However, make sure the new container is only slightly larger (one to two inches) than the original pot. Use a mix that is well drained. Fertilize three times in summer. Spider mites may be a problem if humidity is too low. Prune only selectively when grooming. Propagate by seed.

SELECTIONS *H. forsterana* (Kentia Palm, Sentry Palm) A slow-growing palm that outgrows its space in width faster than height. It grows to ten feet or more in a container, but frequently reaches ten feet in width by the time it's seven feet tall. Rich gray-green leaf stems burst into many long, somewhat arching pinnae (leaflets). Kentia palm is tolerant, easy to grow, and retains its attractive looks even in dark, cool locations for extended periods. This is a great entrance specimen for large, wide-open spaces, such as atriums. Unfortunately, kentia palm fronds are sometimes tied together because they have grown too wide for their space. Kentias frequently tend to be pricey because they grow slowly.

HOYA WAX VINE *Asclepiadaceae*

This group of stiff-leaved vines or climbers from southeast Asia and the Pacific isles is grown for colorful or textured foliage as well as artificial-looking clusters of thick waxy flowers that resemble milkweed flowers, one of their relatives. The stems contain a sticky, milky sap. Hoyas may be easily trained on supports and do well in hanging baskets.

Hoyas are easily grown as long as water is not offered too frequently and they receive medium light and average to warm temperatures. Allow the soil to dry between soakings and avoid cold drafts. Higher than average humidity ensures flower production. They need to be fertilized three times in the summer and should be repotted infrequently–put it off as long as possible. Spent flower stems should not be removed because the next season's flowers are formed on them. Propagate by stem cuttings and watch for mealybugs and aphids. Mealybugs can be a real problem on curly-leaved varieties.

PLANTS NAMED FOR PEOPLE

Begonia Michel Begon, governor of French Canada, 1638-1710, patron of botany.

Billbergia J.G. Bilberg, Swedish botanist, 1772-1844.

Fittonia Elizabeth and Sarah Mary Fitton, authors of *Conversations in Botany*, c. 1850.

Fuchsia Leonard Fuchs, German botanist, 1501-1566.

Gardenia Dr. Garden, eighteenth-century American physician and naturalist.

Hoya Thomas Hoye, gardener to the duke of Northumberland at the end of the eighteenth century.

Poinsettia Joel R. Poinsette, gardener, botanist, diplomat, first ambassador to Mexico.

Saintpaulia Walter von Saint Paul-Illaire, district governor of German colony of East Africa and discoverer of the plant in an East African jungle.

Sansevieria Raimondo de Sango, prince of Sansevieria.

Trandescantia John Tradescant, gardener to Charles I of England (died 1637) and his son, John Tradescant, gardener, botanist, explorer (died 1662).

Hoya carnosa on a wire frame.

SELECTIONS *H. bella* A tidy, small-leaved type, susceptible to mites. This water-demanding species will produce clusters of fragrant flowers in a north window.
H. carnosa Plain waxy green leaves to three inches in width have distinct midribs. The undersides of the leaves are much paler than the top. The wiry new growth is leafless initially. The clusters of creamy white flowers have pinkish-red centers and are fragrant at night. Performs particularly well in a hanging basket as long as it is supported, or does well trained on a wire form. Because of succulence, stems become heavy with time.
H. carnosa 'Compacta' (Hindu Rope) Slow grower, leaves are contorted and seem to be crumpled and turned inside out.
H. carnosa 'Crimson Queen' A tricolored variety of *H. carnosa*—slow growing.
H. carnosa 'Krinkle Kurl' Brightly colored red, cream and green leaves are similar in shape to *H. carnosa* 'Compacta'.
H. longifolia var. *shepardii* (Long-Leaved Hoya) Leaves are narrow and similar in size and shape to young green beans. The plant is visually linear as it ages. The stems are light grayish with many bumps that are the remnants of old flowers. It flowers easily and profusely, although the flowers are smaller than other hoyas. They are dirty white or pink with darker centers. This one is not frequently seen in cultivation.

LIGULARIA *Asteraceae*

This genus contains almost 100 species of herbaceous perennials. Native to Europe and Asia, they grow in moist, sunny places and flower in summer when grown outdoors. The typical aster family flowers are generally yellow to orange.

Grow in bright light in winter and in shade outside in summer—a good plant for north light. Ligularia tolerates cool night temperatures. Keep evenly moist; wilts easily if allowed to dry out. Pot in regular potting soil and repot as the plant becomes potbound. Ligularia responds well to monthly fertilization. Propagate by division.
SELECTIONS *L. tussilanginea* 'Aureo-maculata' (Leopard Plant) has showy, large round shiny leaves with irregular yellow spots or flecks; multiple bright yellow flowers appear atop stiff wiry stems above the foliage. Will grow eighteen to twenty inches in height and width.
L. tussilanginea 'Argentea' Lovely cultivar with shades of white and green mottling throughout leaf; mostly white at margins. Softer leaves and less vigorous than *L. tussilanginea* 'Aureo-maculata'. (BLITHEWOLD)

MIMOSA *Fabaceae*

Mimosa contains about 400 species of plants from tropical and subtropical America, Australasia, Africa and Asia with just about every habit imaginable. Most have bipinnate leaves that visually link them with other members of the legume family (Fabaceae). Round heads of tubular, small flowers pop out of the bud accompanied by the emergence of long stamens. The fruits are typical legumes—almost flat beans.

The species listed requires frequent watering and should be treated as an annual—keep the soil evenly moist. Allowing it to dry out causes yellowing and dropping leaves. Give the plants medium light and average to high tem-

HOMALOMENA WALLISII (SPECKLED DROP TONGUE) Eight inches long; medium to low light and average to high temperatures; high humidity; evenly moist; fertilize infrequently; moderate growth rate.

HOWEA FORSTERANA (KENTIA PALM, SENTRY PALM) Ten feet tall; ten feet wide; medium to low light and cool temperatures (will tolerate average temperatures); evenly moist; hold back on watering in winter; fertilize three times in summer; slow growing.

HOYA CARNOSA CV. (WAX VINE) Leaves three inches wide; medium light and average to warm temperatures; dry between soakings and avoid cold drafts; high humidity ensures flower production; fertilize three times in the summer; slow growing.

HOYA LONGIFOLIA VAR. SHEPARDII (LONG-LEAVED HOYA) Eight-inch hanging basket; leaves the size of young green beans; medium light and average to warm temperatures; dry between soakings and avoid cold drafts; high humidity ensures flower production; fertilize three times in summer. (SHOWN WITH UNIDENTIFIED GESNERIAD.)

PLANTS FOR CHILDREN
Two plants that are particularly popular with children at Chicago Botanic Garden are *Mimosa pudica* (sensitive plant) and *Dionea musipula* (Venus flytrap). Plants naturally move in the breeze, but these two plants respond to human touch. Other plants that attract attention are *Hypoestes phyllostachya* (pink polka dot plant), *Kalanchoe tomentosa* (panda plant), and *Musa* x *paradisiaca* (banana).

peratures. Fertilize infrequently and avoid high-traffic areas—these plants are spiny. Pot into an average, well drained potting mix. Potting into a larger pot once the plant becomes woody does not improve the vigor. They are prone to mealybugs, mites, and thrips. Pruning is seldom needed—only when grooming. New plants are easily propagated from seed, which is prolifically produced after flowering.

SELECTIONS *M. pudica* (Sensitive Plant) Grown as a small, stiffly branched spiny plant, it generally has an untidy habit. It is often grown because of its response to touch or movement: the leaves fold and the petiole collapses, only to open easily in a few minutes. The flowers are round pink "puffs." Children love these plants.

MUHLENBECKIA PLATYCLADA [HOMALOCLADIUM PLAYCLADIUM] *Polygonaceae*

Called ribbon bush, centipede plant, or tapeworm plant, this single species is from the Solomon Islands. It has flat, segmented stems that make this a curious plant to grow. The tiny leaves come and go virtually unnoticed. As the stems mature, they become somewhat rounded and then woody and brown. At this point, they break easily. Ribbon bush can grow to five feet in a container. The flowers are like the leaves—hardly noticeable. This is a good plant for quizzing students on plant morphology since the stems look like leaves.

Grow in medium light preferably, although it will tolerate high light (gardeners at The New York Botanical Garden find it performs best in high light). Ribbon bush will also tolerate cool, average, or hot temperatures. Keep the soil evenly moist and repot frequently in average, well-drained potting mix when young because they show damage from dehydration readily. Fertilize three times in summer and avoid high-traffic areas because the stems are brittle. Watch for mealybugs, thrips, and scale; they are also susceptible to powdery mildew. Prune only when needed for grooming because they branch sporadically and abnormally when cut. Propagate by stem cutting or seed every few years to insure vigor.

MYRTUS MYRTLE *Myrtaceae*

Myrtles, from Europe, Africa, and Florida, have been grown as decorative plants for thousands of years. After a time of not being popular, myrtle, especially the dwarf, is in favor again—as a traditional herb and for training as topiary or bonsai. The delicate but decorative flowers are followed in many species by edible fruits.

Grow myrtle in medium to high light. Myrtles demand water and may die from one missed watering. Repot frequently in average, well-drained potting mix. Myrtles are good candidates for topiary—they may be pruned to woody stumps and under the right conditions will leaf out again. Root pruning may be necessary to keep them vigorous; this must be followed by pruning foliage of an equal percentage of the plant. Fertilize three times in summer or use

LIGULARIA TUSSILANGINEA 'AUREO-MACULATA' (LEOPARD PLANT)
Eighteen to twenty inches; bright light in winter, shade in summer; tolerates cool night temperatures; keep evenly moist; fertilize monthly; slow growing.

MIMOSA PUDICA (SENSITIVE PLANT) Will grow to eighteen inches tall; medium light and average to high temperatures; evenly moist; fertilize infrequently; grown for its response to touch–the leaves fold; fast growing.

MUHLENBECKIA PLATYCLADA (RIBBON BUSH, CENTIPEDE PLANT OR TAPEWORM PLANT) Can grow to five feet in a container; medium light (will tolerate high light); cool, average or hot temperatures; evenly moist; fertilize three times in summer; moderate growth rate.

MYRTUS COMMUNIS (GERMAN MYRTLE, COMMON MYRTLE, GREEK MYRTLE) Grows to six feet in a pot but may be kept much smaller with frequent pruning; medium to high light and average to cool temperatures; evenly moist; fertilize three times in summer or use dilute fertilizer at every watering; slow growing. (Shown trained as a topiary standard.).

Fern fronds vary in size and appearance, but the most commonly recognized is that of the feathery Boston fern, whose fronds are long and graceful and are divided into many leaflets. Other ferns have straplike or leaflike fronds. *Nephrolepis exaltata* 'Dallasi', commonly known as Dallas fern (shown above), is similar to the Boston fern, but its fronds are half the length.

dilute fertilizer at every watering. Give them average to cool temperatures. Mealybugs, thrips, whitefly, mites, and scale may be problems. Propagate by stem cuttings or seed.

SELECTIONS *M. communis* (German Myrtle, Common Myrtle, Greek Myrtle) Found in southwestern Europe and the Mediterranean region, this plant is referred to in the Bible as symbolizing peace and justice. It is an aromatic shrub that grows to six feet in a pot but may be kept much smaller with frequent pruning. Pointed dark green leaves make a perfect background for the tiny "fireworks"-type of off-white flowers and small purple fruits. Pruning inhibits flower production since flowers form on new growth. Bark on older plants is decorative, reddish, and peeling. Chicago Botanic Garden has two specimens that are over 100 years old and came from the wedding bouquet of one of the garden's first benefactors. Rooted cuttings trained into spiral forms over fifteen years grace the entrances to the Educational Greenhouses.

***M. communis* 'Variegata'** Much slower growing although similar to the species. The leaves have creamy-yellow margins. This cultivar is more difficult to train since the branching is unpredictable.

NEPHROLEPIS SWORD FERN *Polypodiaceae*

These plants from the tropics and subtropics have been grown since Victorian times. There are thirty species of these terrestrial clump-forming ferns. The fronds are evergreen and adapt well to indoor cultivation. A commonly available group of ferns, much work is being done in the lab on new varieties for mass production.

Grow nephrolepis in medium light and average temperatures. Pot in a peaty, moisture-retentive mix and keep the soil evenly moist at all times. Multiple plants per pot make a full plant quickly. Repotting into larger pots encourages the plants to grow larger. To maintain a particular size, divide frequently. Fertilize three times in summer or with dilute fertilizer solution at every watering. Prune only as needed for grooming, but root-prune often to maintain vigor. Watch for scale and mealybugs and avoid drying winds and high-traffic areas. The plants spread by runners, or stolons, and propagate easily by division. Species can be propagated by spores.

SELECTIONS *N. exaltata* 'Fluffy Ruffles' (Fluffy Ruffles Fern) A reliable cultivar that stays relatively small. The leaf edges are cut and ruffled, yet maintain a neat decorative appearance. Easy to grow, it tolerates less than perfect conditions (except dehydration).

***N. exaltata* 'Dallasi'** (Dallas Fern) Dense, compact form, similar to *N. e.* 'Bostoniensis' but fronds are half the length.

***N. exaltata* 'Silver Balls'** New growth uncurls with round silver balls along the edge of fronds–quite decorative. Has an erect habit.

PAPHIOPEDILUM LADY SLIPPER *Orchidaceae*

These orchids are native to Asia, Malaysia, and the Philippines. The flowers range from one inch to six inches, depending on the species or cultivar. The flowers vary from green, yellow, or brown to burgundy, pink, or purple, and spotted. The flowers have a slipperlike lip that gives the plant its common name. The leaves are green or grayish mottled and straplike. Lady slippers are easy to grow, and there are hundreds of hybrids available.

Lady slippers perform best in medium light–a window with morning sun is best. If possible, provide 75-85° F. days and 50° F. nights. Keep them evenly moist, but keep water out of the plant crown–the most common cause of death is overwatering. To check moisture level, stick a sharpened pencil one-third of the way into the potting mix and twist. If the wood comes out wet, don't water. If it comes out dry or slightly moist, water. Pot lady slippers in fine-grade fir bark; they can be transplanted any time of year. Fertilize with high-nitrogen fertilizer once a month all year long. Propagate by dividing large established plants or by separating offshoots. Watch for occasional mealybugs.

SELECTIONS *P. insigne* (Lady Slipper) Green strap leaves with yellowish-brown spotted flowers; grows to six inches high. An easy plant with many flowers that can be grown quickly.

P. x maudiae Nice burgundy and white striped flowers with mottled leaves; there is also a green and white flowered form available. Attractive even when not flowering because of the mottled leaves. (University of California Botanical Garden)

PELLAEA *Polypodiaceae*

Native to temperate and cool tropical regions, these are small ferns with rich dark green fronds growing in tufts or creeping among rocks. The pinnae are tougher than most ferns, suggesting they can tolerate more dryness. This is not the case. Pellaea is from *pellaios*, Greek for "dark." Many of the frond stems are almost black.

Grow pellaeas in medium light. Repot in peaty, moisture-retentive mix as often as necessary to keep up with the watering demands. Keep the soil evenly moist (they will not tolerate drying out) and grow in average to cool temperatures since it is difficult to keep watered in high temperatures. Fertilize three times in summer or with dilute fertilizer at every watering during growing period. Prune only selectively as needed for grooming. Avoid drying winds, drafts, and low humidity. Scale can be a problem. Propagate by rhizome division or spores.

SELECTIONS *P. falcata* (Australian Cliff Brake) A leathery-looking fern similar in overall appearance to nephrolepis except that is is much more compact. Rich, elegant, shiny pinnae stand on dark erect arching fronds. Tolerates cool drafts and lower light than other pellaeas. Grows to fourteen inches in height and is not well-suited to a hanging basket. A fresh-looking fern–a nice change from the over-used nephrolepis.

P. rotundifolia (Buttonfern) Native to New Zealand, Australia, and Norfolk Island. Offered in the trade as perfectly round little plants, but as they grow the rhizomes creep around, upsetting the symmetry. Dark reddish brown scaly fronds support pairs of glossy dark green roundish pinnae. Fronds arch over the edges of the pot, commanding attention–a fern that at first glance doesn't look like a fern. This is a good fern for the frequent waterer–do not let

FERNS

Ferns differ from other houseplants in that they do not produce flowers or seed. They reproduce by spores and their leaves or "fronds" arise from rhizomes that grow below or on top of the soil. The spores are borne on the undersides of some of the fronds in tiny brown, red, or black spore cases called sori.

Although some ferns are epiphytic (see sidebar, page 93), others are terrestrial, usually inhabiting shady, moist places. This is the key to successful culture–give them plenty of humidity, rich soil, and medium or bright, filtered light. Ferns do not do well in low light. Direct sun can damage tender fronds.

Most ferns are easily propagated by dividing underground rhizomes, but a more challenging method is to propagate by spores. Propagating by spores is a slow process and it will often take up to a year to have a plant that resembles a fern. When the spores are ripe (tapping the frond should release a fine dust of spores), distribute them over a moist, sterile medium. Cover with glass or plastic and put them in a warm spot with bright light. After several months, the surface will appear as if covered with moss. Remove the cover and keep the medium moist. After a few more months, you will begin to see tiny ferns, which can be potted. It is critical to keep the humidity high and even during this entire process.

An old but effective method of spore propagation is to set a brick in a saucer of water and sprinkle spores on the surface of the brick. The water moves through the brick and the spores grow.

Peperomia caperata 'Red Ripple'.

it dehydrate. If it does, remove damaged fronds and resume watering. The plant may show new signs of life, but will never look quite the same.

PEPEROMIA *Piperaceae*

Peperomia represents a large group of plants from the worldwide tropics and subtropics. Plant producers have tapped this genus for many species and cultivars suitable for interior use. Many have fleshy, shiny leaves and propagate easily. A palette of color and texture is available from this varied group of shrubby, succulent, epiphytic, and groundcover-type plants.

Grow peperomia in medium to low light. Repot as needed in average, well-drained mix. Most tolerate drought well, although they perform best if watered as soon as they dry out. (Some gardeners find that overwatering and poor drainage lead to root rot and keep their peperomias somewhat on the dry side.) Fertilize three times in summer and provide average temperatures. Peperomia tolerates pruning quite well. Avoid cold drafts and high-traffic areas since the succulent leaves scar easily. Peperomia has few problems with insects or disease, although it will occasionally have mealybugs. Propagate by stem cuttings and rhizome division.

SELECTIONS *P. argyreia* (Watermelon Peperomia) Grows in rosette; leaves are green with bands of silver running from the center of the leaf to the tip.

P. caperata **'Red Ripple'** (Red Ripple Peperomia) A free-branching peperomia that grows in a dense mound. All parts of the plant are red. The dark leaves are deeply corrugated and crinkly. The stems are bright red but are almost invisible on a well-grown plant. New plants are started easily by removing the plantlets, much like African Violets. This peperomia is tolerant of low light and is one that will hold its color in low light. Old leaves whose petioles have elongated may be removed to reveal many new leaves held close to the crown. Avoid overwatering, especially in low light, for compact, dense plants.

P. magnoliifolia **'Jellie'** *(P. clusiifolia* **'Jellie')** (Jellie Peperomia) A vividly colored cultivar with broad, pointed, spoon-shaped leaves that at times seem to sag from their own weight. Pink edges the cream and green leaves; the stems are also bold pink. The color is intensified in strong light. Prune only selectively since pruning old stems leaves unsightly scars, and it takes time for new branches to form and hide the scars. This peperomia grows well in medium to high light, a good plant for year-round color. There is no need to wait for flowers since the color is in the foliage. The flowers are inclined to give the plant an untidy appearance and may be removed as part of grooming.

P. obtusifolia (Baby Rubber Plant) Common, easy to grow. Plain green spatulate leaves; grows bushy.

P. pereskiifolia A good basket peperomia from Venezuela, Brazil, and Colombia. Thick, wiry stems have long internodes between whorls of three to six leaves. The firm leaves have a distinct midrib from which the leaf edges slightly fold upward. Medium green leaves seem to be strung in pierced bunches along a reddish stem that is slightly arching. One of the more unusual habits for peperomia. Overwatering can be a problem; the plant branches well from the base in high light.

NEPHROLEPIS EXALTATA 'FLUFFY RUFFLES' (FLUFFY RUFFLES FERN)
To ten inches; medium light and average temperatures; fertilize three times in summer or with dilute fertilizer solution at every watering; moderate growth rate.

PAPHIOPEDILUM GREX VAR. LEYBURNIENSE 'MAGNIFICUM' To one foot; medium light; Average days and cool nights; evenly moist; keep water out of crown; fertilize once a month all year; average growth rate.

PELLAEA ROTUNDIFOLIA (BUTTONFERN) Leaves to one foot long; medium light and average to cool temperatures; evenly moist (they will not tolerate drying out); fertilize three times in summer or with dilute fertilizer at every watering during growing period; moderate growth rate.

PEPEROMIA CAPERATA 'RED RIPPLE' (RED RIPPLE PEPEROMIA) To twelve inches; low light and average temperatures; tolerate drought but perform best if kept moist; fertilize three times in summer; moderate growth rate.

Phalaenopsis 'Pink Zebra' x 'Memoria Yoshimo Mishima'.

P. polybotrya (Coin-leaf Peperomia) A South American species with felted leaves; somewhat prostrate growing.

PHALAENOPSIS MOTH ORCHID *Orchidaceae*

Moth orchids are graceful orchids that are native to southeast Asia and Malaysia. They have green, wide, straplike leaves that come off the stem opposite one another. The rounded flowers are borne on arching spikes up to a foot high. A spike can have from three to twenty long-lasting flowers in white, pink, yellow, and purple. The flowers can also be spotted or striped. A plant can flower for up to eighteen months. If you can bring an African violet into flower, you can easily grow moth orchids. Hundreds of cultivars are available to suit all tastes.

Moth orchids perform best in medium light. Provide 75-85° F. days and 50° F. nights. Keep them evenly moist but be careful not to overwater, the most common cause of death. To check moisture level, stick a sharpened pencil one-third of the way into the potting mix and twist. If the wood comes out wet, don't water. If it comes out dry or slightly moist, water. Pot in fine- or medium-grade fir bark; they can be transplanted after flowering. Repot every two to three years (when bark has broken down). Fertilize with high-nitrogen fertilizer once a month all year long. Propagate by separating plantlets that may form on spike after flowering. Propagating orchids by seed is difficult, and should be left to experts. Watch for occasional mealybugs.

SELECTIONS *P. lueddemanniana* Fragrant two-inch flowers have pinkish stripes on white petals. Flower stems are shorter than many phalenopsis culivars. ***P. sanderiana*** Typical large flowers that look like the broad white moths that gives the genus its common name. (University of California Botanical Garden).

PHILODENDRON *Araceae*

Native to tropical America, this is a varied group of commonly grown indoor foliage plants. Easy to grow, these plants are available in a wide variety of sizes, colors, and textures. Most philodendrons grown in the home remain in their juvenile state and never flower. In their native habitats, many philodendrons are clambering vines that use other plants for support as they work their way toward the light. Juvenile leaves look much different than mature leaves, and often the vine must be grown vertically to achieve mature leaves.

As a rule, the more colorful varieties require higher light than the plain green varieties. For example, an old-fashioned variety such as *P. scandens,* which everyone's grandparents grew and is part of our childhood memories, will take very low light. Otherwise, philodendrons grow well in medium to low light and average temperatures. Allow the soil to dry briefly between soakings and avoid cold drafts and drying winds. The roots are thick and heavy as with most epiphytes, so repot with an average mix when the pot is totally filled with roots, or when the plant begins to climb out of the pot. Fertilize three times in summer or reduce fertilizer to control growth. Most philodendrons tolerate pruning well, but it is seldom necessary aside from

PEPEROMIA MAGNOLIIFOLIA 'JELLIE' (JELLIE PEPEROMIA) To twelve inches; medium to high light; average temperatures; tolerate drought but perform best if kept moist; fertilize three times in summer; moderate growth rate.

PHALAENOPSIS (MOTH ORCHID) Arching spikes up to two feet high; medium light; provide 75-85° F. days and 50° F. nights; evenly moist but be careful not to overwater; fertilize with high nitrogen fertilizer once a month all year long; slow growing.

PHILODENDRON GLORIOSUM (SATIN LEAF PHILODENDRON) Leaves to one foot; medium light; average temperatures; dry between soakings; fertilize three times in summer; slow growing.

PHILODENDRON 'BLACK CARDINAL' (BLACK CARDINAL PHILODENDRON) To five feet across in time; medium to high light and average temperatures; dry briefly between soakings and avoid cold drafts and drying winds; fertilize three times in summer or reduce fertilizer to control growth; fast growing.

PHILODENDRON SELLOUM (TREE PHILODENDRON) Twelve- to eighteen-inch leaves on eighteen- to twenty-four-inch stalks; medium to low light; average temperatures; dry between soakings; fertilize three times in summer; slow growing.

PILEA 'MOON VALLEY' (MOON VALLEY PILEA) Leaves grow to four inches long; medium light and cool to hot temperatures; dry slightly between soakings; high humidity; fertilize infrequently; fast growing.

PILEA 'SILVER TREE' (SILVER TREE PILEA) To eight inches; medium light and cool to hot temperatures; dry slightly between soakings; high humidity; fertilize infrequently; fast growing.

PLECTRANTHUS PURPURATUS (PURPLE SWEDISH IVY) Twelve inches long; medium light and average temperatures (will tolerate cool temperatures); evenly moist; fertilize three times in summer; fast growing.

grooming. Mealybugs may be a problem; mites and thrips occasionally appear. Wet, cold soil invites disease and should be avoided. Propagate by stem cuttings or by seed. Stem cuttings root easily in water or in soil.

SELECTIONS *P. gloriosum* (Satin Leaf Philodendron) Large creeping philodendron with huge heart-shaped leaves over one foot long; leaves are deep green with prominent white veins. For shady locations–bleaches out in bright light.

P. martianum Thick spongy petioles, eighteen inches long, support pointed leaves of similar length; becomes large. Undemanding.

P. scandens var. *oxycardium* Commonly found in mixed gift planters.

P. selloum (Tree Philodendron) grows large; gradually reduce water in winter.

P. 'Black Cardinal' (Black Cardinal Philodendron) A striking addition to the interior landscape, although the color fades in low light. Dark burgundy in color, broad-leaved and stately, this cultivar grows quite large in time. The main stem tends to wander as it ages. It is sensitive to physical damage–the midribs are easily broken, causing unsightly leaves. This is one of many varieties developed by Bamboo Nursery in Florida. This series of introductions makes a whole new palette of colors and textures available for medium to bright light situations. Some are climbers that require support, and others are self-heading types that get fuller and bushier with age.

P. 'Emerald Prince' A broader-leaved, emerald green type similar to 'Black Cardinal'.

PILEA *Urticaceae*

Native to worldwide tropics and subtropics, many species of pilea have heavily textured pairs of rounded leaves. Colorful patterns frequently mark the surface of the leaves while the undersides tend to be plain and hairy. Plants may vine or trail or can be mounded and shrubby. These easy-to-grow decorative plants are frequently seen in dish gardens and are rewarding, even for the non-green thumb.

Provide pileas with medium light and allow the potting mix to dry slightly between soakings. They will tolerate cool to hot temperatures. Avoid drying winds and low humidity. Fertilize infrequently and pinch to keep plants full–cuttings will easily start new plants whenever older plants get leggy. Pileas will tolerate the same pot for a long time–a ten-inch pot is about as large as you can safely go before plants become unsightly. Use an average, well-drained potting mix. Propagate by stem cuttings. Watch for spider mites, easily detected by tapping leaves over white paper. Mites cause the edges of the leaves to turn brown, disfiguring the plant. Mealybugs and scale can also be problems.

SELECTIONS *P. depressa* (Creeping Jenny) Small, smooth-leaved vining type; good for terrariums, dish gardens, or hanging baskets.

P. microphylla (Artillery Plant) Arching stems of tiny round leaves–shoots its seeds everywhere and inhabits greenhouses and southern gardens as a benign weed.

P. 'Moon Valley' (Moon Valley Pilea) Deeply quilted leaves grow to four inches long. Coffee-colored areas bleed from the three prominent veins on the top

Pilea 'Moon Valley'.

For indoor decoration, we have nothing to equal ivy. It will endure more hardships, flourish under more unfavorable circumstances, and endure darkness, gas, and dust better than any plant we think of at present.
FROM *VICK'S MONTHLY MAGAZINE*, 1879

sides of the leaves. Undersides are highlighted red and as heavily quilted as the tops. Tops and bottoms are hairy. Benefits from regular pinching.

P. nummulariifolia (Creeping Charlie) Good basket plant with coin-sized and -shaped bright green textured leaves.

P. 'Silver Tree' (Silver Tree Pilea) Native to the Caribbean; stiff wiry stems to six inches support pairs of serrated leaves that taper to a point. A silver band marks the midrib with the remainder of the leaf a dark olive green. The undersides of the leaves are reddish with hairy veins. The stems are red also. Tiny flowers cluster tightly to the crown–not very decorative, but they add another texture. Can have problems with scale, mites, mealybugs, and whitefly. Attention to small changes in the overall appearance will allow for early pest detection. In low light plants become leggy and unsightly. A good plant to try your hand at propagation.

PLECTRANTHUS SWEDISH IVY *Lamiaceae*

Native to Old World tropics, Africa to east Asia, Australia, and the Pacific Islands, these vining candidates are great for hanging baskets. They have wiry, mostly four-angled stems. Opposite pairs of rounded leaves vary in color and size. Several species flower readily, and all propagate easily. They are tolerant of less than perfect conditions and flourish in spite of the grower.

Provide medium light and average temperatures. Plectranthus will also tolerate cool temperatures. Keep the potting mix evenly moist and fertilize three times in summer. Pinch tips of stems to keep full. Swedish ivy tolerates pruning well. Pot in average, well-drained potting mix. Repot infrequently–start plants over soon after they are moved into an eight- or ten-inch pot or basket. Propagate by stem cuttings in soil or water (beware–the sap will turn your fingers orange). Occasional problems may occur with mealybugs and whitefly.

SELECTIONS *P. australis* (Swedish Ivy) Waxy bright green leaves with other habits the same as *P. purpuratus*.

P. oertendahlii Another velvety, smaller-leaved variety with silver veins.

P. purpuratus (Purple Swedish Ivy) A velvety-looking plant that gushes over the edge of its pot. Dark purplish leaves hang off dark purplish green stems. Flowers are bright white with fine reddish markings. Many-flowered racemes are produced at growth points of stems and are held vertically above the foliage. Purple Swedish ivy benefits from occasional tip removal to keep it full. It is easy to grow and rewarding.

PODOCARPUS *Podocarpaceae*

Native to the mountains of Australasia and South America, the West Indies and Japan, this genus includes coniferous evergreens of a stately nature. Some have weeping habits, while others are stiff and bristly-looking. Some are valued for timber, growing to 100 feet. Tolerant of cool temperatures, the slow-growing cultivated species do well at entrances of buildings and in large, bright, less than comfortably heated spaces.

Provide medium to high light and average to cool temperatures. Keep potting mix evenly moist and hold back on water during winter. Fertilize infrequently and prune only as necessary (seldom needed). Podocarpus seldom needs repotting because of slow growth. Use an average mix that is well-drained. Podocarpus can be propagated by stem cuttings, but it is slow and difficult. It is best to purchase one rather than try to propagate. These plants have no serious problems but may have occasional scale and mealybugs.

SELECTIONS *P. gracilior* (African Fern Pine) Native to East Africa, this valuable timber tree grows to seventy-five feet in the wild, but makes a beautiful weeping specimen for the home. It can be easily kept in bounds by annual pruning. The graceful stems seem to hang from the weight of the many flat four-inch-long leaves that surround the stems. Dark green in color, this plant easily attracts attention to itself in a large bright room. Leaves at the center drop naturally as it grows and light is cut off from the inner reaches of the plant. Bark is warm reddish-brown.

P. macrophyllus (Japanese Yew, Buddhist Pine) Similar to *P. gracilior* but less weeping, more bristly and brushlike.

P. macrophyllus '**Maki**' More compact than *P. macrophyllus*; stays small and has more vertical habit; slow-growing.

P. nagi (Broadleaf Podocarpus) Easy to grow; leathery leaves.

POLYSCIAS *Araliaceae*

These highly attractive, elegant plants for the interior are native to tropical Asia and Polynesia. Foliage colors and textures vary greatly, and most have attractive stems as well as leaves. This is an advantage because chances are good that they will drop a lot of leaves before you get all environmental and cultural conditions adjusted for healthy growth. These are not good plants for beginners or the faint-hearted. Once established, however, the plants are worth the effort.

Give polyscias medium light and average to high temperatures. High humidity and soil warmth are essential. Avoid drying winds and cold drafts. Let the soil dry between soakings and ease off on watering in winter. Fertilize at normal strength three times or more in summer or with dilute fertilizer every watering during active growth. Polyscias will tolerate pruning, but it is usually necessary only as part of grooming. Pot in an average, well-drained potting mix and repot infrequently—only when you can't keep up with the demand for water. Propagation is difficult—use rooting hormone and put stem cuttings in warm soil or air layer. It is much easier to buy an established plant. Be alert for scale and spider mites.

SELECTIONS *P. balfouriana* (Dinner Plate Aralia, Balfour Aralia) An upright type with broad, rounded leaves. Sometimes leaves are segmented into three parts. Leaf margins are white and toothed. Bark becomes grayish with age; an old plant can grow to six feet and is usually multistemmed. One of the more tolerant types, this plant still drops leaves at any transgression in care. Watering too frequently shows up first as dark shiny spots on the undersides of leaves and then as yellow falling leaves. High humidity, frequent misting, and allowing the soil to dry between waterings will help this plant along. Warm tem-

UNUSUAL PLANTS

LITHOPS These unusual succulents have only two leaves. They are called living stones or stonefaces because that's just what the leaves resemble. This camouflage makes the plants visually disappear into the gravel, protecting the plants from grazing animals. The two leaves are fused and have a slit in the top from which a single daisylike flower emerges. These leaves then begin to die, providing moisture to two newly forming leaves. The plants should not be watered while the old leaves are shriveling. These are truly conversation pieces that are not easy to grow and must have direct sun and little water.

CHENILLE PLANT (ACALYPHA HISPIDA)

This plant has rather plain foliage and spectacular long pinkish tassels or tails of tiny flowers. Another striking conversation piece.

WHISK FERN (PSILOTUM NUTUM)

Besides having a Latin name that is fun to say and curious to look at, this prehistoric plant does not have roots or true leaves. Once you have one, you'll have many, as the spores shoot out and sprout in pots of other plants! At Chicago Botanic Garden, a whisk fern is growing at the base of a euphorbia in an area separated from the original plant by two greenhouses and a public hallway.

JATROPHA This cousin of the poinsettia has the unusual habit of shooting its seeds when they are ripe. This inhibits competition for water, light, and nutrients between mother and baby.

peratures are essential.

P. crispatum (Chicken Gizzard Aralia) Crinkly rounded dark green leaves with highly contrasting light beige bumpy stems.

P. fruticosa (Ming Aralia) Delicate cutleaf type–has an Oriental look and is sometimes used for bonsai. Keep more to the dry side; will tolerate low light.

PSILOTUM *Psilotaceae*

Easy-to-grow curiosities left over from the age of dinosaurs, these epiphytes are widely distributed throughout the tropics and subtropics. They are fern-like leafless, rootless spore producers that show up in places unexpectedly (such as pots of other plants) once you have an established parent plant. They are not offered frequently in the trade.

Psilotums will thrive in low to high light and tolerate cool to hot temperatures. They should be allowed to dry out briefly between waterings and fertilized infrequently. (Gardeners at The New York Botanical Garden find they perform better when kept evenly moist.) Pruning is necessary only as part of grooming. Pot in coarse, fast-draining soil and repot only when the stems begin to run around the inside edge of the pot. Most psilotums are pest-free and can be propagated by rhizome division or by spores.

SELECTIONS ***P. nudum*** (Whisk Fern) A wiry, stemmy, brushlike plant native to the southern United States that grows to about two and a half feet in nature but stays about one foot in a pot; a good conversation piece grown for its character. Spores are formed in small round bumps near the ends of stems. The name is fun to say and easy to remember after you have entertained friends by showing off your knowledge of Latin. Many other types are known, but few are readily available.

PTERIS TABLE FERN, BRAKE FERN *Pteridaceae*

These are decorative terrestrial ferns mostly with long stalks supporting branched pinnae. Many have delicately cut fronds, bright silver or white coloration, and may be ruffled or curly. Spores form in marginal lines, making fronds heavy and droopy with age.

Give table ferns medium light–the plants will languish in low light. Gardeners at The New York Botanical Garden find that table ferns do fine in low light and thrive in warm temperatures; at Chicago Botanic Garden they do much better in medium or bright light and tolerate average to cool temperatures. Avoid drying winds. Keep the potting mix evenly moist and fertilize infrequently or use dilute fertilizer in every watering during the growth period for lush plants. Prune only selectively when grooming. Pot in a peaty, moisture-retentive potting mix and repot before the plant begins to dry out faster than you can keep it watered. Propagate by rhizome division or spores. Pteris can have trouble with scale, mites, and mealybugs, but if plants are well cared for, there should be no problems.

SELECTIONS ***P. cretica*** (Cretan Brake Fern, Cretan Table Fern) This species and its cultivars are the most commonly available pteris ferns. Fronds grow six to twelve inches long. The graceful look and habit is distinct and easily recogniz-

PODOCARPUS GRACILIOR (AFRICAN FERN PINE) Can be kept to twelve feet or less (commonly around eight feet); medium to high light and average to cool temperatures; evenly moist and hold back on water during winter; fertilize infrequently; slow growing.

POLYSCIAS GUILFOYELEI Can grow to six feet; medium light and average to high temperatures; dry between soakings and ease off on watering in winter; fertilize at normal strength three times or more in summer or with dilute fertilizer every watering during active growth; slow growing.

PSILOTUM NUDUM (WHISK FERN) About one foot; epiphytic; low to high light and cool to hot temperatures; dry out briefly between waterings; fertilize infrequently; slow growing.

PTERIS CRETICA (CRETAN BRAKE FERN, CRETAN TABLE FERN) Fronds six to twelve inches long; medium to high light and average to cool temperatures; evenly moist; fertilize infrequently or use dilute fertilizer in every watering during the growth period; moderate growth rate.

able from other types of ferns. Provide more light than is commonly required by ferns. This is an easy fern to grow for those who like to water; once it dries out, though, it's never the same. May be difficult to locate the species; cultivars are readily available.

***P. cretica* 'Albo-Lineata'** Broad pinnae have a wide white central band.

***P. ensiformis* 'Evergemiensis'** Delicate variety with bright white lines and curly ends.

***P. quadriaurita* 'Argyraea'** (Silver Brake Fern) Green with a broad band of silver enclosing the midribs; fronds up to three feet long. Keep humidity high by placing on saucer of wet pebbles and spritzing foliage frequently.

RHIPSALIS WICKERWARE CACTUS, MISTLETOE CACTUS *Cactaceae*

This delightful group of leafless epiphytes is native to tropical America, Brazil, Africa, and Sri Lanka. They are hardly recognizable as cactus. Most have pendant branches—leafless stems that may be rounded or broad and flat. Flowers are generally small but sparkle brightly and are frequently followed by small berries. These plants do well in hanging baskets or on stands where their stems are allowed to hang freely.

Provide medium to high light and average temperatures. Allow the soil to dry between waterings (it's kept evenly moist at The New York Botanical Garden) and fertilize infrequently. Pot in a coarse, fast-draining potting mix and repot only when needed to encourage growth and delay the stems from becoming woody. Rhipsalis will tolerate the same pot for many years. Prune only selectively when grooming and propagate by stem cuttings or seed. Rhipsalis can be prone to mealybugs.

SELECTIONS *R. baccifera* (Mistletoe Cactus) gets its name from the white translucent berries that are formed after flowers that are easily overlooked. The rounded branched stems reach incredible lengths in nature, but commonly stay shorter than three feet in a pot. It is a curious leafless plant that does best

African violet cultivars.

in a hanging basket or on a simple pedestal with plenty of room for its arching stems. Visually it is linear.

R. pilocarpa (Erythrorhipsalis pilocarpa) A favorite–this plant has erect new growth that elongates and becomes pendant. The joints in the stem are covered with white bristly hair, giving the plant an overall sparkly look. Flowers explode off the tips of all the stems–a real treat. Looks very different when grown indoors year-round as compared to those taken outside for the summer. If grown indoors, plants remain pristine with the white hairs staying bright and fluffy. Plants taken outdoors become gray–the hairs cling to the stems.

R. salicornioides (Hatiora salicornioides) (Drunkard's Dream) Interesting segmented stems resembling small bottles–hence the common name. It has yellow flowers in spring if provided a cool, dry winter.

RHOEO MOSES-IN-A-BOAT, BOAT LILY *Commelinaceae*

Only one species occupies this genus. *R. spathacea* is native to Mexico, the West Indies, and Guatamela and has been grown in homes for years. The leaves of rhoeo are eight to ten inches long and blue-gray on top with reddish-purple undersides. They are whorled around the stem, giving the appearance of a vase. Small white flowers are borne inside small bracts–the "boats." It is an easily grown, attractive plant in most conditions.

Rhoeo tolerates low to medium light and average to warm temperatures. Keep it evenly moist and pot in rich, organic potting soil. A mature plant does well in a six-inch pot. Fertilize once a month with a balanced fertilizer. Propagate by seed, offsets, or cuttings. As the plant elongates, the top part can be cut off and rooted and the cut stub will produce offshoots.

SELECTIONS *R. spathacea* See description above.

R. spathacea 'Variegata' Very slow-growing; stiff dark green leaves with longitudinal fine white to pale yellow stripes. (UNIVERSITY OF CALIFORNIA-BERKELEY)

SAINTPAULIA AFRICAN VIOLET *Gesneriaceae*

Native to East Africa, particularly Tanzania, African violets are grown for the masses of flowers that can cover the entire plant. These herbaceous perennials grow in tufts or rosettes. Plants can vary in size from two inches to eighteen inches wide or more. Leaves are fuzzy and rounded on short or long petioles. Leaf edges may be serrated or wavy and crinkly. The flowers may be single, semidouble, double, frilled, multicolor, or bicolored. Most inexpensive cultivars available are forms of *S. ionantha*. The popularity of this plant has driven hybridizers to use other species in conjunction with *S. ionantha* to come up with exciting new looks. The resulting plants are pendulous, trailing, "basket" types and the ever-popular mini types.

Provide medium light and average to warm temperatures; the more light provided, the flatter the plant will be. Keep the soil evenly moist and avoid getting water on the leaves. Tepid water is a must. Use dilute fertilizer every time you water and avoid cold drafts and low humidity. African violets do quite well in self-watering pots. Pot in average, well-drained soil and pot into larger-size pot only if you want to increase plant size. For most cultivars, a five-inch pot is the maximum size before the plant becomes "stemmy" and

Rhoeo's flowers are borne within small bracts almost hiding the flowers–hence the name "Moses-in-a-boat."

RHIPSALIS BACCIFERA (MISTLETOE CACTUS) Under three feet; medium to high light and average temperatures; dry between waterings; fertilize infrequently; slow growing.

RHIPSALIS SALICORNIOIDES (DRUNKARD'S DREAM) Under three feet; medium to high light and average temperatures; dry between waterings; keep cool and dry in winter to promote flowering; fertilize infrequently; slow growing.

RHOEO SPATHACEA (MOSES-IN-A-BOAT, BOAT LILY) Leaves are eight to ten inches long; low to medium light and average to warm temperatures; evenly moist; fertilize once a month; slow growing.

SAINTPAULIA IONANTHA 'YELLOWSTONE' (AFRICAN VIOLET) Two to eighteen inches wide and tall; medium light and average to warm temperatures; evenly moist; avoid getting water on the leaves; dilute fertilizer every time you water; avoid cold drafts and low humidity; slow growing.

needs to be started over. Prune only selectively after flowering. Propagate by leaf cuttings, stem cuttings or seed. Leaf cuttings are the most popular and easiest method. Mealybugs and cyclamen mites can be a problem; thrips and aphids easily infest the flowers. Leaf spots are common when the plants are watered from above with cold water. Stem rot and petiole rot are not uncommon on poorly cultivated plants. Powdery mildew appears as a result of water standing on the leaves.

SELECTIONS *S. ionantha* (African Violet) Virtually all plants offered to the public are cultivars. Flowers on the species are small and vary from light blue to violet or white with a violet center. The foliage is plain compared to the colorful and texturally exciting cultivars. Finely cultivated plants available at shows and plant sales quickly pale and become average and tired looking unless the grower is attentive and fusses over them. If you can grow one well, chances are you can grow any of them well. Hundreds of cultivars are offered–take your pick.

SAXIFRAGA SAXIFRAGE, ROCKFOIL *Saxifragaceae*

This large group of clustering plants from northern temperate zones and the South American mountains has been broken down into several categories according to physical characteristics. The ones discussed here are grouped together by irregular, unequally marked flowers, hairy leaves, and runners, or stolons.

Provide medium light for saxifrages and average to cool temperatures. Keep the soil evenly moist while actively growing and hold back on water in the winter. Pot in average, well-drained potting mix–bulb pans or hanging baskets are appropriate containers. Repot annually when the soil is covered with plantlets and stolons hang in a mass over the edge of the pot. Prune after flowering and only selectively as part of grooming. Propagate by runners. May be used as groundcover under large container plants.

SELECTIONS *S. cuscutiformis* (Minature Strawberry Begonia) This is a spritely species, brightly marked with white veins on medium green leaves with scalloped edges. Young leaves are held at an attractive angle, gradually laying on top of one another. The flowers are small and white and dangle off an upright raceme. Delicate threadlike stolons produce many little plantlets. Performs well on large topiary forms or in terrariums. May have a problem with mealybugs.

S. stolonifera (Strawberry Begonia or Geranium) Hairy round leaves have silver markings along and in between veins. Undersides of leaves are red. Runners (stolons) are red and produce new plants at the tips.

S. stolonifera '**Tricolor**' (Tricolor Strawberry Begonia or Geranium) An intensely colored plant with the same habit as *S. cuscutiformis* and *S. stolonifera*. Hairy leaves are dark green and white with an obvious pink wash. The underside is reddish, and the stolons are bright reddish pink. This plant is slow growing and more sensitive to overwatering. It needs higher light than *S. stolonifera*.

PLANT PRODUCER PRACTICES

Marketing plays as big a role in selling plants as it does in dish detergent. Plants are frequently labeled to attract impulse buyers; not for the botanist or serious grower. Often only a common name (or no name at all!) is offered, and it may be a name not usually associated with the particular plant. If you are interested in correct scientific names or at least an accepted common name, purchase plants from a reputable greenhouse–not at a tent sale in a parking lot.

Some members of horticulture industry are forever looking for ways to make things "better" and faster. Often this mean producing plants that do not resemble their namesakes found in nature. These quickly produced "clones" frequently change as they grow and adjust to a home environment. The potted rhipsalis (*R. salicornoides*) on the previous page may elongate and thin out eventually. The compact hibiscus purchased covered with flowers will be difficult to keep in bounds and less floriferous after some time in the home.

S. stolonifera 'Tricolor' (Tricolor Strawberry Begonia or Geranium).

SCHLUMBERGERA *Cactaceae*

Native to Brazil, these epiphytic cactus have flat segmented stems that are often confused as leaves. The segments are toothed and have hairs or bristles at the aeroles located along the margins. Flowers are produced on new growth and have reflexed petals. Many of the newest cultivars have large iridescent "yawning" flowers.

Give schlumbergera medium to high light and average to hot temperatures. Allow the soil to dry between soakings and hold back on water in the winter. Avoid high-traffic areas because the stems are brittle and break easily. Use an average, well-drained potting mix and keep the plants in the same pot for as long as possible. It is, however, possible to pot up to a larger-size pot to increase the plant's growth. Fertilize at full strength in summer and use dilute fertilizer for every watering during the growing period. Prune only selectively when grooming. Propagate by stem cuttings. Stem rot is common if kept too cool and too wet. Mealybugs are always a possibility.

SELECTIONS *S.* x *buckleyi [S.* x *bridgesii]* (Christmas Cactus) A commonly grown hybrid hardly recognized as a cactus. Most plants offered are cultivars. Waxy segmented stems may be toothed or not, depending on the cultivar. Some cultivars will flower twice a year. Flowering is dependent on light duration and temperature. If temperatures are held at 50-59° F., the plants will flower regardless of light duration. Temperatures over 60° F. during long days produce vegetative growth. The same temperatures during short days produce flowers. In other words, provide cool temperatures into fall to produce flowers during its natural flowering time, late fall and early winter. Always allow the plant to dry a little between waterings during its vegetative growth. During flower bud formation, allow the plant to begin to dry out but do not let it dehydrate or it will drop its buds. There is a palette of colors from which to choose.

S. x *buckleyi* 'Jingle Bells' Shiny reddish flowers.

S. x *buckleyi* 'Christmas Fantasy' Iridescent white with a red mark in the throat.

SCIRPUS *Cyperaceae*

These are mostly grassy clump-forming or tufted, semiaquatic perennials that inhabit moist places all over the world. The tiny flowers are tightly grouped into clusters.

Provide medium to high light and average to cool temperatures. Keep the soil evenly moist—in fact, they can actually sit in water. Avoid drying winds and prune only selectively as needed for grooming. Fertilize three times in summer. Plant in peaty, moisture-retentive potting mix and repot when plants fill the pot. Divide the rhizomes regularly to keep the plants productive.

SELECTIONS *S. cernuus* A delightful, unusual, tufted, grassy plant that explodes from its pot. A well-grown specimen has threadlike new bright green stems shooting out from the soil. Older stems droop over the edge of the pot. When in flower, the plant sparkles with small globular flowers suspended on the ends of stemmy filaments. Must be kept moist at all times. Keep out of

SAXIFRAGA CUSCUTIFORMIS (MINATURE STRAWBERRY BEGONIA)
To six inches in hanging basket; medium light and average
to cool temperatures; evenly moist while actively growing
and hold back on water in the winter; medium growing.
SHOWN WITH S. STOLONIFERA (LARGER, DARKER LEAVES).

SCHLUMBERGERA X BUCKLEYI CV. To twelve inches; epiphytic;
medium to high light, average to hot temperatures; dry
between soakings and hold back on water in the winter;
fertilize at full strength in summer, use dilute fertilizer during growing period; slow growing.

SCIRPUS CERNUUS Six- to eight-inch hanging basket; medium to high light and average to cool temperatures; evenly
moist (they can actually sit in water); fertilize three times in
summer; fast growing.

SELAGINELLA UNCINATA (CLUBMOSS) To three inches tall with
creeping stems; medium light, average temperatures; evenly moist; dilute fertilizer at every watering; slow growing.

Most of the failures experienced with houseplants are due to attempting to grow them under unsuitable conditions. In other words, the environment is at fault. The chief job, therefore, of the would-be grower of houseplants is to provide the right growing conditions. . . if the environment cannot be changed, plants must be selected which will endure the environment.
MONTAGUE FREE, FROM *ALL ABOUT HOUSEPLANTS*, 1955

pounding rain or wind for the most pristine growth. Makes a great six- to eight-inch hanging basket. Works well as "hair" on a topiary form as long as you are a faithful waterer.

SELAGINELLA CREEPING MOSS, CLUBMOSS *Selaginellaceae*
Selaginellas come in trailing and upright forms, and vary from blue-green to pale green to yellow-green to variegated. They have been popular since Victorian times and are a superb plant to use in a terrarium. These plants are in the clubmoss family, whose members produce spores rather than seeds. They not ferns, however.

Grow selaginella in medium light and average temperatures. Keep the soil moist at all times and mist the leaves with tepid water to keep the humidity high. The leaves are very delicate and will shrivel if put in a drafty or dry spot. Fertilize with a dilute solution at every watering. It's easily grown in a shallow pot with well-drained potting mix. Repot only if necessary in spring and propagate by stem cuttings in spring or summer.
SELECTIONS *S. martensii* **'Albomarginata'** Broad feathery fans of medium green are irregular, blotched with patches of ivory or yellow. Stems creep along soil surface, slowly filling pot.
S. krussiana A common type that will mysteriously move from its own pot to others. Soft medium green feathery stems fill a pot fairly quickly.

SERISSA *Rubiaceae*
This is a single species of decorative pot plants native to southeast Asia. Many cultivars have been developed and are readily available through mail-order sources. These plants are desirable because of long flowering periods and attractive foliage.

Give serissa medium to high light and average to cool temperatures. Keep the potting mix evenly moist and fertilize three times in summer. Prune after flowering–serissa tolerates pruning quite well. Pot in average, well-drained potting mix and repot when it sends up stems from the roots, indicating it is potbound. Serissa tolerates root pruning if done with care and if a similar percentage of foliage is removed at the same time. Propagate by stem cuttings. Outstanding for training as a tree-form standard or bonsai.
SELECTIONS *S. foetida* Tiny dark green leaves and produces four-petaled white flowers.
S. foetida **Longwood Clone** Foliage is similar to species, but the larger flowers are pink with five recurved petals–stemmy with tiny leaves.
S. foetida **'Plena'** *[S. foetida* **'Floreplena'***]* (Snow Rose) Double white flowers slightly larger than a pencil eraser cover this plant, usually in winter. It will produce flowers year-round, but in less profusion. Undemanding and rewarding; delicately pointed elliptical leaves are dark green. Newer growth is held on wiry whitish stems; older growth yellows and becomes fissured. Mites may be a problem in dry conditions. Slow growing so prune with care. The plant flowers on new growth so prune if necessary after flowering.

***S. foetida* 'Sapporo'** Similar to the species but more compact and slower growing.
***S. foetida* 'Variegata'** Broad leaves, edged creamy white, single whitish pink flowers. Vigorous.

STREPTOCARPUS CAPE PRIMROSE *Gesneriaceae*

Native to Africa and Madagascar, this group of plants is related to the African violets although they vary greatly in habit. The delicate flowers are tubular or funnel-shaped and appear to bounce on thin wires. The five flower lobes spread wide and come in blue, red, white, pink, and purple. Seeds are readily produced in slender twisted pointed capsules. *Strepto* means "twisted" and *karpo* means "fruit." If you grow African violets well, this plant will do well for you also.

Cape primroses benefit from warm temperatures, tepid water, and high humidity. Avoid drying winds, cold drafts, and high-traffic areas. Provide medium to low light and allow the top of the soil to dry between waterings. Don't allow water to get on the leaves. Fertilize with a dilute solution at every watering. Pot in average, well-drained potting mix and repot annually if you have problems with root mealybugs. Otherwise, it will grow well in the same pot for several years. Prune only selectively after flowering. Propagate by stem cuttings, leaf cuttings, rhizome division, and seed. Mealybugs and thrips may be a problem—watch for patches of flowers that look like the color has been rubbed off. If thrips become a problem, removing all flowers is the first step in control.

Streptocarpus saxorum.

SELECTIONS *S.* x *hybridus* (Cape Primrose) Long, broad fuzzy leaves are held by a distinct midrib that is susceptible to breakage. Flowers are held on long, wiry stems above foliage. Several flowers appear on each stem and open in succession. The throats of the flowers are frequently striped with a contrasting color—perhaps acting as directional signals for pollinators. Cultivars offer many flower sizes, colors, and textures. Removing spent flowers rather than letting them go to seed keeps the plants flowering for longer periods.
***S.* x *hybridus* 'Constant Nymph'** Common and rewarding—dozens of navy blue flowers appear simultaneously and continue for several months.
S. saxorum A stemmy plant that performs well in a hanging basket as well as a pot. Put it out in warm weather in a protected bright spot. Leaves are elliptic or oval, hairy, and gray-green and may appear in twos or threes. Flowers are powder blue or lilac and are produced abundantly. Flower stems are mere "wires" so that the flowers seem to float over the foliage. Start baskets annually from cuttings. Propagate in fall when you bring it in for the winter.
***S.* 'Good Hope'** More succulent, pointed leaves.

SYNGONIUM [NEPHTHYTIS] *Araceae*

This group of twenty climbing vines is native to tropical America and the West Indies. The leaves vary in size and shape as the plants mature (like epipremnum). Many of them have arrow-shaped leaves on heavy stems. They produce aerial roots so can be grown on a slab or in a basket. Many

SERISSA FOETIDA LONGWOOD CLONE To two feet; medium to high light and average to cool temperatures; evenly moist; fertilize three times in summer; slow growing.

SERISSA FOETIDA 'PLENA' (SNOW ROSE) To two feet; medium to high light and average to cool temperatures; evenly moist; fertilize three times in summer; slow growing.

STREPTOCARPUS X HYBRIDUS CV. (CAPE PRIMROSE) To one foot; medium light and warm temperatures; dry between waterings; use tepid water and don't get it on the leaves; high humidity; fertilize with a dilute solution at every watering; moderate growth rate.

SYNGONIUM PODOPHYLLUM CV. (ARROWHEAD VINE) Stems to ten feet; medium to low light; average temperatures and high humidity; dry between waterings; fertilizer thre times in summer; slow growing.

cultivars are available, some of which are produced by tissue culture, which makes them shorter and denser.

Give syngonium medium to low light and allow the plant to dry between waterings. Provide average temperature, high humidity, and fertilize three times in summer only. Syngonium tolerates pruning well. Repotting is seldom needed; pot in an average, well-drained mix. Propagate by stem cuttings and watch for problems with scale.

SELECTIONS *S. podophyllum* (Arrowhead Vine, Goosefoot Plant) Young leaves are three-lobed with silver or white markings–older leaves become large and dull. Prune frequently to control vining and induce more growth. Many cultivars are available and they are hard to identify since the leaves change as they age.

S. **'Emerald Gem'** Most commonly available; arrowhead shaped leaves with light-colored veins.

S. **'Bold Illusion'** Broad arrowhead-shaped leaves that are cream with pink veins. They lose their color in low light.

S. **'Infra Red'** Severely three-lobed leaves, blushed with rich pink.

SYZYGIUM *Myrtaceae*

This is a large group of plants native to the Old World tropics of which a few are desirable as houseplants. These have nice foliage characteristics as well as the bonus of edible fruits. Flowers consist of many stamens, giving the overall fuzzy look of the myrtle family.

Grow in medium to high light and average temperatures. Keep the soil evenly moist and fertilize three times in summer. Use an average, well-drained potting mix. Repot every couple of years and disturb or prune the roots a little when potting into a larger container. Scale can be a problem because it is difficult to see against the brown bark. Be suspicious of sticky areas around the pot or on the foliage. Mealybugs and mites can also infest poorly cultivated plants.

SELECTIONS *S. paniculatum* Grows large quickly; similar in appearance to *S. paniculatum* 'Compacta'.

S. paniculatum **'Compacta'** (Dwarf Brush Cherry) Opposite pairs of simple pointed leaves and distinct branching habits make this a tidy plant to grow. It is extremely tolerant of pruning because of good self-branching, making it an excellent candidate for topiary. This selection makes a great tabletop or floor-sized ball or poodle shape. It naturally grows in a strict cone shape, making a delightful Christmas tree. The new growth is highlighted with bronze-red changing to rich dark green with age. The midrib is distinct, seeming to fold the leaf in half. White flowers are round with many stamens protruding with a sparkle on the end. Rosy pink irregular roundish edible fruits follow. It flowers on new growth, so take care in pruning. Flowers appear in late summer into fall.

TRADESCANTIA SPIDERWORT *Commelinaceae*

These somewhat fleshy perennials are native to North and South America.

HANGING BASKETS AND VINING PLANTS

Climbing, vining, and trailing plants are all excellent candidates for hanging baskets, and some of them also work well if trained up on a frame or trellis. Plants trained in this manner will take more care and pruning to keep them attractive, so a favorite method of easy care is to grow them in hanging baskets. When planning a hanging basket, also consider plants that have arching forms such as ferns–these are graceful basket plants.

Containers range from wire baskets filled with sphagnum moss (only suitable for outdoor use because of watering) to decorative baskets on their own hangers to plastic pots with wire hangers. Regardless of the type you choose for indoor use, the most critical element is that the pot drain well and the water be captured in a saucer of some sort. Generally, six- to eight-inch baskets are commonly used because of their ease of handling. Ten-inch and larger baskets can be extremely heavy.

Some plants will fill a basket with only one plant while others will look full and healthy if several plants are planted together. If using only one, plant it in the center of the pot and let the vines or trailers hang down around the pot. If using several plants, put one in the center and space the others around it, letting the trailers hang over the sides.

See page 23 for a list of plant choices for hanging baskets.

Above: Callisia (Bolivian Jew). The commonly called "tradescantia group" includes callisia, zebrina, setcreasea, and tradescantia. These plants all thrive under similar conditions and are excellent subjects for hanging baskets because of their trailing nature.

They have alternate leaves that wrap around the stem and three-petaled flowers. There are many colorful varieties available that are easy to grow and propagate. They make excellent hanging baskets.

Grow tradescantia in medium light and average to cool temperatures. Allow the soil to dry between soakings and fertilize three times in summer only. Repot infrequently and pinch often to keep the plant full. Propagate by stem cuttings in soil or water. Tradescantias are generally pest-free.

SELECTIONS *T. albiflora* **'Albovittata'** (Wandering Jew) Irregular white stripes on leaves; delicately hairy on margins.

T. fluminensis (Wandering Jew) Trailing stems to two feet; fleshy, glossy leaves are oval and pointed. The leaves are blue-green on top and purple on the underside.

T. fluminensis **'Variegata'** Variable cream or white stripes in the leaves.

T. sillamontana (White Velvet) Stiff, succulent and somewhat upright plant; the plant is covered with dense white wool; pinkish flowers; keep on dry side in winter.

Zebrina pendulosa (Wandering Jew) A closely allied plant with habit similar to *T. albiflora* 'Albovittata'. Leaves are marked with glistening silver stripes on top and purple on the underside.

TREVESIA *Araliaceae*

This group consists of four to ten species native from India to the Malay Peninsula and Polynesia. Shrubs or small trees in nature, they tend to be prickly along the stems with leaves cut in unusual patterns, some reminiscent of snowflakes or ice crystals.

Grow in medium to high light and allow the soil to dry slightly between soakings. Fertilize three times in summer and give the plant average to hot temperatures. Prune selectively and avoid drying winds, cold drafts and low humidity. Pot in average, well-drained potting mix and repot annually. Watch carefully for scale and mites–infested leaves will be shed so treat the plant quickly if you find these pests. Propagate by stem cutting or seed.

SELECTIONS *T. palmata* **'Micholitzii'** (Snowflake Aralia) A favorite, this is a distinctly-leaved plant that deserves its name. Leaves are borne at the tips of prickly stems, emerging as small snowflakes that are totally covered with white felt. As the leaves enlarge, the felt gradually disappears, but the shape remains, becoming more deeply cut with the inner webbing between the veins more pronounced. The leaves can grow to be two feet across in a humid, bright environment. Most plants can be maintained at less than six feet tall with ten- to twelve-inch leaves. The erect stems are aralia-like with prickles and large leaf scars that are reminiscent of a "smile." Lower leaves are shed over time, exposing prickly but attractive stems. Old plants will branch near the base. This plant needs a fairly large space. It may be difficult to find.

SYZYGIUM PANICULATUM 'COMPACTA' (DWARF BRUSH CHERRY)
To ten feet, can keep pruned to eighteen inches; medium to high light and average temperatures; evenly moist; fertilize three times in summer; moderate to fast growth.

TRADESCANTIA ALBIFLORA 'ALBOVITTATA' (WANDERING JEW)
Vines to three feet; medium light; average to cool temperatures; dry between soakings; fertilize three times in summer; slow growing.

TREVESIA PALMATA 'MICHOLITZII' (SNOWFLAKE ARALIA) Less than six feet tall with ten- to twelve-inch leaves; medium to high light and average to hot temperatures; dry slightly between soakings; fertilize three times in summer; slow growing.

ZEBRINA PENDULA (WANDERING JEW) High light; average to cool temperatures; dry between soakings; fertilize three times in summer; fast growing.

LOW LIGHT

East or north exposure or room interior

A plant that grows in low light can be placed in an east, northeast, or north window. It does not require any direct sun and will survive in predominately filtered light. There are, however, dark areas indoors that simply are not suitable for plants. For example, if there is not enough light by which to read comfortably, a plant will not grow well. Supplemental lights or growing carts offer the opportunity to grow plants in poorly lighted situations and are discussed on page 210. Incandescent light, particularly if shaded, offers no real value as a light source for houseplants. Other options for low-light areas are seasonal plants that are rotated in and out of a greenhouse or well-lighted spot, short-term plants that are disposed of after blooming, and preserved or silk plants.

PLANTS IN MEDIUM-LIGHT SECTION (PAGES 74-137) THAT ARE SUITABLE FOR LOW-LIGHT SITUATIONS

Anthurium
Aucuba
Curculigo
Ficus
Homalomena
Howea
Peperomia
Psilotum
Pteris
Rhoeo
Streptocarpus
Syngonium

PLANTS IN HIGH-LIGHT SECTION (PAGES 24-73) THAT ARE SUITABLE FOR LOW-LIGHT SITUATIONS

Hypoestes
Nolina

LOW LIGHT

AGLAONEMA CHINESE EVERGREEN *Araceae*

The Chinese evergreen is native to tropical and subtropical Southeast Asia and the Philippine Islands. Although adaptable to several light levels, the all-green forms of these shrubby plants perform particularly well in low light. The great variety in size, shape, and coloration of leaves makes this the plant of choice for low-light areas in homes and commercial settings, such as malls and office buildings. They are reliable, easy to maintain, and relatively free of disease and insect problems.

Aglaonemas grow best in low to medium light in average home temperatures (65-80° F.). A coarse root system allows them to tolerate a short dry period between soakings. Leaves tend to yellow if allowed to stand in water or if watered before drying out. They do not tolerate drying winds or cold drafts.

Aglaonemas seldom need repotting, especially in low light, where they grow slowly, although an increased demand for water indicates a need for repotting. Use an average-weight potting soil with good drainage and fertilize infrequently (gardeners at New York Botanical Garden find they need frequent feeding). Aglaonemas are self-branching so the only pruning needed is removal of older unsightly canes and an occasional yellow leaf. Remove the canes at two inches above the soil level to produce offsets, giving the plant a fuller appearance. Propagation by stem cuttings in soil is the preferred method, although they can also be divided or propagated by stem cuttings in water. Watch for mealybugs at the bases of leaf stalks; spider mites can be a problem in bright light.

SELECTIONS *A. commutatum* **'Maria'** is particularly suited to low light; this slow grower requires little attention. The rich dark leaves are marked with white. Smaller in size than many of its cousins, the leaves are held at a pert angle to the petiole. The plant grows into a neat, dense mound with inconspicuous flowers appearing on mature plants. In most cases, flowers should be removed as they appear because if left on the plant, the flower stems become unattractive (and slimy) as they deteriorate. If the plant is allowed to flower, red fruits will sometimes form. Frequently, this plant appears in mixed dish gardens and is often the one that lingers after others in the dish have perished. With little attention, this lovely plant will stand elegantly on its own.

A. **'Silver Queen'** Another tough, reliable plant frequently used in difficult areas, and an excellent plant for low-light areas of the home. The decorative, narrow, pointed leaves are heavily marked with dull silver-gray surrounding green zones between the veins. The plant grows dense and full, reaching a mature height of two feet. Spider mites or mealybugs may be a problem if the plant is stressed as with too little water or too much sun.

ASPIDISTRA CAST IRON PLANT *Liliaceae*

Popular since Victorian times, these plants from east Asia maintain their simple beauty in spite of neglect and other abuse. Vertical evergreen leaves are generated from horizontal rhizomes. These plants are slow growers that usually don't get noticed until there is a thick layer of dust on the leaves. These are

AGLAEONEMA COMMUTATUM 'MARIA' (CHINESE EVERGREEN) One to two feet tall; low to medium light and average temepratures; dry briefly between waterings; fertilize infrequently; easy to grow; moderate growth rate.

AGLAEONEMA 'SILVER QUEEN' (CHINESE EVERGREEN) Two feet tall; low to medium light; average temperature; dry briefly between waterings; fertilize infrequently; easy to grow; moderate growth rate.

ASPIDISTRA ELATIOR (CAST IRON PLANT) To two and one half feet; low to medium light and cool to average temperatures; dry between soakings and reduce watering in winter; fertilize infrequently; slow growing.

CALATHEA MAKOYANA (PEACOCK PLANT) To twenty inches; low light and average; will tolerate hot areas as long as the humidity is high; daily misting helpful; evenly moist; reduce watering in winter; fertilize infrequently; slow growing.

Plants for low light: calathea, dracaena and caladium, a disposable plant.

excellent low-light plants–they could almost grow in a closet but perform best in low to medium light and cool to average temperatures (52-80° F.). They should be allowed to dry between soakings and will not tolerate drying winds. Water as needed in spring, summer, and fall, and reduce watering in winter.

Aspidistra requires average-weight potting soil and will tolerate the same pot for many years. Potting to a larger-size pot encourages growth. Aspidistra should be fertilized and pruned infrequently. If the plant sits dry for extended periods of time, spider mites will be a problem. Otherwise, mites and mealybugs appear only infrequently. To propagate, divide the rhizome and replant in fresh soil.

SELECTIONS A. elatior (Cast Iron Plant) Visually rather uninteresting plants, making them suitable as filler in dark corners or busy hallways. The clump-forming dark green plant sends leathery pointed leaves to three feet. One annual spurt of growth sends fresh bright green tubes of growth up from the rhizome. They unroll and darken among the older leaves. The flowers are almost never seen by the passerby since they are rather flat and held at soil level. New cultivars with interesting markings and the same tolerance for abuse are becoming commonly available.

A. elatior 'Minor' (Milky Way Cast Iron Plant) much smaller, dwarf type with creamy-white spots on the leaves.

A. elatior 'Variegata' A full-sized aspidistra with white marks running the length of the leaf. High light will cause the variegation to fade.

CALATHEA PEACOCK PLANTS *Marantaceae*

These tropical plants vary in size from small plants suitable for home culture to large conservatory types. They are tuberous clumping perennials with attractively marked leaves. Some species are challenging to grow and may take a couple of tries to achieve success. Elevated humidity levels will improve the growth of most calatheas, and many perform really well during the hot, humid days of summer. Many species and cultivars are offered in the trade, all of which are distinctly marked; most are suited to the home.

Calatheas perform well in low light at average home temperatures. They will tolerate hot areas as long as the humidity is high. Frequent daily misting keeps calathea leaves healthy. If the leaves become unsightly, remove them, adjust the cultural conditions, and the new growth should appear in an improved state. Plant growth slows in winter and plants may look unsightly; reduce watering at this time. When new growth begins in spring, prune the plant accordingly. It is commonly called the second chance plant owing to its initial forgiveness, allowing the grower to try again. Keep the soil evenly moist (except in winter), fertilize infrequently, and avoid drying winds, cold drafts, and direct sun. Pot in an average, well-drained soil and repot before water stress becomes a problem–the leaves are damaged by dehydration. Mites and thrips can be a problem; mealybugs will appear occasionally.

SELECTIONS C. lancifolia [C. insignis] (Rattlesnake Plant) is native to Brazil. As with many calatheas, the leaf markings add a great deal of visual interest–it has

CALATHEA ORNATUM Eight-inch-long leaves; low light and average temperatures (will tolerate hot areas if humidity is high); daily misting helpful; evenly moist; reduce watering in winter; fertilize infrequently; slow growing.

CHAMAEDOREA METALLICA (MINIATURE FISHTAIL PALM) Three feet tall; low to medium light and average temperatures; dry slightly between soakings; fertilize three times in the summer; slow growing.

DRACAENA DEREMENSIS 'JANET CRAIG' (JANET CRAIG DRACAENA) May reach ten feet (can prune to shorten); low light and average temperatures (cold sensitive); dry briefly between soakings; fertilize infrequently; slow growing.

DRACAENA DEREMENSIS 'LEMON LIME' (STRIPED DRACAENA) Grows to four feet; low light and average temperatures; dry briefly between soakings; fertilize infrequently; very slow growing.

textured narrow leaves with undulating edges. The plant forms a clump that stays dense and upright.

C. makoyana (Peacock Plant) The leaves are reminiscent of a peacock's tail, hence the common name. The peacock plant's broad, oval, pointed leaves decoratively marked with linear patches of green are asymmetrically attached to the midrib. The undersides are marked with purple in the same pattern. Once you have adjusted your cultural habits to the needs of this plant, you will be well rewarded.

C. picturata This is a decorative plant that is moderately difficult to grow but worthwhile if its cultural conditions are correct. It is round-growing, and the broad leaves are marked with silver along the midrib and parallel to the leaf margin. The undersides are solid purple. If it goes dormant because the conditions are not right, adjustments in care will often bring it back from the "dead."

C. picturata 'Argentea' Dark green leaves with silver margins.

C. picturata 'Vandenheckei' has a silvery midrib with irregular edges.

CHAMAEDOREA METALLICA *See page 85 for main* Chamaedorea *entry*

C. metallica (Miniature Fishtail Palm) This native of Mexico is an uncommon dwarf palm growing to three feet with dark bluish-green forked leaves. The leaves are broad and coarse compared with slender stems. It is commonly sold in groups of three stems per pot and is quite appropriate for small spaces. It is generally underused because of its scarcity. It may have a problem with mites and mealybugs, especially during flowering.

DRACAENA *Agavaceae*

Dracaenas are staples of the foliage industry. Widely used for many years, these palmlike plants from tropical and subtropical Africa and Asia have earned a solid reputation. They have great variety in leaf color and texture and vary from shrubby types to tree forms. Most are easy to grow and rewarding because they grow quickly in adequate light.

Dracaenas will tolerate low light in average home temperatures, and most varieties should be allowed to dry briefly between soakings. They will not, however, tolerate drying winds or low humidity. Most dracaenas perform best in pots that are small in proportion to the plant size. They should be repotted in an average, well-drained mix when they become top-heavy. Dracaenas should be fertilized infrequently and although they tolerate pruning quite well, it is usually necessary only for grooming. Dracaenas can be propagated by stem cuttings or by seed. Watch for mealybugs on the flowers, and mites can be a problem in low humidity.

SELECTIONS D. deremensis 'Compacta' Give the same culture as *D. deremensis* 'Janet Craig'. The dark-green leaves are only five inches long and are tightly clustered along the slow-growing stems.

D. deremensis 'Janet Craig ' (Janet Craig Dracaena) This plant is second only to the corn plant in the history of interior landscaping. Glossy dark green leaves are held in graceful curves along the stems. It may reach ten feet. Withholding water slows the growth and keeps the stems stronger. High fluoride levels in city water cause tip burn. Trimming removes brown tissue only to have the cut edge turn brown over time. Do not allow water to stand in the crown.

'Janet Craig' does not tolerate cold temperatures, especially when wet. It may have a problem with mealybugs, mites, and thrips, but is generally pest-free.

D. deremensis 'Warneckei' (Striped Dracaena) One of the most colorful plants for low light, and it is not as susceptible to tip burn as *D.* 'Janet Craig'. The leaves are striped with white and are much narrower than *D.* 'Janet Craig' or *D. fragrans.* It grows to four feet eventually. This has become another frequently used mall plant because of its color and low light tolerance. It has no problems if well-cultured. Otherwise, it may have a problem with mealybugs, mites, and thrips.

D. fragrans 'Massangeana' (Variegated Corn Plant, Mass Cane) A durable plant, commonly planted with three canes to a pot. Variegated corn plant has tufts of broad leaves striped with yellow that cluster at the tips of stiffly erect woody canes or stems. The canes will resprout if they are cut and put in good light–often done in the foliage industry to encourage multiple "breaks" or tufts along the canes, which give the plant a more lush appearance. Mass cane does best if kept somewhat dry though the winter as the plant tends to lose many roots. The broad leaves should be dusted frequently to avoid buildup. Mealybugs love the sweet-smelling flowers, although flowers rarely appear in low light. They are also prone to mites and thrips. *D. fragrans* is the same in appearance as 'Massangeana' but without the yellow banding on the leaves.

D. marginata (Madagascar Dragon Tree) An interesting plant architecturally. Light-colored stems meander gracefully, ending in tufts of narrow maroon and green pointed leaves, giving the plant an exotic look. Some growers encourage unique bends in the stems by suspending weights when the plants are young or by tilting the pot first at one angle and then another. Can be prone to spider mites; keep on the dry side.

D. marginata 'Tricolor' This plant offers an unusual and architecturally interesting look in the right low-light situation. It grows to eight feet or more in a container. Cream and reddish variegated narrow pointed leaves gather in tufts at the end of twisted, irregularly growing stems. The light color of the bark is a great contrast to the leaves. This undemanding plant changes its look over the years as the stems meander in various directions. This adaptable plant will also do well in full sun with more frequent watering. Spider mites are a frequent problem. There are many new varieties available that differ from 'Tricolor' only in leaf color.

D. reflexa (Pleomele reflexa) (Song of India) Native to Madagascar and Mauritius this is a less rigid, more flexible-stemmed dracaena that holds its leaves all the way down to the soil level in sufficient light. Four-inch medium green leaves spiral around the stem–the newest growth points upward and then becomes horizontal with age. Some feel song of India is hard to grow, but this is not so. It is used well for a large mass of refreshing indoor greenery that is fairly trouble-free.

D. reflexa 'Variegata' The leaves are yellow-edged and require only slightly more light than *D. reflexa.*

EPIPREMNUM *Araceae*

Native to tropical Asia, epipremnum contains about ten species of climbing vines. The leaf shape and size change dramatically (up to thirty inches

It's that way with houseplants. Beyond their present beauty lie the deeper realms of love and memory. If you're an indoor gardener, I'm sure you have at least one plant, given to you in love or inherited from a friend or relative, whose very sight evokes pleasant recollections. I understand these emotions well because I have plants that my mother once cherished and each time I see them she comes alive again in my mind, full of laughter and the love of family and flowers.

JAMES UNDERWOOD CROCKETT, FROM *CROCKETT'S INDOOR GARDEN,* 1978

long) when the plant goes from a juvenile to mature state. In order for this change to occur, the plant must grow vertically. Indoor species are grown for their foliage–they will not flower in pot culture. These plants make a lovely hanging basket or can be trained onto a bark slab–they have aerial roots and will climb readily. This plant is closely related to the split-leaf philodendron, which has the same juvenile/mature changes.

Provide epipremnum with medium to low light, average temperatures, and allow the soil to dry between soakings. Avoid cold drafts and provide high humidity if possible. Repot only when root-bound (infrequently) into average, well-drained potting mix. Fertilize infrequently and pinch often to keep the plant bushy. Propagate by stem cuttings kept in the dark until rooted. Watch for scale.

SELECTIONS *E. aureum* (incorrectly referred to as *Scindapsis aureus* or *Pothos aureus*) (Golden Pothos, Devil's Ivy) Commonly grown; many offered in trade are grown on a support and treated with growth regulators to broaden the leaves. When grown in the home, they will have the more typical heart-shaped leaves on long vines.

E. aureum **'Marble Queen'** (Marble Queen Pothos) Slower growing; white marbling on the leaves.

FATSIA *Araliaceae*

Fatsia is native to Japan and is generally a large, coarse evergreen shrub, suitable for large spaces in the home or conservatory. They are excellent plants to use in drafty spots, such as entryways or near sliding glass doors, because of their tolerance of temperature extremes.

Fatsias will also tolerate low light. The soil should be allowed to dry briefly between waterings and repot only when the plant becomes out of proportion with the pot. Use average potting soil that is well-drained. Fertilize three times in summer and prune only to improve the plant's appearance. Severe pruning is seldom needed. Scale can be a serious problem. Aphids may appear on new growth; mites, mealybugs, and thrips may appear infrequently. A vigorous plant will avoid all these problems. Propagate by stem cuttings, seed, or air layering.

SELECTIONS *F. japonica* (Japanese Fatsia) A strong-growing shrub that does particularly well near a drafty spot that few other plants can fill. Although the leaves are large, it presents itself with dignity and grace. Japanese fatsia has broadly palmate leaves with light venation. The leaves coarsely group together to make a six-foot shrub, although it may be kept shorter with selective pruning. The flowers are small and whitish-yellow. This plant is sure to make you feel like you have a green thumb because it is rewarding and easy to grow.

F. japonica **'Variegata'** (Variegated Japanese Aralia) Similar to species except the leaves are boldly variegated with creamy yellow.

FICUS *See page 97 for main* Ficus *entry*

SELECTIONS *F. lyrata* (Fiddle-Leaf Fig) Native to tropical West Africa, this is an elegant plant that serves as a focal point in any room and works well in low light. The fiddle-leaf fig has broad dark green leaves that are light green

DRACAENA FRAGRANS 'MASSANGEANA' (VARIEGATED CORN PLANT, MASS CANE) To ten feet tall; low light and average temperatures (cold sensitive) ; dry briefly between soakings (keep somewhat dry though the winter); fertilize infrequently; slow growing.

DRACAENA MARGINATA 'TRICOLOR' (MADAGASCAR DRAGON TREE) Two to six feet or more; low to medium light and average temperatures (full sun with more frequent watering); dry briefly between soakings; fertilize infrequently; slow growing unless fed frequently and in bright light.

EPIPREMNUM AUREUM (GOLDEN POTHOS) Four to six feet tall if grown as an upright; low to medium light; average temperatures; dry between soakings; high humidity; fertilize infrequently; average growth rate in medium light.

FATSIA JAPONICA (JAPANESE FATSIA) Can grow to six feet; low light; tolerant of temperature extremes; dry briefly between waterings; fertilize three times in summer; slow to moderate growth rate.

underneath and have a slightly rippled edge. The bark is dark red-brown with raised meandering ridges in beautiful contrast to the leaves. It grows quite large over time. The fruits are about the size of a golf ball and are dry and wrinkled like the trunk. It tolerates pruning well and should be pruned in late spring or summer. Mealybugs may be a problem, especially when the plant is fruiting. This is sure to be a conversation piece in any large room. Stately and exotic, this slow grower deserves your consideration.

F. mclealandii 'Alii' This a refreshing change from the typical ficus (*F. benjamina*, *F. nitida*). Narrow, long leaves grace the head of this tree, giving it a fountain-like appearance and the bark becomes decorative with age. It can become quite large but can be controlled with pruning; can be bushy or tree-like. It is virtually problem-free although thrips, mealybugs, and scale are possible. This is an excellent choice for large spaces.

MARANTA *Marantaceae*

Native to tropical America, marantas are rhizomatous, low-growing plants grown for their colorful foliage or food purposes. Arrowroot (thickener in cooking) comes from *M. arundinaceae*. Marantas are closely related to the calatheas, but are a more difficult group of houseplants to grow.

Provide low to medium and average to hot temperatures. Avoid drying winds, cold temperatures and low humidity; if you have difficulty growing these plants, increase humidity. Keep the soil evenly moist. Fertilize three times in summer or with dilute fertilizer at every watering during the growing season. Repot in average potting mix only every two years or so. Propagate by stem cutting or rhizome division. Watch for spider mites.

SELECTIONS *M. leuconeura* (Prayer Plant) gets its name because its leaves fold upward along the midrib in the evening. This plant is slow growing and makes a low mound of six inch green leaves.

M. leuconeura var. *erythroneura* Light green leaves with silver and red veins that follow the curve of the leaf.

MONSTERA WINDOWLEAF *Araceae*

Monsteras are climbers that are native to tropical America. Their long peti-oled leaves will change from juvenile to mature shapes if the plant is grown upright. Unfortunately, this is often impossible in the home since the plants are so large. The aerial roots may be up to an inch in diameter on old plants.

Provide low to medium light and allow the plant to dry between soak-ings. Give longer periods of dryness between soakings in winter. Fertilize three times in summer and prune regularly to maintain size. Repot infre-quently in an average potting mix and propagate by stem cuttings. Potential problems are scale, whitefly, and mites.

SELECTIONS *M. deliciosa* (Swiss Cheese Plant, Mexican Bread Fruit) will grow to ten feet or more in a pot; the leaves can be ten to thirty-six inches long. The medium green leaves are deeply cut. It has heavy clambering stems with long pink aerial roots. It may develop edible fruits following strange but beautiful green and creamy white flowers. Fruits should be very ripe

FICUS LYRATA (FIDDLE-LEAF FIG) Four to twelve feet; low light and average temperatures; milky sap or latex; dry between soakings; fertilize three times in the summer or less frequently if you are trying to control growth; moderate growth rate.

FICUS MCLEALANDII 'ALII' Can grow to ten feet or pruned to shorten; low or medium light and average temperatures; fertilize three times in the summer; sap may permanently stain clothing; moderate to fast growing.

MANTARA LEUCONEURA (RED PRAYER PLANT) To twelve inches. Low to medium light; average to hot temperatures; evenly moist; fertilize three times in summer; slow growing.

MONSTERA DELICIOSA (SWISS CHEESE PLANT) Vines to ten feet; low to medium light; average temperatures; dry between soakings; fertilize three times in summer; slow growing.

Philodendron 'Xanadu'.

before eating–taste like pineapple custard but may be irritating to some people.

PHILODENDRON *See page 118 for main* Philodendron *entry*
P. Scandens var. oxycardium Commonly found in mixed gift planters.
P. 'Xanadu' Long petioles gracefully support the deeply lobed glossy green leaves. Compact and broader than tall, it stays tidy and full in medium light but performs well in low light even though it thins out a bit. This appealing cultivar is widely available and stays of reasonable size for the average home. Larger specimens are also cultivated.

PYRROSIA FELT FERN *Polypodiaceae*
These ferns from Asia and the Malay Archipelago have unusual habits–creeping, brittle rhizomes support long pubescent leaves. Because they are brittle, they are easily damaged, particularly in high-traffic areas. They perform well in hanging baskets because of their epiphytic nature.

Felt ferns perform well in low to medium light in average temperatures. Keep the soil evenly moist and provide a peaty soil mix that is moisture retentive. They will not tolerate drying winds or cold drafts. Fertilize three times in summer or add dilute fertilizer in every watering during its growth period. Felt Ferns tolerate pruning well, but it is seldom necessary. An added bonus is the virtual lack of pests. Propagate by rhizome division or spore.
SELECTIONS P. lingua (Tongue Fern) Native to China, Japan, and Taiwan, this epiphyte tolerates pruning and short periods of dryness. This plant thrives in cooler temperatures. Hairy reddish stems wander vigorously, supporting long, tonguelike fresh green leaves. It does well in a hanging basket or shallow bulb pan. There is confusion in the trade about this plant and its name.
P. lingua 'Cristata' Decorative, broad, pubescent fronds with crested leaf tips; underside of leaves distinctly contrasting to upper sides.

RHAPIS LADY PALM *Arecaceae*
Natives of southern China and southeast Asia, these elegant, clump-forming, multistemmed palms grow slowly and add an oriental flair to any room. The variation between many available species is slight to the casual observer.

Rhapis palms are extremely tolerant of low light and actually perform better in this situation. Keep the soil evenly moist. They perform best in average temperatures, but tolerate cool situations. Rhapis palms will not tolerate drying winds and low humidity. Repot with a peaty, moisture-retentive mix when new growth appears around the rim of the pot. Fertilize three times in summer and let the plant rest for the winter. Prune only selectively when grooming the lady palm. Rhapis palms are susceptible to scale, mites, and mealy bugs. Propagate by rhizome division or by seed.
SELECTIONS R. excelsa (Lady Palm) Desirable palms for slow-growing, dense, pleasantly textured habit. Lady palms are elegant, small, clump-forming palms with deeply segmented fronds. Fibers surround the stems, adding another texture. Lady palms grow to five feet or more in a container. Their stiff, wiry stems tolerate traffic areas well. Acquiring palms of a size to use as a floor plant requires a considerable monetary investment because of their

PHILODENDRON SCANDENS VAR. OXYCARDIUM (PARLOR IVY) Low to medium light; average temperatures; dry between soakings; fertilize three times in summer; slow growing.

PYRROSIA LINGUA (FELT FERN) Leaves to fifteen inches long; medium to low light; thrives in cool temperatures; epiphyte; tolerates short periods of dryness; fertilize three times in summer or add dilute fertilizer in every watering during growth period; slow growing.

RHAPIS EXCELSA (LADY PALM) Five feet; low light and average temperatures (tolerates cool); evenly moist and high humidity; fertilize three times in summer; extremely slow growing.

SANSEVIERIA CYLINDRICA (DEVIL'S TONGUE) Three feet; tolerates low light but performs best in medium or high light; cool to hot temperatures; dry out between soakings; fertilize infrequently; slow growing; sharp leaves may be dangerous in high-traffic areas.

Sansevieria trifasciata 'Futura', a compact, short growing broad type that mimics *S. t.* 'Laurentii'.

lengthy production time.

R. humilis has longer, narrower leaves and similar habit.

SANSEVIERIA MOTHER-IN-LAW'S TONGUE, SNAKE PLANT

Agavaceae

Sansevierias are native to Africa, Madagascar, and southern Asia. The genus contains many varied plants. Sansevierias were in private residences long before houseplants became popular. They grow in spite of the worst possible cultural conditions (that's not to say these plants look great, but they survive). Variety in color and texture make this genus worthy of consideration for interior landscape design.

Sansevierias will tolerate low light but perform best in medium or high light. Allow them to dry out between soakings. They will also tolerate cool, medium or hot temperatures. Repot sansevierias infrequently since they have an extremely reduced root system; plant them in a coarse, fast-draining soil mix. Fertilize sansevierias infrequently and prune only when grooming. Sansevierias are virtually insect-free and can be propagated in summer by rhizome division or by leaf cuttings. The only problem we have had in the Chicago Botanic Garden greenhouse is weevils on *S. trifasciata* 'Laurentii'. They once scalloped the leaf margins of a group of plants for a week and then disappeared.

SELECTIONS ***S. cylindrica*** (Devil's Tongue) Native to tropical Africa, its leaves leap from the ground in sparse numbers at first, filling out in time. The devil's tongue has rodlike, sharply pointed leaves that are dark green and three feet in height. This culturally tolerant plant is a showstopper in the right location. It is definitely a plant for the design attitudes of the twenty-first century with its great architectural qualities. Its sharp leaves may be considered dangerous in high-traffic areas.

S. parva Great hanging-basket plant.

S. trifasciata **'Futura'** Broad and short leaved, this winner is a refreshing trade-off to the commonly known mother-in-law's-tongue. Its leaves grow to fourteen inches tall and up to five inches wide. It is easy to grow and pleasant to look at—a personal favorite.

S. trifasciata **'Golden Hahnii'** Similar in every way to 'Hahnii', but very sensitive to overwatering and physical contact and requires medium to high light.

S. trifasciata **'Hahnii'** (Bird's Nest Sansevieria) The habit of this sansevieria makes it distinctly different from other species in the genus. It is medium green in color and grows to eight inches across. It is an excellent candidate for small pots and spots. It is also easy to divide and share with friends. Its only problem is stem rot if water is allowed to chill in the crown of the plant.

S. trifasciata **'Laurentii'** Good old standby. It has a little more color than the standard *S. trifasciata.* Grows to four feet tall.

S. trifasciata **'Moonshine'** is a light gray, broad-leaved variety that grows to eighteen inches; the leaves scar easily. An elegant cultivar.

SPATHIPHYLLUM PEACE LILY *Araceae*

Native to tropical Central and South America, this group of dark green-leaved, low-light plants has the added interest of frequent flowering. The

SANSEVIERIA TRIFASCIATA 'GOLDEN HAHNII' To six inches across; tolerates low light but performs best in medium or high light; average to hot temperatures; dry out between soakings—no forgiveness here, rots easily; fertilize sansevierias infrequently; very slow growing.

SANSEVIERIA TRIFASCIATA 'HAHNII' (BIRD'S NEST SANSEVIERIA) Six inches across; tolerates low light but performs best in medium or high light; cool to hot temperatures; dry out between soakings; fertilize sansevierias infrequently; very slow growing.

SPATHIPHYLLUM WALLISII (PEACE LILY) Extremely low-maintenance plant; eighteen inches high; extremely tolerant of low light; average temperatures; low humidity; dry out slightly between soakings; fertilize three times in summer; moderate growth rate.

XANTHOSOMA LINDENII (INDIAN KALE) Grows to three feet; low light and average temperatures; evenly moist soil; fertilize infrequently; tropical appearance; moderate growth rate.

Above: Xanthosoma lindenii. Opposite: A collection of sansevierias at Chicago Botanic Garden.

flowers are usually fragrant. This group is tolerant of a wide range of conditions and ranges from twelve inches to four feet in height. Larger-leaved varieties should be carefully placed because passersby may easily bend or tear the leaves.

Most of these plants are extremely tolerant of low-light conditions and subsequently do best if allowed to dry out slightly between soakings. Gardeners at University of California at Berkeley find they perform better if kept evenly moist. These characteristics as well as the tolerance of low humidity are desirable in mall environments—several cultivars have become used almost exclusively for this. They perform best in average temperatures and will do well in the same pot for many years. Repot with an average, well-drained mix only when the leaf stems begin emerging from the soil around the sides of the pot. Fertilize three times in summer and prune only selectively. Under average conditions, these plants are virtually pest-free. Propagate by dividing the clump.

SELECTIONS *S. floribundum* This is a small Colombian species that puts on a beautiful show of delicate flowers with tiny leaves. Should be kept evenly moist.

S. wallisii Native to Colombia and Venezuela, this peace lily is a low-maintenance plant that stays small enough to sit on a table for many years. Its leaves have undulating edges and are a rich dark green. The flowers appear frequently and are greenish in high light or white and pointed in low light. This is a "must" for the non-plant person. It performs well in self-watering containers, and the most maintenance it requires is occasional dusting.

S. x 'Mauna Loa' This spathiphyllum needs medium light to perform well and is much larger than *S. wallisii*. Medium-sized and compact with showy flowers. One of the best for a wide range of conditions.

S. 'Sensation' Large and spectacular; probably best suited to malls or large spaces.

XANTHOSOMA *Araceae*

These are surprisingly easy to grow aroids from Mexico and tropical America that add color to low-light areas. They are allied closely to alocasia (elephant ears), a group of plants that can be hard to grow in the North. Xanthosoma is tropical and exotic-looking, and many species are grown for their edible tubers. Xanthosoma requires evenly moist soil and thrives in average temperatures—it will not tolerate drying winds or cold drafts. Repot only when the rootball dries out too frequently to keep up with watering, using a mix that is peaty and moisture-retentive. Fertilize infrequently and prune selectively when grooming. Spider mites can be a problem if the plant is allowed to sit dry for extended periods. Propagate by rhizome division or seed.

SELECTIONS *X. lindenii* (Indian Kale) is native to Colombia. It is tropical in appearance and quite undemanding in its needs. Indian kale has highly contrasting dark green arrow-shaped leaves with distinct white markings. The leaves are borne on long wiry petioles that originate from the soil-covered stems. Grows to two-and-one-half feet. It is becoming more available and widely accepted. It is seen frequently in habitat plantings in modern zoos and may be listed as caladium by some botanists.

SEASONAL BLOOMING PLANTS
Some flowering plants are grown by florists and greenhouse operators for temporary display purposes only. These plants are forced to bloom by very carefully controlled temperature, humidity, and light regimes, and are often treated with growth regulators. These plants are beautiful when in bloom, but are very difficult to virtually impossible to bring back into bloom by the household gardener; some are annual and die after flowering. In these instances, the plants should be enjoyed and discarded after the bloom period is finished. For the gardener up to a challenge, we have noted which plants can sometimes be revived and how to go about doing it in the home. Disposable blooming plants usually come in five- or six-inch pots. Do not expect them to grow larger; expect some leaf drop from environmental changes. Remove leaves as they yellow, remove spent flowers to prolong display. Keep evenly moist in bright light and in cool temperatures for longest blooming period.

Chrysanthemums come in a wide range of sizes and colors.

SEASONAL BLOOMING PLANTS

CHRYSANTHEMUM MUM *Asteraceae*

This group of 200 species is native to northern temperate zones and has daisy-like flowers as a common characteristic. Annuals, perennials, and shrubs are represented in this genus. Many hybrids have been developed, exhibiting a myriad of flower types and colors. The Japanese have worked with this group of attractive plants for centuries and have developed spectacular cultivars, often offered at collector's prices.

Provide medium to high light for pot mums; keep the soil evenly moist. Mums will tolerate average to cool temperatures. Keep out of high-traffic areas because leaves, flowers, and stems all break easily. Mums should be treated as disposable plants–it is not advisable to try to keep them as houseplants after they have bloomed. They can be propagated, however, by stem cuttings.

SELECTION *C. vestitum* (Florists' Chrysanthemum, Mum) This species has been used with others for hybridization to create a palette of color and texture not offered by many other pot plants. Flower sizes range from one inch across on the popular mini-mum types to several inches across on the large football mums used in corsages. Petals may be stumpy and rounded to threadlike and tubular or straight, curved or spoon-shaped. Multiply the variations with the many colors and sizes available and it is easy to come up with the right look to fit the occasion. Easy to maintain and long-lasting, these have become staples in the floral industry. At one time offered only as a Thanksgiving or fall-blooming plant, now you can get mums every month of the year. Florists' mums are not hardy, so will not survive the winter in cold climates if planted outdoors. For the longest blooming period, keep them in bright, indirect light, cool and evenly moist.

CYCLAMEN *Primulaceae*

Cyclamen are perennial plants from Europe and the Mediterranean region that offer five-petaled reflexed flowers standing above dense mounds of blue-green leaves. The flowers look almost like butterflies in flight. A woody corm is formed at soil level from which leaves, flowers, and roots are generated. Spent flowers should be removed. Seeds are easily produced and will shorten the flowering period if not removed.

Provide medium light and allow the soil to just begin to dry before soaking. Avoid watering directly on the corm. Provide cool temperatures for maximum blooming (50-60° F.) and avoid drying winds. Use dilute fertilizer at every watering from fall until bud set. Plant in an average, well-drained potting mix and repot in fall. Propagate by seed.

SELECTIONS *C. persicum* (Cyclamen) A species that offers great variety in flower and foliage color that has allowed for selection of preferred types over the years. Breeding has produced many flower colors and plant sizes but has almost eliminated fragrance. The species has white to rose flowers with a

CHRYSANTHEMUM (MUM) Twelve inches high; medium to high light; average to cool temperatures; evenly moist; florists' mums are not hardy, so will not survive the winter in cold climates if planted outdoors; considered disposable plants–very hard to bring back into bloom.

CYCLAMEN PERSICUM (CYCLAMEN) Medium light and cool temperatures (50-60° F.); dry slightly before soaking; dilute fertilizer at every watering from fall until bud set; can try to bring it into bloom again by summering outdoors.

EUPHORBIA PULCHERRIMA (POINSETTIA) Bright light; cool temperatures (55-65° F.); evenly moist; can be brought back to bloom by summering outdoors and following photoperiodic regime beginning in October.

EXACUM AFFINE (PERSIAN VIOLET) To ten inches tall; medium light; average to cool temperatures; evenly moist; dilute fertilizer at every watering; slow growing.

Christmas poinsettias have been bred in many shades of red, pink, yellow, and white, and in marbled and polka-dotted patterns.

delightful fragrance that will fill an average room overnight. Cultivars of the species, such as the modern mini-cyclamen, occasionally have some fragrance.

A well-grown plant will be a large mound of firm, distinctly mottled heart-shaped leaves that appear almost lacy with a large crown of flowers held on erect stems over the foliage. Colors range from white to pink, mauve, purple, and red, sometimes with ruffly petals. Most plants offered are at least a year old from seed, making them relatively expensive. They are prone to crown rot and cyclamen mites, which take a percentage of the crop and push the price even higher. Plants fade quickly in a warm room—yellowing leaves indicate too high temperatures, too much water or a plant that has severely wilted at one time.

The cyclamen is held over for rebloom by some intrepid growers. Place it outside, turned on its side, under a shrub for the summer and let the rain water it for you (the foliage may disappear altogether). Don't forget it in fall—a freeze will turn the corm to mush. Cool fall temperatures and reduced light will trigger the plant into new growth. Repot and begin fertilizing. Keep it in a cool, bright location and water as the soil begins to dry out. Fertilize regularly with a flower-inducing fertilizer. Unfortunately, the ones held over for the second year seldom look as good as those that are professionally grown. Good luck!

EUPHORBIA *Euphorbiaceae See page 50 for main* Euphorbia *entry.*
SELECTIONS *E. pulcherrima* (Poinsettia) One of the most widely produced seasonal plants, the poinsettia is known to everyone as a holiday gift plant. Breeding now produces cultivars that are shorter (growth regulators are used in production) and offer larger, more colorful leaflike bracts. Colors of red, pink, white, yellow, marbled, and polka-dot are available for the Christmas season. The true flowers of the plant are small and typical to the genus. The color is provided by leaves (bracts) that change from green in the shortened days of fall. For attractive foliage, place plants in bright light and keep them evenly moist. This plant is strictly "photoperiodic." Fourteen hours of uninterrupted darkness each day must be provided for a minimum of ten weeks to bring the plant to color. Temperatures in the mid-fifty to mid-sixty range are desirable. Treat them with dilute fertilizer frequently until the color is well developed. After the holidays, you can try to hold the plant over, but it never has the same impact the following year as one grown from cuttings. If you must try to bring the old plant into bloom a second time, cut it back when your floor is littered with curled crispy leves. Leave four to six inches of stem above the soil level. Keep it relatively dry and in a bright spot—long days promote healthy foliage growth. Repot in early summer and increase watering. Feed regularly and thin out any weak stems—leave about five sturdy stems. Pinch one or two more times, but not after August 1. At the end of September, start the fourteen hour darkness routine, making sure that the plant gets ten hours of bright light. Expect the bracts to be smaller the second year. May have problems with whitefly, which is hard to control without pesticides.

The idea that it is necessary to possess a mysterious power in order to grow good plants is ridiculous. The only secret power the indoor horticulturist really needs is a true interest in plants. This will lead you to work a great deal around them. As you do so, you will breathe out carbon dioxide; this is a great stimulant to all plant growth and is probably the origin of the legend about the green thumb. Neither humans nor animals can thrive if basically they are unwanted. They sense this from the attitude of the people around them. I suspect that plants have something of the same capacity, for it is always obvious when they are grown only as part of the decor and not because the owner cares for them.

THALASSA CRUSO, FROM *MAKING THINGS GROW*, 1969

EXACUM *Gentianaceae*

This genus has approximately 40 species of annual, biennials and perennials. They have opposite, simple, very small leaves and blue or white flowers in clusters at the leaf axils.

Grow in medium light and average to cool temperatures. Keep soil evenly moist and provide dilute fertilizer at every watering. Propagate if desired by seed.

SELECTIONS *E. affine* (Persian Violet) Up to ten inches tall, the foliage is bright green and shiny. Grown for its lavender to purplish fragrant flowers with contrasting yellow stamens. It is a profuse bloomer —remove spent flowers to prolong blooming. Discard when finished blooming–almost impossible to bring back into flower in the home. Purchase plants with tight buds and keep cool to prolong blooming.

PRIMULA *Primulaceae*

This is a group of clump-forming evergreen or deciduous short-lived perennials from the northern hemisphere. Leaves may be long and narrow with indistinct midribs or rounded with wavy or ruffly edges. Most blooming "pot" types are treated as annuals, although some delightful species are perennials to be planted in the outdoor garden after they bloom as pot plants.

Provide primula with medium light and evenly moist soil. Fertilize with a dilute solution at every watering during the growing period and keep the temperatures cool. Plant in an average, well-drained potting mix and propagate by seed or rhizome division.

SELECTIONS *P. acaulis* Also offered as a blooming pot plant. It may be planted out in the garden after threat of frost and will come back the following year if well watered and fed over the summer. It is available in many bold colors. The flowers are coarser and are held closer to the foliage than *P. malacoides*.

P. malacoides (Fairy Primrose) Soft, hairy, rounded leaves on long petioles go virtually unnoticed when this bloomer is in full flower. The tall inflorescences tower above the foliage with many small rounded flowers held to the main stems by thin, wirelike pedicels. Colors range from white (the most fragrant) to pink, red, and lavender. Some double forms and dwarf varieties are also available. These are early spring bloomers that like it cool. Temperatures of 55-60° F. will hold the plant in suspended flowering for four weeks or more. Treat *P. malacoides* as an annual–purchase plants when flowers are tight ball-like buds on well developed flower stalks. Most are offered in four- or five-inch pots and make a nice presentation when several pots are arranged in a basket or mixed with small pots of ivy or other spring bloomers. They may have occasional aphids and will almost always have problems with spider mites. Propagate from seed sown in early summer.

P. obconica (German or Poison Primrose) Large showy heads of blue, pink, lavender, or salmon flowers; rounded cupped leaves; some people have an allergic reaction if they touch the leaves.

PRIMULA (PRIMROSE) Most blooming "pot" types are disposable although some can be planted in the outdoor garden as perennials; medium light and cool temperatures; evenly moist; fertilize with a dilute solution at every watering.

RHODODENDRON INDICUM (AZALEA) Two and a half feet tall; medium light and cool temperatures; evenly moist; fertilize three times in summer with acid fertilizer; prune immediately after flowering; fall and winter temperatures of 50-60° F. encourages bud set.

SENECIO X HYBRIDUS (CINERARIA) Medium light and cool to average temperatures; evenly moist soil; disposable–difficult to bring back into bloom without greenhouse.

SINNINGIA SPECIOSA (FLORIST'S GLOXINIA) Twelve-inch-tall stems; bright light, average temperatures with high humidity; evenly moist; fertilize infrequently; fast growing from seed.

Flowering plants fill this sunroom with color; included are azaleas, impatiens, gloxinia, and geraniums.

RHODODENDRON, AZALEA *Ericaceae*

This is a diverse group of evergreen or deciduous trees and shrubs found in most temperate regions, particularly the Himalayas, China, and Malaysia. They are grown for their spectacular seasonal floral displays. Some species grow quite large in their native habitats. Others, many of which have been used in hybridization, are small, mounded shrubs whose foliage virtually disappears from view when the plant is in flower.

Most azaleas perform best in humid, cool situations with acid soil. Provide medium light and keep the soil evenly moist. Azaleas should be potted in a peaty, moisture-retentive potting mix that has acid qualities (large amounts of peat moss). They should be repotted only after flowering. Fertilize three times in summer or with a dilute acid solution at every watering during the growing period. Azaleas tolerate pruning, which should be done immediately after flowering to shape the plant. Azaleas can be propagated by stem cuttings or seed.

SELECTIONS *R. indicum [R. simsii, Azalea indica]* (Azalea) Seasonally available blooming pot plants offering flower colors from white to pink to salmon, lavender and bicolors in single, semidouble, and double forms. Long-lasting flowers are held above rich green oblong leaves. Many cultivars are available from florists or at the local supermarket. Purchase plants with dark green leaves and lots of flower buds that are beginning to show color. Bud drop is common when conditions are changed drastically before flowers begin to open. Also, larger specimens in large pots are easier to keep watered than small ones in tiny pots, which dry out quickly. Some people can grow these plants effortlessly year-round in their homes and bring them into flower every winter. This makes the sizable investment worthwhile. Forcing azaleas to reflower is much easier than cyclamen, poinsettia, or many other gift plants. Bright, indirect light year-round is ideal. If you put them outside for the summer, place them under a shrub or against the foundation of the house. Constant soil moisture is essential. Distinct temperature differences between summer and winter are the key to flowering. Holding at fall and winter temperatures of 50-60° F. encourages bud set. Elevated humidity is recommended but not essential. Fertilize regularly in summer. Prune after blooming to invigorate and control plant size—plants can easily become two-and-one-half feet tall and wide in a few years. Collect friends' azaleas after they finish flowering and save yourself the investment. These can also be trained as bonsai.

SENECIO *Asteraceae*

This genus contains 2,000 to 3,000 species, including annuals, perennials, climbers, trees, and shrubs. The common characteristics are alternate leaves and the typical composite or daisylike flowers. Foliage can be succulent, pubescent, finely dissected, to broad and coarse, and white to yellow to green. In other words, it is almost impossible to relate senecios to one another by their foliage. Many of the senecio flowers are pungently scented.

Provide flowering senecios with medium light and evenly moist soil. They perform best in cool to average temperatures. Propagate by seed.

SELECTIONS *S. x hybridus* (Cineraria) A group of decorative hybrid cultivars grown for their large clusters of intensely colored, vibrant, daisylike flowers. This is one of the few blooming plants that is available in blue. Other colors are pink, white, yellow, rust, maroon, and bicolored. Foliage is coarse—large (up to eight inches) hairy leaves mound over the top edge of the pot and hang down over the sides. Plants must be kept evenly moist and in a cool room. Temperatures above 65° F. cause the flowers to open and fade quickly. They are relatively easy to grow from seed if temperatures of 45-55° F. are maintained. Try to purchase pest-free plants, not easy because of their susceptibility to aphids. Aphids are a "given" on cineraria. Much research is being done on biological controls for aphids using these plants. Mites are another problem in hot, dry situations, and whitefly is another possibility. Check the undersides of the leaves and the flower buds for insects before you buy. It is best to purchase the plants as quickly as possible after delivery from the grower. They are frequently available in late winter and early spring. Look for lots of tight buds with a couple of open flowers. Well-grown plants in a good environment will entertain you with great color for four to six weeks. After bloom, dispose of the plants.

SINNINGIA SPECIOSA FLORIST GLOXINIA *Gesneriaceae*

These plants are related to the African violet and should not be confused with the genus *Gloxinia*. Sinningia contains about 75 species of plants native from Mexico to Argentina and Brazil. The foliage and leaves are borne from a tuber and the leaves are hairy. *Sinningia speciosa* is a common gift plant, best known for its large showy flowers of white, pink, red, blue, or purple.

Provide bright, filtered light during active growth and provide average temperatures with high humidity (a tray of moistened pebbles works well). Keep the soil evenly moist but not soggy and never allow water on the leaves. Fertilize infrequently. Although not easy for the novice gardener, florist gloxinia can be allowed to go dormant after it blooms and then brought back into bloom. After blooming, reduce the watering (allow the top inch of soil to dry) and fertilize every two weeks until the foliage dies. When the foliage is yellow, stop watering altogether. Store the tuber in its pot of dry soil at about 50° F. In spring, repot the tuber and place in a warm spot. Water sparingly until leaves appear. Then begin the regular care listed above.

Cupressa macrocarpa 'Goldcrest'

OTHER PLANTS The range of houseplants is much too large to cover in a book this size; we could actually fill several books with selections that perform well indoors. On the following pages, we will list just a few of the other plants that merit attention.

CONIFERS Several slow-growing conifers make fine houseplants; pruning their roots in early spring helps keeps them small. They do not require much care, and make fine backdrops to other specimens. Most need bright light, average warmth, and frequent watering; cut back on water in spring. *Cupressa macrocarpa* 'Goldcrest' (Cypress), which can grow to a forty-foot tree outdoors, and *Chamaecyparis pisifera,* (False Cypress) a smaller shrub, are particularly suitable for the home.

GRASSES Among the grassy plants which will thrive in pots are acorus, miscanthus, carex, and fescue. Most need cool conditions, bright light, and fertile soil.

ALPINA An easy to grow member of the ginger family. *A. zerumbet* 'Variegata' has bright yellow markings on the leaves. The vertical stems arise from underground rhizomes. Flowers are China white with red and yellow.

ALTERNANTHERA A colorful commonly grown group of small-leaved plants that perform well in a bright window or indoors and may be bedded out in warm weather.

BOWIEA An unusual succulent plant whose stem closely resembles an onion. A fine waxy vine emerges from center of the "onion" forming a dense curtain. The plant is toxic, but is a curious addition to a collection of succulent plants.

BRIGHAMIAINSIGNIS A Hawaiian endangered species grown from seed collected from cultivated plants in botanical institutions. A bizarre, easy-to-grow plant that has been described as a "bowling pin with a cabbage on top."

BRUNFELSIA A genus in the nightshade family that is known for its profuse production of ivory to white to purple flowers that cover the shrub in a color. Keep plants potbound and offer cool nights to encourage flowering.

CLERODENDRUM Shrubs or vines that are grown for their spectacular flowers. The bleeding heart vine has red flowers and white calyces, the lava glorybean has a large vertical inflorescence of bright red-orange that is in bloom almost continually. The blue glory bower is a rangy shrub but produces blue flowers; it is somewhat more difficult in the home than others.

CLUSIA ROSEA (Balsam Apple) Has broad stiff leaves on a tree that grows advanticious roots; makes an unusual tree for the house.

CORREA Very showy small-leaved shrubs that are covered in pink to reddish flowers in spring and summer.

CRINUM Easy-to-grow plants that grow from bulbs and produce showy flowers. Some get very large, to six feet; most remain manageable in the home. The evergreen types are particulary desirable as the foliage may be dark green to burgundy in color.

DORSTENIA Cousins to ficus, these odd succulent plants come in a wide variety of sizes and textures. Some have weak, wandering stems that are dark olive green with small leaves. Others have large broad dark green leaves with thickened stems. All have flat podlike flowers that shoot their seeds when ripe.

EICHHORNIA (Water Hyacinth) A noxious weed in the South, clogging waterways. As a nonhardy containerized aquatic it performs well floating in warm water and flowers like a spring hyacinth; shiny rounded leaves are attached to buoyant expanded petioles. Roots into the bottom of the container.

MURRAYA PANICULATA (Lakeside Jasmine) A fast growing shrub with sweet-smelling clusters of white flowers that are followed by red fruits. Flowers are small.

NERTA (Bead Plant) A tiny-leaved mat-forming terrarium-type plant that produces orange fruits. Good companion plant for venus flytraps and sundew.

OSMANTHUS FRAGRANS A slow-growing shrub for medium to bright spots. Flowers frequently; flowers are delightfully fragrant and used in perfuming.

OTACANTHUS CORULEUS Soft blue flowers with white centers are produced in large numbers this somewhat rangy plant. Frequent dilute fertilizer applied regularly will insure long periods of flowers. Pruning after flowering helps control and direct shape.

PACHYPODIUM A spiny stem succulent that forms interesting caudexes. Flowers are borne on a new growth and range from white to pink and reddish and yellow.

PANCRATIUM MARTIMUM (Sea Daffodil) Broad tapering leaves emerge from large bulbs. Flowers are large, spidery, and very showy. Easy to grow. Rest dry through winter.

PASSIFLORA Passion vines produce marvelously curious flowers but are a bit difficult to control. The vines produce curly tendrils that help it manuver upwards. There is much variety in flower color and size. Leaves exhibit egg mimics that represent butterfly eggs. These mimics have evolved over time to inhibit butterflies from laying eggs on the leaves and the resulting larvae from consuming the plant.

PIPER Members of the pepper family with great variety of habits. *P. ornatum* is a very colorful coarse vine. *P. nigrum* is a dark green vine, the source of black and white pepper.

POLYPODIUM A group of ferns, many of which are easy to grow. Many become large with age, some have furry rhizomes that creep over edge of pot.

SEDUM Several sedums thrive in the home. *Sedum burrito,* shown at right, makes a spectacular hanging basket.

TIBOUCHINA A woody shrub with long internodes. Leaves are covered with white silvery hairs. Rich purple flowers are produced on new growth. Lanky growth can be controlled by growth regulators and pruning after flowering.

Sedum burrito.

DESIGNING AN INDOOR GARDEN 3

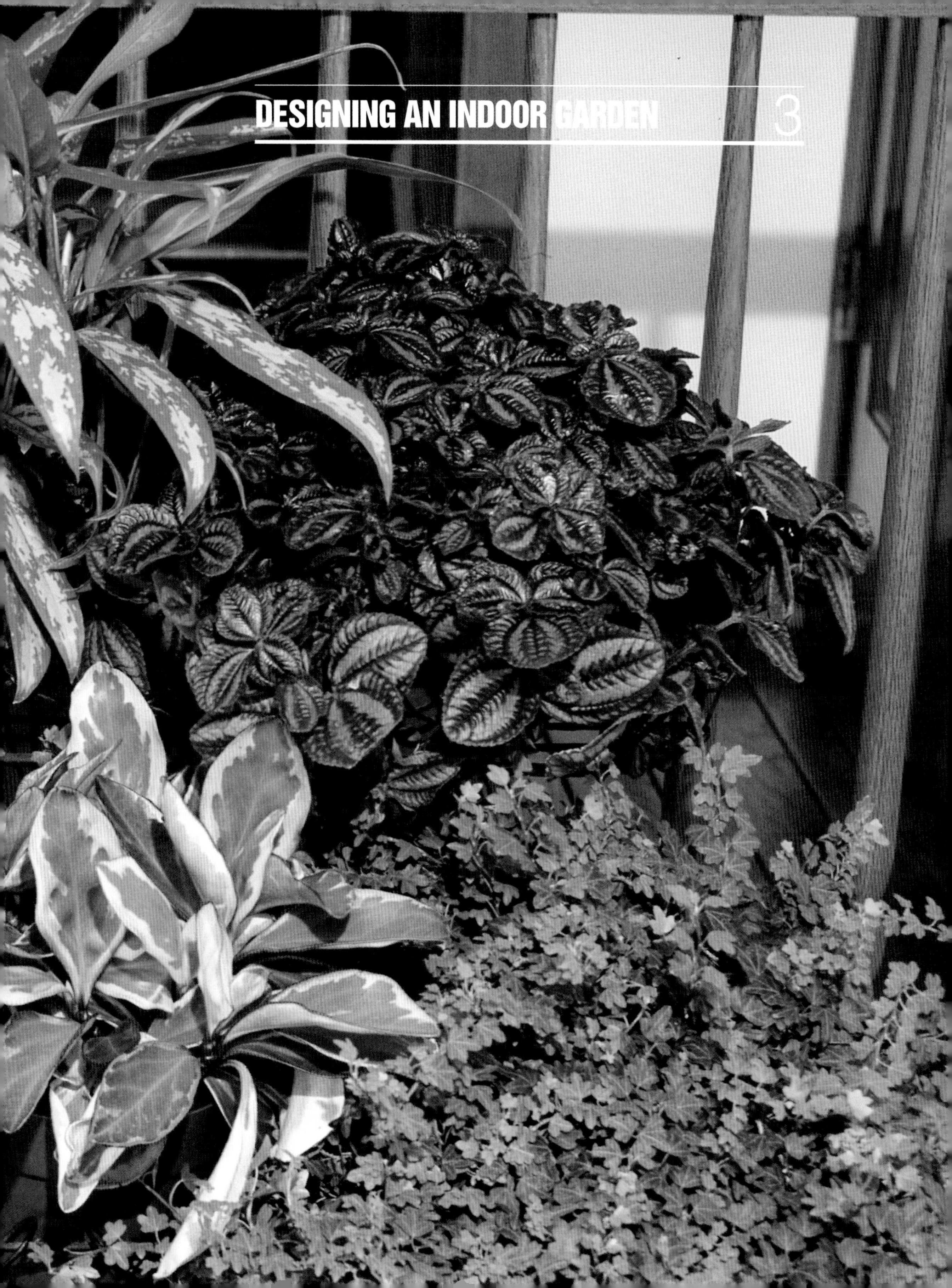

Houseplants come in an extraordinary range of shapes, sizes, and colors. Some good color combinations:
• The vertical yellow-edged leaves of *Sansevieria trifasciata* 'Laurentii' work well when combined with the broad medium green palmate leaves of *Fatsia japonica;* this can be complemented with with the vining habit of the yellow variegated *Epipremnum aureum.*
• The pink polka dot plant (Hypoestes phyllostachya) has active markings that are enhanced by using blooming plants such as *Pentas lanceolata* 'Rose Pink' or pink primulas. To this, add *Calathea* 'Sanderiana', which has board, dark, almost black leaves with pinkish lines, and a plain green ivy.
The best design advice is to keep it simple. Too much variety in color and texture becomes confusing to the senses. Squint at the grouping of plants to eliminate distractions and give you a true view; if anything stands out glaringly, it probably doesn't work well in the combination.

Plants add a certain warmth to a room by providing subtle yet delightful sensory elements and often serving to soften the overall setting. Just as it is outdoors, a collection of indoor plants, no matter how varied and well grown, does not necessarily create a garden. By combining design, style, and an awareness of aesthetics, it is possible to create a gardenlike setting indoors that is both a pleasure to be in and a productive place for growing. When practiced commercially this is sometimes referred to as interior–or plantscaping.

The first consideration in designing a house garden is whether the place indoors will be used temporarily for plants–to display seasonal flowering ones, such as chrysanthemum, poinsettia, or primrose–or permanently, as a place to nurture and display a variety of fascinating foliage and flowering types.

Temporary-occupancy plants require only enough light to be seen in a flattering manner. Permanent indoor residents cannot be treated as other nonliving design accents such as sculpture or placed in a location that does not meet their growing requirements. Plants require light of sufficient strength and duration to foster ongoing healthy growth. This subject is discussed on pages 210-211, and light requirements are listed with the discussion for each of the plants included in the plant selector.

PLACES AND PLANTS The traditional and simple way to grow houseplants is to place the pots on a windowsill or to hang them in the window by ceiling hooks or wall-mounted brackets. Since today's windows often have no sills, resourceful indoor gardeners also appropriate almost any surface that can hold a plant, such as the floor, a tabletop, pedestal, or shelf. Surfaces that are off limits to potted plants include the television, speaker boxes, or any other equipment or place that could be damaged by water spills. Also, the mantel above an active fireplace is usually too hot for living plants.

Indoor garden design must take practicality into account; the enjoyment of a beautiful plant is often ruined by having its pot leak water until the carpeting or wood floor beneath is destroyed. Even glazed pots and saucers may "sweat" sufficiently to mar a delicate surface unless they are placed on top of a cork coaster, the purpose of which is to dissipate moisture before it collects to the point of causing a problem.

It is also important to recognize the difference between service or growing pots–usually plain plastic–versus decorative containers, which can be of almost any material, including plastic, glass, ceramic, clay, wood, metal, wire, or woven. Clear plastic saucers and liners sold for waterproofing pots and flower arrangements in baskets come in handy as basic equipment for gardening indoors. (See page 174 for more information about containers.)

It is also critical to stabilize indoor plants so that normal household air movement doesn't result in their being toppled. Tree-form standards and large-flowered Dutch amaryllis in full bloom are especially prone to top-heaviness and will fare better in heavy clay or ceramic planters rather than in lightweight plastic. Also be sure that plants are positioned so that they will not be brushed by people passing, which can result in mechanical damage to leaves. Some plants have dagger-sharp spines at the leaf tips–certain members of the

Light source is the single most important determining factor in choosing and placing plants. The picture at the left shows plants placed near their light source. The picture above shows plants rotated into the interior of a room; they will spend most of their lives in a better-lighted situation.

genus *Agave* for example–that might cause harm unless placed for safety.

There are as many ways to design and arrange an indoor garden as there are gardeners and plants. It is a constantly changing, movable feast that can be attained from something as basic and ordinary as growing avocado pits into an indoor grove to as complex and fascinating as collecting only foliage plants with variegated foliage or only flowering kinds with delightfully scented blooms.

When designing a room, attention to color, texture, size, shape, proportion, and balance must be considered–with plants just as with any other design feature. The color of the foliage, flowers, even the container in which the plant is grown must be considered. The color scheme in a room may dictate the selection of plants and some notice should be given to the color relationship of plants to each other.

The color features of a plant can match, blend, complement or contrast but should not conflict with each other. Generally, plants grown for their foliage are the easiest to include in a design because green is a pleasing and calming natural color to the eye. Bold flower colors such as those of bromeliads and orchids offer an interesting focal point to a room but usually require much more careful placement.

Secondarily, but no less important, texture provides interest and can be as effective as color in making a statement. Texture refers to the feel of the foliage and flower surface. It can be serrated (like *Polyscias crispatum,* the chicken gizzard aralia or *P. guilgoylei* 'Quercifolia', the oak leaf aralia), frilly or curly (such as *Nephrolepis* 'Fluffy Ruffles'); smooth (like *Spathiphyllum clevelandii*); bumpy (like *Kalanchoe* 'Fang'); fuzzy (like *Cyanotis kewensis*); or shiny (such as *Camelia sinensis* cultivars). Texture may also relate to the size of the leaves and stems. Large leaves give a very coarse appearance and small leaves and stems appear very finely-textured. These elements should

The many moods of houseplants: traditional (above); modern (right); classic (opposite page).

be used to complement and contrast with each other, and to emphasize the plants' location in a room. Textures add energy to a space; broad, plain, strap-like leaves can calm or give relief to a busy room.

A plant's size, habit (outline), or character will also play a role in the overall design. Plants may naturally relate to a particular design scheme such as Victorian, contemporary, or Southwestern style. For example, although cactus or succulents can be grown in any room that has the right growing conditions, they are particularly well-suited when grown with Southwestern decor because of the inherent assocation with the setting. Ferns and vines are frequently associated with Victorian style; contemporary style can be accented with the exotic architectural characteristics of *Dracaena marginata* or *Ficus lyrata*. Rhapis palms and aralias are perfect accents in an Oriental room. If the growing conditions limit the selection of plants, containers can be selected to match the dominant style.

The size and stature of a plant should be in proportion first to its own container and ultimately to its surroundings. A frequent mistake that indoor gardeners make is using an inappropriate-sized container. Generally, in order for a plant to appear visually balanced, the container should be no more than one-third of the plant-and-container combination. A pot too tiny or excessively large is awkward. Size plays a role within a room as well. Small plants should be placed amid other smaller features. For example, a small African violet appears much more at home nestled on a narrow window ledge than placed in the center of a large, sprawling dining table where it will appear dwarfed and out of scale. Similarly, a large tree fits best in a larger space such as in an atrium or wide open entryway.

Among indoor plants there some floor-to-ceiling trees available, but woody bushes and short palms can also serve as trees if they are set on a pedestal of sufficient height. There are also vines that can be assisted in climbing on trellising, string, or wire to frame a window or adorn an indoor arbor; others can spill naturally and gracefully from a shelf or hanging position.

Plants can be used individually as specimens, or clustered and arranged in a grouping to create a pleasing unified appearance. When placing them, however, keep in mind each plant's physical needs.

A specimen plant is one that can stand alone. It has a distinctive character or habit that demands one's attention. It may be a large tree with architectural features or a plant whose foliage is unique in shape or color, a distinctive flowering plant or a stunning cascading plant. Selection of the specimen plant is dependent upon the situation. Although almost any well-grown plant can take center stage in the right location, a specimen should be hand selected, noting individual plant characteristics that fit the space. It may take some searching to come up with the right character for your space. Good examples of potential specimens: *Ficus lyrata*; *F.* 'Green Gem'; *Dracaena marginata*; *Spathiphyllum* 'Sensation', *Schefflera* 'Amate'. Placement of specimens should complement the surroundings while still providing appropriate growing conditions. When displaying a plant individually, the pot becomes a dominant feature and requires careful selection. When in doubt, use a neutral container of the appropriate proportion to allow the plant to command the greatest attention.

Plants in individual pots can be arranged together to form an island or community of plants which together are more pleasing and interesting than if placed individually. The best groupings include plants of varying heights, habits and textures to add to the overall diversity and balance. Varying bloom times keep the group interesting for longer periods. Plants with weak habits or one-sided plants can be masked by foliage of other plants in the group. Groupings of individual pots are versatile and can be arranged easily. The closeness of the pots to one another becomes a matter or personal preference and can be adjusted as a reflection of the plants' needs. Staging plants means to arrange plants in varying heights and dimensions. Inverted empty pots function as stages or pedestals to artificially vary heights. Additionally, trailing plants can be used as facer plants to provide a clean front or to mask pots. Some plant groupings are further connected by using similar or identical pots.

Design needs are sometimes accommodated by growing two (or more) plants that are the same. While one is doing decorative duty in less than ideal conditions the other can be recuperating in a place where its cultural needs take precedence.

A vast majority of indoor gardens are filled with essentially the same plants. The world is filled with extraordinary plants that adapt miraculously to living indoors and consistent care. This book offer the everyday as well as the unusual characters from the plant world that are the most favored for growing in house gardens. Every new plant lends adds its character to your indoor garden.

HIGH LIGHT

SOUTH OR WEST EXPOSURE

A plant needing light at the high end of the high-light category can be placed in an area receiving direct sun for much of the day. To decrease the amount of light, place plants in a combined exposure, such as a southeast window, or place up to two feet from the light source.

MEDIUM LIGHT

WEST OR EAST EXPOSURE

A plant that grows best in medium light is one that receives some direct light, is placed in a brightly lighted spot such as a west or east window, or is placed in filtered southern light. Medium light is the ideal situation and many of the plants suggested in this book will accommodate it readily.

LOW LIGHT

EAST OR NORTH EXPOSURE OR ROOM INTERIOR

A plant that grows in low light can be placed in an east, northeast, or north window. It does not require any direct sun and will survive in predominately filtered light. There are, however, dark areas indoors that simply are not suitable for plants. For example, if there is not enough light by which to read comfortably, a plant will not grow well. Supplemental lights or growing carts offer the opportunity to grow plants in poorly lighted situations and are discussed later. Incandescent light, particularly if shaded, offers no real value as a light source for houseplants. Other options for low-light areas are seasonal plants that are rotated in and out of a greenhouse or well-lighted spot, short-term plants that are disposed of after blooming, and preserved or silk plants. Remember that plants in low light usually have low water requirements.

Let there be light! This section is the most important in this book because it is essential to evaluate the available light before choosing plants.

When deciding placement for indoor plants, available light is the most critical consideration. Evaluate the following: What natural light is available? How close will the plant be to the light source? Are there any objects that may limit light from this source, such as trees or buildings, shades or curtains? Determining or measuring light duration, intensity, and quality can be difficult with the naked eye. One deceiving aspect is that a situation only inches from the light source can drastically differ in intensity from a spot a foot away from the light source.

The quality of light will also vary with the direction of exposure and with changes in the season. A window with a southern exposure typically provides the greatest amount of light in winter since the sun shines here directly for much of the day. In summer, however, the sun's angle is higher in northern climates, so a southern window gets intense sun for a much shorter period. A southern location can be intense and hot, so these spots are good for sun-loving plants that tolerate heat, such as cactus or colorful bromeliads. A more diverse selection of plants can be grown in a southern exposure if they are placed at varying distances from the window, since distance quickly diminishes the amount of sunlight and temperature. A sheer curtain also lessens the intensity of a southern exposure.

A west window also provides intense sunlight but not for the same duration as a south window. A west window receives most of its direct sun in the afternoon, resulting in a hotter situation than a south window in the afternoon.

An east window provides morning light, making the location more moderate and cooler, the perfect situation for African violets and other gesneriads. A northern window will provide only minimal light and effectively sustain a few low-light foliage plants. Plants in this situation should be as close to the window as possible. Mirrors, light-colored walls, and supplemental light will help improve the situation. Supplemental light is an effective way to increase the amount of light a plant is exposed to.

As one might guess, a plant's light requirement directly relates to the plant's native environment. For example, aloe is native to many parts of Africa. It is adapted to very high light and dry soil, so in order to keep it healthy, we must try to replicate that situation as best we can—a south or west window and dry soil. Plants with a wide adaptability of light exposures, such as ponytail palm, may fall into more than one light category. The chart at left qualifies light types and provides a standard terminology by which this book identifies light requirements in the Plant Selector. In the most simple terms, plants are categorized as needing high, medium, or low light. There are some gradations within these broad groups, so any variables are mentioned in the plant description. Also, these categories reflect average indoor conditions. Plants requiring specialized greenhouse conditions have not been included, although all plants listed normally perform well in a greenhouse. Additionally, even though a plant may be listed as tolerating low light, it may perform better given more light. These categories provide a starting point -- experience and experimentation will help you determine how plants will perform in your particular situation.

SELECTING A LOCATION Just as in real estate, location is everything! Within a home, there can be great variance in temperature, air circulation, light, and humidity. Be conscious of these differences, identify existing microclimates and place plants in locations that offer the best growing conditions. Most plants perform well in temperatures near 75° F. during the day and 65° F. at night, but many plants tolerate more extreme temperatures.

Avoid locations with obvious extremes—these can be problematic. For example, a cold porch is limited in the temperatures it provides. Upper floors tend to be warmer than main floors. Rooms with south-facing windows tend to be warmer than those with north-facing windows. A foyer has inherent problems with drafts from the door. In summer, the foyer may be windy with bursts of heat from the outside; in winter plants can be damaged because of quick and drastic temperature changes when the door is opened. During winter months, avoid placing plants in the direct air flow from heating vents, which can be as drying and harsh to plants as air conditioning can be in the summer. Also in winter, heated air lacks the humidity plants need. Temperatures can drop several degrees near cold windowpanes, chilling plants or actually freezing foliage that touches the panes (although cold in winter may actually be good for some cactus and other plants that require dormancy for flowering). Kitchens and bathrooms tend to offer slightly more humidity, and older homes with steam heating tend to have more humidity than those heated with gas or electric heat.

SOIL Soil is a critical factor in plant growth and one that can be easily altered in indoor gardening. Since roots require air and water, the soil should allow plenty of air space and drainage, while at the same time retain water and nutrients. Garden soils respond differently when taken out of their natural setting and used in containers than they do in a garden setting. They often bring with them existing disease and insect problems that can become much more problematic indoors than outdoors. In general, avoid garden soils for houseplants.

Because of the physical limitations of the container and the indoor setting, today most indoor plants are grown in a soil-less potting mix. Prepared potting mixes don't have the complexity of outdoor soils, which are rich in soil organisms and minerals, but a soil-less potting mix can be customized for the qualities needed to benefit houseplants. Most soil-less mixtures include three common ingredients—peat moss, vermiculite, and perlite—in various proportions, and they are sterilized to be free of pests, diseases, and weeds. Although it is possible to mix your own, commercial mixes are readily available, easy to use, and relatively inexpensive. Some potting mixes also contain slow-release fertilizers.

Specialty mixes are available and vary in their ingredients according to plant needs. For specialized plants, more expensive mixes are worth the investment to keep a plant in top shape. A potting mix for foliage plants will

SEASONAL CHANGES

Remember that as the sun changes its position with the seasons, the temperature and humidity also change. During the winter months, when light is much reduced, most plants cease active growth and simply maintain themselves. Less light and slow growth indicate a need for less water. Overwatering is a common problem in low-light situations and during the winter months. Fertilizer should generally be withheld during winter months. Also, plants that cannot tolerate high light in the summer often benefit from exposure to winter sun.

Three components of potting soil: peat moss, vermiculite, and perlite.

PLANT PRESENTATION

A solid visual combination of the right plant in the right pot can be perfected by the appropriate top dressing. Top dressing can be any number of neutrally colored materials such as aquarium gravel, pea gravel, fine bark chips, long-fibered sphagnum moss, green sheet moss, or coarse silica sand.

Top dressings must remain loose and open, allowing water to drain through. They also need to match the texture of the plant and pot combination—a large, coarse combination requires a coarser top dressing than a small, delicately-marked succulent plant—and the color of the top dressing should be appropriate.

Top dressing also serves to contain soil particles that would otherwise wash out during watering. The plant's water requirements must be monitored closely after top dressing has been applied as the soil color is no longer available as a visual indication of water needs.

be all-purpose with approximately equal parts of each ingredient. A mix for flowering plants tends to have more organic matter that retains water since flower buds are particularly sensitive to drying out. A mix for cactus and other succulents will have the least amount of organic matter and will usually have sand, charcoal, or calcined clay as one of its components. Cactus and other succulents need a medium that drains quickly since they are prone to rotting in organic soils. Orchids and other epiphytes thrive in a medium of bark chips, which gives the specialized roots plenty of air. Some epiphytes will also grow on slabs of bark, much as they grow in the wild.

Avoid choosing a potting mix that is heavy in peat moss or one that is extremely lightweight. Peat moss dries out readily and shrinks, making it difficult to rewet and causing the water to run down the sides of the pot, missing the roots altogether. A mix that is too lightweight may cause a top-heavy plant to tip over and possibly uproot.

SELECTING CONTAINERS Plants can be grown in nearly any type of container as long as it has drainage holes to release excess water and is of adequate size to provide plenty of room for soil and roots. The height of the container also comes into play when determining how much room is left for watering and when deciding how the container looks in proportion to the size of the plant. A good general rule for an attractive plant is a visual proportion of two-thirds plant to one-third pot (or less). A container should not detract or compete with the surroundings or the plant itself and can be either completely neutral or a specific addition to a room's decor.

The most common pots are plastic or clay (terracotta). Plastic pots are easy to handle, do not break easily, and are fairly inexpensive. They do not allow soil to dry out as quickly as clay pots and have less tendency to accumulate mineral salts from fertilizer or hard water. They are easy to clean, store, and reuse. The size of the plant must be taken into consideration—plants requiring a ten-inch pot or larger are best potted in plastic pots as ceramic containers become extremely heavy and difficult to handle over ten inches. A disadvantage is that because of its light weight, plastic offers less stability for large or tall plants. Also, plastic is not visually as attractive or as natural-looking as clay (although this could be debated with the wide array of plastic pots now available).

Clay pots are porous, readily exchanging air and moisture through the sides. This provides good aeration for the roots, but also causes the soil to dry out fairly quickly. They are ideal for plants that need drier soil, such as cactus and other succulents. Clay pots are heavy and lend stability to large or tall plants, but they are more expensive, breakable, and are harder to clean and store than plastic pots. Turning clay pots upside down outside for two or more seasons will usually leach out any salt residue and make them look as good as new.

Whichever type of pot is chosen, drainage is essential. Most pots come with drainage holes in the bottom and are intended to be used with a saucer to catch excess water. Saucers prevent messy watering and damage to furniture or floors. Some saucers are attached to the pot, and others are separate units. They should be emptied of excess water within an hour after watering (a turkey baster is superb for removing the water if the pot is too heavy to lift easily). Pots in greenhouses, on the other hand, usually drain freely onto gravel or cement floors and into floor drains.

Although the ideal pot has plenty of drain holes, there are many beautiful pots that do not. In order to prevent overwatering and problems with standing water, double-potting is a functional way to solve a drainage problem with an attractive pot. The plant is potted in a functional pot with drain holes, and this is then placed inside a decorative pot without drainage holes. The decorative pot catches excess water in place of a saucer, can provide some bottom watering, adds weight and stability to the plant, and can be chosen to suit the decor.

Double potting: a plastic pot inside a decorative container.

Self-watering containers are specially-made units that are decorative and provide water for an extended period. They are often used in offices and malls where it is more difficult to monitor watering. Some function similarly to double-potting, and others have a wicking system for extended watering. Some systems provide a reservoir that releases water as a vacuum is broken by roots drawing up moisture. Self-watering systems are appropriate for some plants, but not all. Dracaenas and similar plants that should sit dry between waterings are not good candidates. Ficus trees and palms, on the other hand, do quite well. Plants in self-waterers require a special fine-textured soil in order to perform well. Some commercial operations have reduced maintenance time on indoor plants by as much as 70 percent with the use of self-watering systems. The initial investment in material is high, but the payoff in some situations is worth it.

CHOOSING PLANTS Look a plant over carefully before purchasing or incorporating it into your existing collection of houseplants. Select a healthy-looking plant with good color and form reflective of that particular species. The plant should be clean, sturdy, and well-potted. It should also be free of insects and diseases. Check the entire plant, looking closely at the undersides and upper sides of the leaves and at the leaf axils for symptoms of potential problems. Avoid plants with poor form, that are leggy or chlorotic (pale color), that have leaves with brown margins or blotches or that are wilted.

TRANSPORTING PLANTS Transporting plants to a new location after purchase is an important consideration, especially for gardeners in extreme climates. Plants transported during mild temperatures between 50-80° F. do not need protection, but in summer and winter, plants can be damaged by heat, cold, and wind. Resulting damage is not always immediate, but may show up several days later as leaf drop, tip dieback, or even death.

During the heat of summer, avoid leaving plants in an unventilated car. With the windows closed, the car heats up quickly and a plant will literally cook. When traveling with plants in the car in summer, cover the parts exposed to windows with newspaper to avoid burning. In winter, plants coming from controlled growing temperatures can be severely damaged by very short exposure to low temperatures, even if the temperature is not below freezing. Plant tissues have a high water content that chills and freezes quick-

DIAGNOSING CULTURAL PROBLEMS

Overwatering and underwatering can cause the same symptoms, usually brown leaf edges and tips and wilting. Overwatering kills small roots that take up water and underwatering causes the root hairs to shrivel and die, so in either case the plant is not getting the water it needs. Some symptoms to look for in specific plants:

Aglaonema

Brown leaf tips: dry air, under- or over-watering.
Curled leaves: air too cool.

Begonia

White, powdery patches: powdery mildew.
Flower buds drop: dry air or underwatering.

Cactus

Corky patches: overwatering, injury, humidity too high, poor air circulation.
Soft spots: overwatering or stem rot, injury, poor soil drainage.

Chlorphytum

Brown tips: underwatering or poor nutrition.

Dieffenbachia

Brown leaf edges: underwatering, possibly cold drafts, mites.

Dracaena

Brown leaf edges and tips: dry air, underwatering, mites.

Ferns

Yellowing leaves, brown tips: dry air, underwatering.

Ficus benjamina

Leaf drop: change in conditions of any sort.

Ficus elastica

Leaf drop: overwatering.

Ficus pumila

Leaf shriveling: underwatering, exposure to direct sun.

ly. Wraps and sleeves are intended to be used for short distances, such as from the store to car and then to the house, but will not provide extended protection. Paper wraps are generally better at insulating than plastic wraps. Also, plants wrapped in protective sleeves can be tricky to handle, so carry them by the pot instead of the sleeve. In cold weather, warm the car before bringing the plant to it and never put the plant in a trunk. One of the most commonly mishandled plants is the poinsettia. These plants are native to Mexico so have no tolerance for cold temperatures. Because they are so popular during the winter holidays, they are often purchased from a florist and sometimes taken to the car without a protective sleeve. Think of the poor doomed plant that is left in the car while someone does some holiday shopping.

Wind is another damaging factor that is not often considered when transporting plants. It causes tattering and desiccation to plants that are not protected, particularly in a moving car. Imagine the college student on the way to school with the weeping fig that is too large to fit inside the car, so is stuck out the window for a trip down the interstate. Any questions why it loses its leaves within the first week in a dorm room? Wind damage is not only a problem when part of a plant is hanging out, but can also occur from wind coming in a window. Sunburn can also occur on plants hanging outside a car. Remember, most houseplants are grown in a protected, moist, warm greenhouse with no extremes. Outdoor weather can be quite a shock to them.

ACCLIMATING PLANTS When moving a plant from one location to another, the light, temperature, and humidity will probably vary, especially when moving from a greenhouse to the home or from indoors to outdoors for the summer. The plant will have to adapt to these differences and go through a period of adjustment. If the conditions are quite different, a plant will benefit from a period of acclimatization or gradual introduction to avoid damage or shock.

Even a plant that is suited to low light, such as weeping fig, needs a period of adjustment when being moved into a home. Tropical houseplants are usually grown in Florida or in high-light greenhouses and none is quite so obvious in its expression of adjustment as the notorious leaf-dropping fig. With any change in conditions, figs shed a good portion of their leaves, are set back temporarily, and later send out new leaves. Adjustments also occur when moving a plant from low to high light. Acclimatization will be discussed again when moving plants from indoors to outdoors for the summer months.

ROUTINE CARE

Once an appropriate plant is selected for the conditions of your home, it will require regular, specific care throughout its life. Although certain general guidelines can be applied to most plants, it is wise to familiarize yourself with each plant in your home in case special care is needed. Treating all plants in the same manner soon results in signs of poor culture, such as slowed growth or pale color, signals that the plants need individual attention. For example, a sunny window is ideal for jade and hibiscus, but the plants differ in the amounts of water they require. Jade is a succulent that prefers to be potbound and stay relatively dry with only occasional soaking of its potting mix. A hibiscus needs frequent watering, especially when in flower, and requires plenty of room in the pot for root growth.

LIGHT Plants grown in windows where light is from only one direction benefit from regular rotation. Every few days to a week give each plant a quarter turn. This will promote even growth on all sides of the plant. Plants that are not rotated regularly become one-sided, unattractive, and may even tip over from being lopsided. Often, a plant that is already one-sided can be pruned and rotated regularly to help reestablish fullness on all sides.

If inappropriate lighting is suspected, move plants to a different exposure or provide supplemental lighting (discussed later). Remember that each time a plant is moved to a new location, it will require an adjustment period of at least three weeks. If the plant responds well to its new location, it is best to keep it there. Continual moving never allows the plant to adjust or thrive in an established spot.

It is possible to have attractive blooming plants in spots receiving inadequate light, as long as they are regularly moved back and forth from a greenhouse or other appropriately lighted spot. This allows a display plant to recover its healthy appearance in high light. Typically two or more plants are rotated every one or two weeks to a low-light spot from a greenhouse or sunny spot. For example, two English ivies can be rotated easily—as soon as the one in the low-light display spot begins to languish, replace it with another that is healthy from being grown in high light. Blooming plants like cyclamen, African violet and gloxinia can also be rotated between grow and show locations. As each comes into bloom, move it from its ideal spot in a bright window or greenhouse to the dining-room table or other interior location. As each finishes blooming, move it back to the light and replace with a fresh plant in bloom.

WATERING Seasonal changes affect the growth of a plant. Be aware of these changes and the plant's growth cycles in order to adjust care accordingly. For example, reduce watering during winter when there is less available light due to shorter days and overcast skies. This encourages plants to take a rest. Plants use less water during this time, sometimes one half or less than during the summer, depending on the type of plant and its light situation. Overwatering occurs most often during winter months when gardeners continue to water houseplants on a summer schedule. Conversely, in extremely cold weather, central heating working overtime can dry out plants quickly because of evaporation.

If you are familiar with your plant and its specific needs you will have a greater understanding of proper care and watering. For example, cactus and other succulents grow best in predominantly dry soil with occasional soakings in summer and very little water during the winter months. African violets and many other blooming plants, on the other hand, should be kept evenly moist year-round, but never wet or soggy. Most foliage plants perform best in alternating moist and slightly dry situations during active growth months.

What are the secrets to successful watering? Water plants thoroughly when they need it. The only secret lies in your ability to notice and respond to

(continued from previous sidebar)

Gardenia
Bud drop: lack of humidity, insufficient fertilization

Hedera
Brown leaf tips, stunted growth: underwatering, dry air, spider mites, insecticidal soap damage.

Orchids
Brown spots: exposure to sun, fungal disease or scale.
Drooping leaves: lack of light, overwatering.
Lack of bloom: lack of light, lack of fertilizer, poor air circulation.

Palms
Brown leaf tips: dry air, spider mites.
Yellowing leaves: underwatering.

Pelargonium
Corky patches on leaves: overwatering,
Gray mold on leaves: fungal disease due to poor air circulation
Reddish leaf edges: air too cool or too much sun

Philodendron
Yellow leaves: overwatering
Brown leaf tips: dry air
Curling leaves: overwatering

Saintpaulia
Spots on leaves: cold water getting on leaves
No flowers: lack of light, lack of fertilizer
Mold on leaves: fungal disease

TOOLS

Here are the tools and equipment that every indoor gardener should have on hand:
- Saucers to catch water
- Long-spouted watering can
- Small pruning shears or scissors
- Gloves
- Trowel
- Spray bottles for misting
- Soap and oil mixtures
- Knife
- Stakes, string, green plastic ties
- Plastic bags
- Top dressing materials
- Pebbles for placing in saucer
- Feather duster
- Turkey baster (for removing water from saucers)

(Topiary, terrariums, and bonsai require other specialty tools, discussed in Chapter 5.

Hold leaves out of the way to make certain the water wets the soil thoroughly (or use a long-nosed spout to reach the interior).

the signals the plants provide. In other words, learn to tell when they need water. There are variables to consider, such as the size of the plant, size of the pot, and type of potting mix, that affect the quantity and frequency of watering, but as long as you are observant, watering can be easy. Watering according to a specific schedule simply doesn't account for variations in weather and seasonal changes. Even in a production greenhouse where many of the variables such as pot size, potting mix, and light exposure, have been standardized, it is still essential to make regular checks of individual plants to monitor and adjust care as needed.

When deciding whether plants need water, check visually first. A well-watered plant is firm and upright because the plant tissues are filled with water (turgid). Wilting, loss of turgidity, can be an obvious signal for water. However, the wilting and poor color associated with underwatering are very similar to the signals of overwatering. In other words, more water is not always the answer. Chronic overwatering causes the plant's roots to rot and die, allowing the plant to take up no water and eventually wilt. If a plant cannot take up water because of lack of roots, giving it more water will not bring it back from a wilting state.

A visual inspection should be accompanied by making note of when it was last watered, and simply checking the moisture content of the soil. It is difficult to get an accurate reading of soil moisture by just looking at it, so get used to sticking your finger into the top one to two inches of soil to feel for moisture. A plant that requires constantly moist soil should be moist on the surface as well as below. If the plant requires the soil surface to dry out between waterings, water only when the soil is dry an inch below the surface. The soil in a pot should never go completely dry because this damages fine roots. Most of the roots tend to be located in the bottom two-thirds, and soil dries out from the top down. As you become more familiar with watering your plants, you may not need to use the finger test every time. Also, many gardeners become familiar enough with their individual plants to tell the amount of moisture by the weight of the pot and soil. This method does take some time to learn, however.

Tests have shown that a plant that has completely wilted from lack of water, even once, doesn't perform as well as one that has not. Try not to even occasionally miss a watering. Many plants flag before they wilt. The leaves just begin to lose their ability to hold themselves in their normal position, similar to a flag in light breeze rather than stiff wind. They may also lose their shine, appear slightly gray, or just not be as perky as normal. Flagging should be avoided because of the stress it places on the plant.

Over time you will acquire a feel for watering as you become familiar with the plants in your collection, their needs, and the variables that affect them. Assessment of your plants' needs will become habit. Many gardeners who have grown houseplants for years automatically check the south window first because these plants tend to dry out the fastest. You will learn that all plants don't need one cup of water on a regular weekly schedule, and that those planted in lightweight mixes in clay pots may dry out twice as fast as others.

Some of the greatest frustration when watering occurs when cleaning up spills and excess drainage. Plants quickly lose their appeal if they create a constant mess or damage furniture or windowsills. Both problems are easily avoided by using a long-spouted watering can that reaches to the interior of the plant and properly fitted saucers that are deep enough to catch run-off.

How to water As a general rule (particularly if no specific information on your plant is available), water plants thoroughly until all of the soil is moistened and excess water runs out the bottom. For many plants, the soil surface should then be allowed to almost dry before watering again. Most plants perform very well in these alternating moisture levels, which is why plants that are somewhat neglected between waterings are often better looking specimens than those that are fussed over and watered too frequently. With experience, watering correctly becomes second nature.

Watering can be done from the top or bottom. Most plants are best watered by pouring water on the surface and allowing it to percolate down through the soil. Generally, this is the easiest and most common method and it also leaches, or cleanses, the soil of fertilizer salt build-up. Bottom-watering is typically accomplished by immersing the pot in water. The water is drawn upward into the soil through the drainage holes. Plants such as African violet, florist's gloxinia, and streptocarpus are often bottom-watered since water on their leaves may cause scarring. Wick-watering and self-watering pots provide a similar watering system. Whether bottom- or top-watered, plants should not be allowed to sit in water for extended periods because saturated soil, with its lack of air, will damage roots. Fifteen or twenty minutes (never more than an hour) after watering, remove any water standing in the saucer.

Troubleshooting with top-watering: If the surface of the soil becomes crusted or impermeable to water, prick or roughen it with a fork. If the water runs down the sides of the pot and out the drainage holes without moistening the soil, immerse the pot in tepid water until the soil is moistened and expanded to fill the pot again.

Water type The type of water needed for plants is generally not critical unless the plant is unique or sensitive or if the water is particularly unusual in its mineral content. Avoid soft or very hard water, and water with high pH (alkaline). Water should be at room temperature or tepid since extremely hot or cold water can shock the plant, harm the foliage, and damage the roots. Leaving water to sit overnight in an open container allows chlorine to dissipate (chlorine can cause leaf spotting if excessive) and lets the water come to room temperature. If a water problem is suspected, it is best to have the water tested at a professional lab.

Special situations Gardeners need not be slaves to their plants and can utilize special watering options while away from home. Self-watering pots, wick watering, and other tricks will help supply moisture in your absence. The following are strictly short-term options and generally not appropriate for long-term care.

1. Have a friend check and water plants once or twice a week. This is the only time a specific schedule is acceptable– it is better than nothing and will

VIEWPOINT
VACATION WATERING

If I am going to be away for ten days or less I water all my plants the night before, and I place the ones that require the highest humidity in the bathtub on trays with pebbles covered with water. The bathroom must have a window to allow some light in. For the rest of my plants I allow a minimum amount of light to enter through curtains. I have not used wicks for longer periods. I need a person to check every so often.
FRANCISCA PLANCHARD-COEHLO
THE NEW YORK BOTANICAL GARDEN

I tend to put my plants in the shower, water them well and go. The coolness of the shower and lower light levels will keep the plants in good shape for almost two weeks.
JERRY PARSONS
UNIVERSITY OF CALIFORNIA BOTANICAL GARDENS AT BERKELEY

I put my plants in the bathtub with about an inch or two of water in it. I invert individual flower pots and place plants atop each. Don't forget to close the door to maintain humidity.
ROBERT BOWDEN
HARRY P. LEU BOTANICAL GARDENS

If I'm away three to four days I simply water well. I have not found wick watering very successful. There are some plants–ferns, gardenia, ficus–that I can overwater so that there is water in the saucer but generally this isn't a good idea. I turn off my artificial lights (for few days only) which helps to keep plants from drying out under lights. I have also put plants in bathtub; it works for a week or so; water well.
JULIE MORRIS
BLITHEWOLD MANSION AND GARDENS

V I E W P O I N T

FERTILIZATION SCHEDULES

Our fertilization schedule is different from the one mentioned in many entries in this book. We feed January through October, except plants under lights which are fed year round.
JULIE MORRIS
BLITHEWOLD MANSION AND GARDENS

My fertilizing schedule is set with the weather pattern in New York. Most plants, except cactus and a few species requiring special treatment, are fertilized every two weeks from January through September (bromeliads and ferns with half strength). This is based on the number of daylight hours at a given time of year. In winter growth is slowed so little or no fertilizer is used.
FRANCISCA PLANCHARD-COEHLO
THE NEW YORK BOTANICAL GARDEN

I tend to fertilize my plants twice a month at half strength during the plants' active growing season. I get good growth and healthy plants with this schedule.
JERRY PARSONS
UNIVERSITY OF CALIFORNIA BOTANICAL GARDENS AT BERKELEY

My fertilization schedule is similar to the one used at Chicago Botanic Garden.
DEBORAH LALUMONDIER
MISSOURI BOTANIC GARDEN

probably not harm plants if done only for a short time.

2. Move plants to a moderately lighted spot–slightly away from their light source. This will slow growth and consequently the need for water. Plants should receive just enough light for maintenance of growth until you return.

3. Cluster plants closely to create a microclimate. They will shade one another, conserve moisture, and moderate temperatures. This helps maintain them while you are gone, but if done for a long period may cause problems because of poor air circulation.

4. Fill the saucers with extra water that can be taken up as the plant uses it. Even though plants can be harmed from extended periods of sitting in water, this may be less damaging over the short run than letting the plants dry out completely.

5. Wick watering offers a continual water source for plants by a wick or string that runs from the soil out the bottom of the pot and to a water reservoir. The wick draws water up by capillary action, providing the moisture needed. This type of watering can saturate the soil, so if the method is used over the long term, it should be monitored carefully. If you suspect saturation, remove the wick and let the soil dry out. Rewet the wick by immersing it before replacing it in the soil. Also, initial top watering is usually necessary to start a successful wicking operation.

6. Self-watering pots are designed to provide watering for extended periods (see description of different types of systems under Selecting Containers, page 174). When setting up a self-watering pot, it is critical to watch for the first few weeks to make certain that the soil is not getting too wet. In other words, the plants in a self-watering system cannot be totally ignored.

7. Plastic tents can be set up to hold in moisture. This method should be a last resort because heat and moisture can build up inside, damaging plants. If you choose this option, make certain that the plastic bag or tent has air holes to allow ventilation, especially during summer months, and move the plants into low light.

FERTILIZATION Fertilization, like watering, varies according to the time of year, available light, and temperature. A plant's use of nutrients is greater during active growth and this use will slack off during the winter months. Also, low-light plants tend to grow more slowly and thus require less fertilizer than high-light plants.

Plants use sixteen elements for various functions and growth. Three of them, nitrogen, phosphorus, and potassium, are used in the greatest quantities. These, along with calcium, carbon, hydrogen, magnesium, oxygen, and sulfur, are referred to as macronutrients. Micronutrients, or trace elements, are used in small amounts and include boron, chlorine, copper, iron, manganese, molybdenum, and zinc. A healthy outdoor soil contains most of these nutrients, but indoor potting mixes often contain no soil and few nutrients. Therefore it is essential that they be added, either into the soil prior to potting or as fertilizer applications.

Nitrogen (N) is associated with the production of foliage. Phosphorus (P) is connected with early root production and flower stimulation, and potassium

(K) aids overall sturdiness, disease resistance, and fruit development. These three nutrients are abbreviated as N-P-K, and the amounts of these nutrients, or the analysis, is found on all fertilizer labels, indicated numerically, such as 20-20-20. If you are growing flowering plants like African violets, you will want a higher amount of phosphorus to stimulate flowers. If your plants are foliage plants only, a balanced fertilizer (equal amounts of N-P-K) is sufficient.

Synthetic fertilizers contain nutrients derived from man-made sources. These usually have a higher analysis than organic fertilizers and are used in smaller amounts. This high analysis can damage plants if not used carefully. Natural or organic fertilizers derive nutrients from natural sources, such as manure, fish emulsion, or cottonseed meal. These fertilizers are almost always low in analysis, making it difficult to cause damage, and they deliver nutrients in a more gradual manner. They work more slowly to improve a plant's appearance or encourage flowers, much like the nutrients delivered in nature.

The most common fertilizers available for houseplants are formulations that are mixed with water and applied when watering. Another popular type is a pellet that releases nutrients slowly because it's encapsulated in gelatin or clay. These are usually mixed with the potting soil before the plant is potted. This method avoids remembering to mix and apply fertilizer, but also does not give the gardener any control over how much fertilizer is released. Pellet types must be reapplied annually. There are also concentrated stick forms available, but these have a tendency to create hot spots where they are inserted into the soil, which damage roots and give uneven distribution of nutrients. Some manufacturers take all the guesswork out of fertilization by offering special-use fertilizers, such as one specifically for African violets. This is convenient, but does not mean that you should have six different fertilizers for six different plants. A formula for African violets is most likely appropriate for other flowering plants as well. The method of delivery and nutrient analysis will determine how the fertilizer is applied and how much is used—there are no all-encompassing rules.

Generally speaking, plants benefit from regular fertilizer applications during active growth in spring and summer, fewer applications in fall, and very little, if any, fertilizer in winter. Time fertilizer application so that the plant is moist and not under water stress! Fertilizing a dry or wilted plant usually results in leaf drop and distorted or damaged foliage. It is important to follow manufacturer's instructions and use all products according to label directions. It is better to slightly underfertilize plants than to risk damaging plants by high amounts. When in doubt, use half the recommended rate and increase or decrease as indicated by the growth response. For the purposes of this book "fertilizer" is commercially available synthetic fertilizer. Any "off the shelf" indoor plant type will work. Look for analysis of 10-10-10 or higher. Fertilizer timing recommendations in this book assume plants are grown in an interior or home environment.

HUMIDITY AND TEMPERATURE Humidity refers to the amount of moisture held in the air— most plants grow best at levels of 40 to 60 percent humidity. Most homes do not provide the amount of humidity plants would receive in their

A tray with moist pebbles will increase humidity. Note the inverted saucer that keeps the plant elevated.

natural outdoor setting, but many plants are adaptable and will tolerate lower humidity levels if all other cultural requirements are being satisfied. Plants that are adapted only to high humidity situations seldom make good house-plants and will be a source of constant frustration to the gardener.

Humidity varies depending on the type of home environment, the heating system, and the season. Changing humidity is difficult in the home compared to a greenhouse setting where it can be carefully controlled. Misting is often recommended to increase humidity, but in actuality seldom provides moisture as needed in the form of water vapor. Instead, it wets the leaves, which can increase disease problems. Room humidifiers help to a certain degree, as does the practice of localizing humidity by grouping plants closely, double potting, with an insulating layer of moist sphagnum moss between the pots, and ele-vating pots on a bed of moist gravel.

Air movement, a normal part of the outdoor environment that is often lacking indoors, is desirable for normal growth of most plants. Studies show that air movement, which causes leaves to move, helps naturally to control plant height, produces sturdier plants and aids in insect control. It is not essential but positively affects the growing environment. Small, inexpensive fans can be placed among a group of plants to increase the circulation.

Nearly all plants can grow within temperatures of 55-75° F., the tempera-ture of most homes. Plants generally perform best if night temperatures are around 5-10 degrees cooler than day temperatures. Cactus and other succu-lents are examples of plants that can tolerate wide fluctuations in day and night temperatures (again, recall their native habitat–deserts are searing in the day and very cold at night).

GROOMING AND PHYSICAL MAINTENANCE Grooming and maintenance actually take very little time and will keep plants looking healthy and at their best. The amount of care will vary according to the plant–plants such as palms require little care since they do not shed leaves readily or need pruning. Plants such Swedish ivy and weeping figs are more demanding.

Remove any old, shriveled or discolored leaves. Leaves that have begun to yellow will not turn green again (unless it is because of a nutrient deficiency, which will occur all over the plant) and should be removed. They offer no benefit to the plant and detract from its appearance. Generally, pinch or prune out the entire leaf. If more than a couple of leaves are shriveled or dis-colored, investigate why this is happening–you may be able to avoid serious problems later. Occasionally you will see a recommendation to cut off (with scissors) the brown tips of leaves. In actuality, this only causes another brown edge to appear. However, if a plant has only a few large leaves, a tapering trim may save a leaf temporarily while new leaves grow.

Large, broad-leaved plants tend to catch a considerable amount of dust. Dust not only looks bad, but can actually block the amount of light reaching the leaves and potentially block small pores on the leaf surface as well. Dust can be removed with a feather duster, by wiping the foliage with a soft cloth, or by rinsing in the tub or shower. If wiping the foliage, support the leaf with one hand while moving lightly across the leaf with the other hand–do not rub. In addition to removing dust, this type of grooming allows you a greater opportunity to look at the plant closely. A close examination helps to detect a disorder or insect problem before it gets out of hand.

Leaf-shine products are designed to provide a healthy shine to the foliage surface, although many products make plants look more like green patent leather than living things. Typically a healthy plant with dust-free leaves doesn't need an artificial shine added. Leaf-shine products can be attractants for dust and may end up exacerbating problems by clogging pores. The only time a leaf-shine product will improve a plant's appearance is if mineral deposits from water detract from the plant's appearance. If you decide to use a leaf shine, be certain to use only a product designed for this purpose. Avoid oils or waxes that leave the foliage greasy and eventually clog the pores and damage the foliage. Follow the directions carefully; diluting is usually recommended for most products.

PRUNING Even under ideal growing conditions, some plants will need occasional pruning. Plants may need pinching to encourage a full and vigorous habit, to promote growth, or to correct poor growth due to low light or other cultural deficiency. Pruning can modify and direct growth, improve structure, remove dead or diseased branches and foliage, and reduce size. It may be hard to bring yourself to remove a part of your favorite plant to promote growth, but it will pay off in the end with a healthier, stronger plant.

Prune with sharp pruning shears or scissors. Scissor-action (by-pass) pruning shears are preferable to anvil-type shears because they slice cleanly through the stem and leave no stubs. Anvil shears tend to crush the stem and leave stubs. If cutting a branch, cut it back flush with the nearest main branch. Good pruners are a sizable investment, but will last a lifetime if cared for properly.

Pinching is pruning on a smaller scale. Fingernails can be used to pinch succulent stems, and this is usually done to remove growing tips that encourages side branching. Regular pinching of some plants helps to develop and maintain a full plant.

Each plant has an inherent growth type that should be considered because it may affect the way the plant can be pinched or pruned. For example, a ponytail palm has one thick woody stem, a woody bulbous base, and long linear leaves originating from the top. It may require the removal of an occasional dried leaf, but will never need major pruning because of its simple structure. A vining tradescantia, on the other hand, can be almost mowed off to grow into a full plant. Columnar cactus should not be pruned, but segmented cactus such as Christmas cactus, can be pruned at natural joints. A dracaena that has become too tall can be pruned because the woody stem has the ability to grow foliage from dormant side buds.

Root pruning is another specialized type of pruning that can restrain or limit growth or can be used to invigorate some plants. Minimal root pruning happens automatically at the time of repotting as roots are untangled. This encourages roots to grow into new soil. Severe root pruning will allow a plant to grow for a long while in a small, shallow container, and may actually be a

Wipe off leaves with a soft, dry cloth to get rid of dust and some insects.

factor in dwarfing a plant as with bonsai. Both methods cause new roots to grow at the pruning cuts. Most root pruning should be done in spring and accompanied by removal of some foliage to compensate for root loss. Root prune with care since the results are more likely to be irreversible than when pruning foliage.

STAKING Staking to improve a plant's appearance should not be done to compensate for the poor cultural practices that make a plant lopsided or unstable. In such instances, staking should be considered a temporary tool to improve the condition of a plant while culture is corrected, not as a crutch to hold up a plant that should be pruned or thrown out. Instead, try to improve the cultural problems that caused the plant to look bad in the first place. There are some special situations, however, that require supporting a plant in one way or another. Use a stake that is at least as thick as the stems you are trying to support. Thin stakes often don't stand up any better than the stem with the problem. Green bamboo stakes and green twine or twist ties for attachment virtually disappear from view. Green plastic tie tape is becoming popular because it is wider than twist ties and less likely to cut into stems. It also stretches a bit so is less likely to girdle an expanding stem. Staking can be done when the plant is young to direct and train growth in a particular fashion. Vining plants can be staked and trained to a trellis or decorative form or they can be left to hang from a basket.

MOVING HOUSEPLANTS OUTDOORS IN SUMMER If properly selected for the existing conditions in a home, there is often no need to move houseplants at all. However, since we often have less than ideal situations in the home, moving plants outdoors for the summer can sometimes be beneficial. If an indoor location is deficient in light or humidity, plants often can be revived and brought back into full health by summering outdoors. Similarly, some gardeners in cold climates bring such plants as geraniums and mandevilla indoors merely to overwinter them and then take them back outdoors where they will put on their spectacular display in the summer. Tropical plants also provide exotic accents on decks and patios as long as they are properly hardened and cared for outdoors. Some plants, such as gardenia and hibiscus, should be moved outdoors in summer where they will receive enough light to signal the plant to flower. Some gardeners like to move their plants outdoors merely to get a summer vacation away from indoor maintenance. Watering with a hose and allowing the wind to blow away brown leaves can be a welcome change.

Although a move outdoors may seem simple and an improvement in conditions for the plant, the plant's response to being moved to a new site can be dramatic and potentially detrimental if not handled properly. A plant's response to change depends on the inherent adaptability of the species and the difference in the old and new sites. A plant being moved outdoors must be toughened up–hardened off–to avoid damage by wind, sun, and temperature fluctuations. After all, in the house, plants live in a fairly moderate situation. (An enterprising gardener, doing good things for the plants by giving them a breath of fresh air outside, moved them out one morning and didn't understand why they were nearly dead within two days–tattered and torn, sunburned and damaged by cold night temperatures.)

Acclimatization is a gradual process that allows a plant to adapt and toughen, avoiding the damage of an abrupt move. After spending the winter indoors, leaves are succulent and stems are soft. They need to build up a layer of cells that is resistant to sunburning, desiccation, and being whipped by the wind. Sun damage can occur in a very short time although the damage won't appear until a bit later–showing up as pale areas or burned blotches. Full sun outdoors is considerably more harsh than high light or full sun indoors.

Steps to harden a plant:

1. Learn the needs of the plant being moved outdoors. For example, spathiphyllum, a low-light plant, will suffer in high light outdoors, regardless of how gradually you move it.

2. Select three or four locations with increasing amounts of light and decreasing amounts of protection. Move the plant to the lowest light and most highly protected situation for one to two weeks. Then move it to the next location. Look for situations that are brightly lighted but not in direct sun; protected from wind, such as an open garage or carport, under a large dense tree, under an arbor or tucked into a shrub border.

3. Water the plant well before moving–moisture levels fluctuate rapidly outdoors and can result in drought stress if a plant is not carefully monitored. Also, a water-stressed plant is more susceptible to sunburn and wind damage.

4. Cover or move plants if night temperatures are predicted to drop below 40° F.–a plant may be able to tolerate more temperature extremes after it is adjusted to its outdoor spot, but when first moved out of its 65-75° F. house it is extremely vulnerable to temperature change.

5. Gradually move plant into its final position and increase the amount of time in that spot every couple of days. Choose the final position according to a plant's light requirements, keeping in mind that a houseplant that does well in high light may not be suited to the intensity of direct sun. Most plants grow best in filtered sun, such as under the open canopy of a shade tree, on a patio with morning sun and afternoon shade, or under a gazebo or arbor.

6. Monitor the plant carefully, particularly for water–plants dry out much more quickly outdoors.

When taken outdoors, plants are exposed to organisms like insects and fungal spores that occasionally develop into problems. Otherwise, bugs like ants may just take up residence in the pot, not really causing any harm to the plants. Repotting in fall just before bringing the plant back indoors will eliminate them. Also, submerging the pot in water for a short period will usually float away most insects.

POTTING AND REPOTTING Repotting is done either to replace poor soil, prune the roots, or move a plant into a larger pot. Although it can be done at any time, it is best done just before active growth in spring. If soil problems, such as depleted nutrients or soil-inhabiting pests, are present, it is best to replace all the soil. Otherwise, it is only necessary to add some new soil. Remove the plant from its pot, disturb the roots somewhat to encourage them to grow into the new soil, place the soil ball in a new container, and add some new

TAKING CUES

Understanding the many factors that affect plant growth allows us to provide for optimum growth and can also be useful in manipulating plants. Plants respond to specific cues from nature to initiate flowering, resting stages, and many other functions. By mimicking the variations in light, temperature, humidity, and moisture, we can bring about these changes artificially indoors. While geraniums and African violets will bloom continually with little coaxing if given the right light and moisture, other plants are dependent on specific cues in order to respond. As examples:

• Poinsettia: the bracts will turn from green to red, pink or white in response to a particular amount of darkness (called photoperiodism).

• Amaryllis: needs a cool and dry dormant stage of several months before sending out leaves and a flower stalk.

• Hardy bulbs: need a cooling period mimicking winter in order to form roots and flower indoors.

• Cactus, agapanthus, clivia: must have dry period followed by wet period to trigger flowering.

• Hibiscus and gardenia: must have high humidity and light levels to flower.

REPOTTING

1. Lift the plant from its pot. This spider plant is potbound.

2. Carefully loosen the roots, shaking off some of the old soil.

3. Prune any diseased or discolored roots.

4. Center the plant in its new pot.

5. Fill soil in around the plant and gently firm it with your fingers.

6. Water the plant well.

soil. If the plant has not outgrown its pot, simply replace the soil and put the plant back in the same container. If repotting is necessary to restrict growth, both root and foliage pruning may be in order. The foliage is directly affected by disturbance of roots. If you disrupt 50 percent of the roots, you need to prune 25 percent of the foliage to ensure that the plant won't self-prune by dropping leaves. Repotting an ailing plant will probably not cure it unless poor-quality soil was the reason the plant was in bad shape.

A plant that has outgrown its pot should be planted in a pot that is only an inch or two larger than the old one. Gradually increasing the size of the pot will result in the best growth–plants that are potted in too large a container tend to do poorly because the soil holds more water than the plant can use and because the plant will put on more root growth than normal, often at the expense of foliage and flowers.

The spider plant in its new pot.

1. Moisten the soil thoroughly the night before repotting so it will be easy to handle and the rootball won't fall apart when it is removed from the pot. Gather supplies needed, such as the new pot, screening or clay shards to cover the drainage holes, and a wooden spoon or other implement for gently tamping the soil around the roots. Plastic window screening works well to cover the drainage holes since it allows water to pass freely out of the pot, does not rot, takes up less room than clay shards, and avoids hiding places for soil-inhabiting pests.

2. Carefully slip the plant from its container. If soil is stuck to the pot, run a knife around the edge to loosen it. With small plants, place your fingers around the plant, holding your hand across the soil surface, and then quickly invert the pot and remove it. Although some plants will tolerate a light tug on the stem to loosen them from the pot, it is best to tap the rim of the pot on the side of the table to loosen it rather than take the chance of damaging the plant. Lay large plants on their side and gently slip them from the pot.

3. If you are making a complete soil change, allow the soil to fall away and loosen and remove as much soil clinging to the roots as possible (this may not be possible with extremely dense root systems). Examine the roots carefully for signs of disease or insects, such as root mealybugs, and to determine whether they need pruning. Prune off any discolored or dead roots and gently tease out any roots that are spiraling in the shape of the pot. In cases where you are not making a complete soil change, it is sufficient to disturb the rootball slightly by probing lightly with your fingers. If the roots are tightly bound, take a sharp knife and make three to five shallow cuts from the top to the bottom of the rootball and an X cut across the bottom.

4. Clean and sterilize the pot by dipping it in a dilute bleach solution and fill it one-third with soil. Clay pots should be soaked in water and planted while wet so they will not pull moisture from the plant.

5. Center the plant. Adjust level so that surface of old rootball is at surface level of new soil in the new pot; be careful not to bury rootball deeper than it was before. Fill soil around it, and tamp slightly, removing large air pockets. Leave at least one inch between rim of pot and soil level to allow for a water resevoir; this space allows water to percolate evenly through rootball.

6. Water the plant well and place it out of direct sunlight for a day to a week, depending on whether it was drastically root pruned.

PROPAGATION

New plants can be grown from old by various methods of propagation, many of which are relatively easy and provide rewarding results. Propagation increases the number of plants in a collection, perpetuates a species, can provide youthful, healthy new plants from an aging plant, and in some cases can rejuvenate an older plant. Propagation is accomplished by seed (sexual) or by vegetative regeneration (asexual). Most houseplants are commonly reproduced vegetatively because it is easier and produces faster results than seed.

SEEDS Seed is produced from a flower after successful pollination. Amazing storehouses of potential plant life, seeds come in all sizes, colors, and shapes. Some plants produce prolific seed, while for others seed is rare. A plant grown from seed takes longer to develop into a mature plant than a plant reproduced vegetatively, but a plant grown from seed has two gene sources (pollen and ovule), providing characteristics from two different plants. Occasionally these genes combine to produce entirely new characteristics, and some plants will exhibit certain physical characteristics only when propagated by seed. Transmission of some fungal, viral, and bacterial diseases can be avoided by using seed propagation.

Although the basic seed structure is similar in all plants, there can be great differences in germination techniques. Specific instructions for individual seeds are found on seed packets and in seed-growing references.

Water, oxygen, light, and heat all profoundly affect germination. The introduction of water stimulates most seeds to begin growth. Moisture continues to be important for the developing seedling, which requires frequent applications of small amounts of water to the germinating medium. Although light is not as critical as moisture, it may stimulate or inhibit growth. Most seeds do not need light to germinate, but some seeds must be planted on top of the medium where they will receive light to initiate germination. Light may also provide some radiant heat to the soil. Once germinated, the developing seedlings must have light to continue growth.

Oxygen must be available during germination—there must be a balance of moisture and air surrounding the seed, which is achieved with a well-aerated growing medium that retains moisture. Temperature also plays an important role in the rate of germination and growth. If the medium or air temperatures are extreme, seeds will not germinate. A range of 65-75° F. is best for most seeds, although some have more specific requirements. Heating mats or cables can be used to provide heat in the germinating medium.

Nature keeps seeds in a state of dormancy, awaiting the right conditions to germinate. Dormancy helps ensure survival after germination, and some plants have evolved very specific requirements for breaking the dormancy of their seeds. Some seed coats require scarification, soaking or mechanically scratching the seed coat so that water can enter. Other seeds require stratification, specific alternating temperature regimes, in order to break dormancy.

Below: **For large seeds, make holes with a pencil.** *Bottom:* **Sprinkle seeds; cover with soil and water.**

Still others must be extracted from a fruit before germination can begin.

The germinating medium should be selected to provide adequate moisture and air. The medium should be very loose, well-drained, and sterile to eliminate potential disease problems. Most germinating mixes contain no soil and are made of equal parts of peat moss and vermiculite, perlite or sand. Frequent light watering or misting help provide ideal conditions. Seedlings need only small amounts of soil, so containers for germination are generally shallow, reducing the volume of soil, which thus retains less water. Once germinated, the young plants can usually be potted and grown like other indoor plants, although some seedlings may require special care until well established.

VEGETATIVE PROPAGATION Asexual, or vegetative, propagation involves producing a new plant from a growing portion of an existing plant. Vegetatively propagated plants bypass the juvenile stages of growth and provide a mature plant in less time than if seed-grown. Most plant cells contain all the genetic information necessary to regenerate complete new plants identical to the plant from which they come. Vegetative propagation, or cloning, ensures exact characteristics with no surprises, which is of value when perpetuating a specific cultivar. There are, however, some exceptions to this. For example, *Sansevieria trifasciata* 'Laurentii' loses its yellow leaf margins when propagated from leaf cuttings.

When a part is removed from a plant, the cells at the wounded end of the cutting often have the ability to regenerate missing pieces. These leaf, stem, or root cells differentiate to produce the missing parts and become a complete plant. For example, roots will eventually grow from a stem cutting, and a single leaf cutting of some plants will eventually produce roots and shoots. However, not all plants have similar abilities to regenerate missing parts. Some plants will produce roots from a leaf cutting, but cannot produce new stems and leaves. Because of this, it is important to know which propagation methods will be successful for each plant.

Cuttings Cuttings of various plant parts are most commonly used for vegetative propagation. Cuttings are classified by the part of the plant from which they are obtained: stem cuttings, leaf cuttings, leaf-bud cuttings and root cuttings.

When selecting cutting material, the stock plant should be free of insects and diseases. Cuttings can be taken from an unhealthy plant in an attempt to save a part of it, but an effort should be made to understand why the plant is unhealthy to begin with. If a plant is diseased the cuttings may also contain the disease and should be rooted in an isolated container and inspected regularly for symptoms of the original problem. If the plant is unhealthy because of cultural conditions, producing a new plant and changing cultural habits will usually provide satisfaction.

Stem cuttings (tip, medial or secondary, and cane—see illustrations) are usually three- to five-inch pieces cut from a stem and contain some leaves. For certain plants, such as dieffenbachia and dracaena, however, a stem cutting can be made from a leafless section of the stem or cane. The terminal, or tip, of the stem will give the most rapid development of a new plant, although mid-

ROOTS

A plant will only be as successful as its roots are healthy. Healthy roots are generally plentiful, firm, and pale-colored. Of course there are exceptions to this, such as an epiphyte's aerial roots. Aerial roots are usually in lesser number, and covered with a tough outer covering to protect them against moisture loss. Some roots are orange, red, or brown. It should be obvious when looking at a plant's roots whether they are healthy or not. Generally, any roots that fall apart when handled or look dark, malodorous, or slimy should be cut off. For roots to maintain their health, they need not only enough water to supply the plant, but also enough air to prevent anaerobic decomposition. This means providing a well-drained porous potting mix—except in the case of water-loving plants such as cyperus. Aquatic plants perform best in soils low in organic matter because organic matter rots if left under water, causing decomposition of roots and foul odors.

STEM CUTTINGS

1. Make stem cuttings and remove lower leaves.

2. Dip in rooting hormone.

3. Stick into hole made with pencil and firm soil.

4. Cover cuttings with plastic bag to retain humidity.

5. A rooted cutting.

dle or basal stem cuttings can also be used. Cuts should be made just below a node, the place on the stem that bears leaves or branches. Nodes contain actively dividing cells where root formation is most likely to occur. Cuttings from ficus, pelargonium, cactus, and other succulents should be left to air dry in a cool shaded area until the cut surface heals over (several hours for leafy cuttings to several days for cactus). This will help prevent disease.

Rooting powders are chemical hormones that increase survival rates, shorten the rooting time, and greatly increase the quality and quantity of roots. The most commonly used hormones are naphthalene acetic acid (NAA) and indolebutyric acid (IBA). These come in ready-to-use powdered form and should be used according to the label directions.

With a clean, sharp knife, cut a portion of stem three to five inches long from the parent plant just below a node. Remove leaves at the base and any flowers. Sprinkle a small amount of rooting powder on a clean dish and dip the end of the cutting into the powder. Tap off excess powder (a large amount is not beneficial). Insert the cutting deeply enough into the medium to hold the cutting in an upright position and so that at least one node is below the soil. Firm the moistened medium around the cutting (more succulent plants, such as peperomia, should have less stem below the medium to prohibit rotting). When making cuttings of large-leafed plants, such as rex begonia, cut portions of the leaves away, leaving only one-third of each leaf. This reduces moisture loss. For a plant like dieffenbachia, sections of cane can be placed vertically or horizontally in the moist medium.

Leaf cuttings consist of the leaf blade and petiole (leaf stalk). This type of cutting must initiate both roots and shoots and will take longer than a stem cutting to develop a mature plant. However, it is an easy way to propagate many common houseplants, such as African violet, gloxinia, and many begonias.

African violets are easily propagated by removing an entire leaf and petiole and inserting the petiole into the medium. New plants will form at the base of the petiole. Jade leaves should be inserted directly into the medium since they do not have petioles. Sansevieria leaves can be cut into three-inch sections and inserted directly into the medium. As you are cutting them, notch the top of each section so you will know which end to insert—if inserted upside down, they will not root. When the new plant has formed, cut away and discard the old leaf section.

To propagate rex begonia, lay an entire leaf on the medium, pin it down to assure contact, and make cuts through major veins. It will form new plants at the wounds. Begonias and streptocarpus can also be propagated by cutting wedge-shaped sections of the leaf that contain a major vein and inserting them upright into the moist medium.

Leaf-bud cuttings consist of a leaf blade, petiole, and a portion of the stem containing a bud. This type of cutting is useful for plants that will not initiate shoots from a leaf cutting and also allows many cuttings to be made from a small amount of plant material. The inclusion of a bud in the cutting provides for quick shoot development. Almost any plant that can be propa-

Making leaf cuttings of sansieveria. Be sure to pot them right (top) side up.

Center and top: Leaf cuttings of begonia and streptocarpus. *Above:* Root cutting that has taken root.

gated by stem cuttings can be propagated by leaf bud cuttings. Simply insert a small portion of stem containing a leaf and bud into the medium.

Root cuttings entail cutting the root of a plant into sections and replanting. Root cuttings take considerably longer to produce roots and shoots, but the procedure is used for plants that are shy to reproduce by other means.

Layering accomplishes the same results as a cutting, but no cutting is done until the new plant has produced roots. Many climbing or trailing vines are easily layered by pinning the trailing stem on top of the soil or burying it slightly. In some cases nicking or wounding the stem hastens root formation. The moisture of the soil causes roots to form, and once fully formed, the new plant can be severed from the old.

Air layering is useful for propagating tropical plants with woody stems that have grown tall and lost their lower leaves. Air layering allows the top portion of the plant to develop roots while still attached and nourished by the parent plant. Cut a notch into the stem at the point where roots are desired and wedge a toothpick between the cut surfaces. Spindly or tall stems should be staked to support the section above the cut, and the wound can be lightly dusted with a rooting hormone to hasten the rooting process. Wrap thoroughly moistened, unmilled long fiber sphagnum moss around the area, making sure the wound is entirely covered to keep it moist and dark. Wrap the moss with plastic to keep it moist throughout the rooting period. Securely bind the plastic in place, top and bottom, with rubber bands, twist ties, tape. or twine and check it regularly to be sure the moss has not dried out.

Within one to three months, roots will appear through the ball of moss. When the roots are well-developed, remove the plastic, cut the plant just below the new roots, remove any loose moss, and pot the new plant. Keep your new plant out of direct sunlight for a few days while it adjusts to being severed from the parent. Some parent plants can then be cut back to within four to six inches of the soil surface and allowed to develop new shoots, although not all plants respond to this treatment.

Specialized structures Stolons and runners are specialized stems that naturally produce new plants. Sometimes these stems move under the soil, sending up shoots away from the parent plant, such as with passion vine, grasses, banana and bamboo. Others run above the soil and produce small plantlets that can be cut off and potted, such as with spider plant.

Many plants also produce plantlets on the parent plant. For example, some forms of kalanchoe form plantlets along the leaf margins. The piggyback plant produces plantlets where the leaf blade joins the petiole. Some agaves produce plantlets on their inflorescences, and the mother fern produces many bulbules on mature fronds. As the small plants develop, the frond bends so that the plantlets come in contact with moist soil and form roots. Many orchids form specialized pseudobulbs or air-borne new plants called "keikis" that are easily separated.

Division Division is another method of vegetative propagation used with plants that have multiple crowns, suckers, fleshy roots, rhizomes, or bulbs. It is simply a matter of pulling or cutting apart large plants and potting the divided

AIR LAYERING

1. Notching a dieffenbachia for air layering.

2. Plant material removed from notch.

3. Wrap notched area with damp sphagnum moss.

4. Wrap moss with plastic and secure with ties.

5. After plant has formed roots, sever it from parent plant. Parent plant will sometimes sprout below the cut.

Spider plantlet.

sections. Dividing helps rejuvenate plants and keeps them healthier, it prevents overcrowding, and keeps plants to a manageable size. Some plants perform poorly and may cease blooming if overcrowded or potbound.

Dividing involves removing the entire plant from the pot and cutting, pulling, or breaking the clump apart into smaller pieces. Plants that produce multiple crowns, such as aloe, can be cut or pulled into pieces. Each piece should contain a crown or eye and have a good piece of the rootball attached. Replant divisions as soon as possible with the crowns placed at the same depth that they were growing before. Simply pull bulb-forming plants, such as haemanthus, apart and pot individually.

Some plants are held together loosely and can be pulled apart easily. Others must be broken apart at natural junctures or cut where needed. Tight or crowded crowns and tough roots require cutting with a sharp knife, saw, or spade. Once divided, pot the plants and water well.

Containers, Medium, and Environment A good propagating container should be sterile in order to avoid disease problems occasionally encountered. Plastic containers are easily sterilized by dipping them in a 10 percent bleach solution, Lysol, or trisodium phosphate bath. Heat clean clay pots in a 180° F. oven for an hour, and then soak them in water just prior to filling with soil. Sterilize cutting tools before and between cuts by dipping in trisodium phosphate or a weak bleach solution.

A good medium will provide physical support, an adequate supply of oxygen and water to the root zone, and proper drainage. Regardless of the kind of medium used, it should be sterile to prevent the introduction of disease organisms. Possible rooting media are peat moss, vermiculite, perlite and coarse sand used alone or in combination, or preformed rooting aids, such as peat pellets and foam rooting cubes. Water is not recommended as a rooting medium because roots that develop in water have a different physical structure than those formed in soil, and they tend to be brittle and do not transplant well. Rooting hormones are readily available and speed the development of new roots; most also help prevent infection.

The cuttings or specialized structures that must form new roots should be watered thoroughly as soon as they are placed in the medium. Thereafter, soil moisture must remain constant without becoming waterlogged. Divisions usually have roots already, so do not need as careful attention to watering as cuttings.

The size of the cutting is important. A cutting that is too large will have a very high demand for moisture and will probably wilt and become damaged. A cutting that is too small will not be able to store food for energy to produce roots. Cuttings of two to five nodes are usually appropriate.

Since cuttings without roots are unable to take up water, the humidity surrounding the cuttings must be kept high to prevent excessive wilting due to water loss from the leaves. The humidity can be kept high by enclosing the propagating container in plastic, using a clear glass or plastic lid, or by intermittent misting. If the cuttings are enclosed, it is necessary to ventilate the area occasionally to prevent overheating and to prevent the rooting medium

DIVISION

1. To divide, sever the root ball and crown with a sharp knife.

2. Pull apart the divisions and pot.

3. After dividing, pot up each section.

4. A tough plant such as aspidistra may require a pruning saw to facilitate dividing.

from becoming too wet, which will promote rot. Divisions do not need the
same amount of humidity.

Light is important for rooting cuttings as it provides the energy source to
develop new shoots and roots. The light source can be fluorescent lighting or
indirect sunlight. Cuttings enclosed in plastic must never be placed in direct
sunlight to avoid temperatures rising to harmful levels.

Temperature is another important factor in successful propagation. The
medium should be kept at 75-85° F. while the air around the cutting is best
kept at 65° F. Lower air temperatures slow moisture loss from the leaves,
while bottom heat will speed the rooting process. Various types of specially
insulated electric heating cables are available through garden centers and cat-
alogs.

INTEGRATED PEST MANAGEMENT

Integrated Pest Management (IPM) has changed the way plant pests are handled.
IPM is practiced by professional horticulturists in outdoor and indoor growing situations, and the system can be adapted for home gardens as well.

An IPM system involves making decisions based on which pests are present
and which factors are influencing pest populations and plant health. IPM is a logical, practical, and responsible approach to troubleshooting and plant care. This
type of system allows evaluation of all the factors in a situation, and then provides
options to keep pest populations at a low enough level to avoid unacceptable or
irreparable damage to a plant. IPM also involves evaluating a plant's value in contrast to the extremity of the control measure. For example, a few aphids on a
cineraria are tolerable. If the cineraria becomes completely covered in aphids, the
logical IPM decision is to throw it out since cinerarias are usually considered to be
disposable plants. However, if a prized orchid gets scale, the gardener may go to
extreme measures to take care of the problem rather than discard the plant.

Once you notice an insect or disease problem, an IPM system will help you
decide the most effective and least invasive cultural, physical, biological, or chemical controls.

PLANT SELECTION The first step in putting an IPM system into place is to choose
plants that are appropriate to the situation in which they will be growing. Take
into account the light, humidity, and temperature levels of the growing site and
choose plants that will thrive in that situation.

Insect and disease problems can be avoided by starting with clean, healthy
plants. Never add plants with existing problems to your collection–always examine new plants carefully before putting them with others. Make yourself aware of
the problems a particular plant is prone to and either avoid these plants altogether or keep a particularly watchful eye out for the problem.

It is a good practice to isolate new plants for a few weeks before introducing them
to your collection. Put them in a place by themselves where you can closely observe
them and take care of any problems before moving them to a permanent spot.

PROPER CULTURE IS THE BEST DEFENSE One of the most important factors in keeping
plants free of problems is proper culture. If a plant is growing in an appropriate

location and is cared for properly, it will respond with vigorous growth. Healthy plants will resist many of the common disorders that afflict plants. Find out all you can about a plant's needs when you purchase it and then try to provide whatever it needs, whether it be high or low humidity, moist or dry soil, or high or low light. Stress from a poor location or improper care predisposes plants to a myriad of problems.

Monitoring Make a habit of regularly observing your plants and be attentive to subtle changes in the way they look or respond. The best way to stay on top of plant health and detect disorders early is to touch and examine your plants regularly—clean the foliage and groom your plants frequently. Focusing attention on the plants gives an opportunity to adapt care, refine watering, detect problems early, and take note of general health. Is the new growth curled, are there shiny or sticky droplets on the leaves or the table on which the plant sits? Note any lack of vigor or discoloration or if it just doesn't look right.

Pest problems are most easily controlled if detected early while populations are small, and the spread of a disease can often be stopped in its early stages. However, if a plant is severely affected or is not valuable, it may be simpler to replace it.

Isolate First If a disease or insect problem occurs, first isolate the plant or plants from other plants to avoid infecting them. Take the time to carefully examine nearby plants to see if the problem has traveled or to discover where it originated. Then evaluate the growing situation and make any changes in the culture or environment that may be contributing to disease or insect problems. Are the humidity levels so low that spider mites have taken over? Are you keeping the soil wet enough to encourage fungus gnats?

Correct Diagnosis Correctly identifying the insect or disease in question is critical. Treatment without a correct diagnosis is not only fruitless but can be harmful. Understanding how the insect feeds and lives will help enormously in determining an effective control. Understanding disease cycles and how the diseases spread will also be necessary for determining an appropriate control.

Once a diagnosis is made, stop to think about tolerance levels. The goal of an IPM system is not necessarily to eradicate all pests, but to keep populations under control and to be willing to accept certain low levels of damage. This often means reexamining our thoughts about bugs. A few aphids will seldom harm a plant. Spider mites are difficult to eliminate completely, so if we can keep populations low enough to avoid obvious plant damage, the insect is considered controlled.

The insects you observe may not be alone. Remember that beneficial insects (predators or parasites) may be present and helping you control your problem. Beneficial insects act differently from pest insects. Through careful observation, you can detect the good from the bad bugs. A blanket spray of insecticide could kill these "helpers."

CHOOSING THE APPROPRIATE CONTROL Be aware of your control options and the appropriate timing to make them effective. Select the control method which is the least disruptive to the situation, and if necessary, work through the following series of steps until you achieve the results you want.

Inspect leaves regularly and prune off those that are heavily infested. This will reduce insect populations.

STEPS TOWARD INSECT CONTROL Use in the order given; if one method doesn't work, move onto the next one. :

  1. Identify the problem. Is it dust or is it mites?

  2. Isolate the problem plant.

  3. If the plant can be pruned without harm, do so. Pruning often removes large populations of insects or removes diseased tissue.

  4. Spray a strong stream of tepid water on the upper and lower surfaces of the leaves. This washes off many insects, and large populations can be reduced this way. Aphids and spider mites can often be kept under control with this method alone. Other insects may not be affected, however. Rinsing also cleans the foliage for more effective coverage if another method of control is needed.

  5. If weather permits, move plant outdoors to let natural predators handle the problem. Keep a careful watch on the plant, though, in case the insect problem gets worse. Watch for other insects interacting with pests. Native beneficial insects often occur with pests on plants placed outdoors. Beneficial insects aid in controlling plant populations.

  6. Remove pests physically with fingernails, tweezers, tissue or a cotton swab dipped in alcohol. Wipe top and bottom of the leaves with a soft, damp cloth. A soft bristled toothbrush can be used to dislodge hard-to-remove insects such as scale. This method will usually need to be repeated often for complete control.

  7. Wash both sides of the leaves, stems, and all infected parts in warm soapy water. Mild dish washing soap or insecticidal soap (see section on insecticidal soaps) can be effective controls for some insects.

  8. Apply horticultural oils to smother insects (see section on horticultural oils).

  9. Repotting will often provide reasonable control for insects affecting the roots, such as fungus gnat larvae or root mealybugs. Rinse the roots and repot into a clean pot with sterile potting mix.

  10. Use biological controls such as predatory and parasitic insects; these insects are called "beneficials." This method is most effective in greenhouses, conservatory rooms, or large enclosed growing areas (see information on predators used with various pests on pages 200-202).

  11. Treat with insecticide. In severe cases that persist, the plant can treated with a botanical or synthetic insecticide. Before using any pesticide, read the label carefully to make certain that it is listed for indoor use on the particular plant you intend to treat. Proper application and coverage are the key to success. Misuse can cause damage to the plant and to yourself. Oils and other chemicals can be especially harmful to plants that are water-stressed, so wait until the plant is back to a reasonably healthy state before spraying. Follow label directions carefully.

  12. Discard plant.

PATIENCE Be patient–the controls will work, perhaps more slowly than if immediately spraying with a potent chemical. These methods are for long-term control, not quick fixes. Be aware of the balance you are trying to achieve, particularly among pests and related beneficial insects.

Insecticidal soaps Because of the growing environmental concern about the impact of chemicals on human, animal, and plant life, insecticidal soaps are gaining in popularity for pest control on houseplants, vegetable gardens, and ornamental

Step 7: Spray the backs of the leaves thoroughly with insecticidal soap or horticultural oil.

plants.

Insecticidal soap is nontoxic to humans, mammals, and birds. It is biodegradable, fairly safe to handle, and generally safe to use on nonfood and food plants. Insecticidal soap kills insects through direct contact. The fatty acid component of the soap solution penetrates the body of the insect and disrupts membrane and cell functions, leading to its dehydration. If the soap does not directly contact the insect, it will not kill it.

Insects with soft bodies, such as immature whiteflies, scale crawlers, mealybugs, aphids, and spider mites, can be killed by insecticidal soaps. Insecticidal soaps are ineffective on insects that occur within the plant tissue (such as nematodes), or for insects with hard shells (such as adult scales).

Insecticidal soap is available premixed in a spray bottle or in concentrate that you mix and put in your own sprayer. Insecticidal soaps lose effectiveness after dilution, so mix only what you will use immediately. Since some plants are sensitive to insecticidal soaps, move the plant out of direct sun and make a test on a few leaves as a precaution. Wait three days to a week to see if an adverse reaction occurs. Then either move the plant outdoors or into a bathtub or protect the floor with a drip cloth. Spray the plant completely, covering the under and upper sides of leaves and stems, until the solution drips off. Keep the plant out of the sun until the solution dries. Repeat application after ten days may be necessary for complete control of pests.

Horticultural oils Horticultural oils are becoming a widely used, effective pest-control method. Like insecticidal soaps, they are safe and easy to use and have very low toxicity to mammals, birds, and beneficial insects. They are biodegradable and kill only what they contact.

Horticultural oils are lightweight, highly refined oils that can be used in the flower, vegetable, and indoor garden. They work by smothering the insect or egg, or by interfering with an insect's metabolism, causing death.

Most oils are petroleum-based, although vegetable oils are becoming available. A wide range of formulations is available so it is essential to read the label to know what you are getting. In general, you need to make sure you understand what the oil will control, which types of plants it can be used on, and how to properly apply.

Oils effectively control aphids, spider mites, scale, mealybugs, whitefly, fungus gnats, and some caterpillars. Oils are sometimes used in combination with insecticidal soaps to give more complete control by making the mixture coat the surface more effectively. Oils work by contact, meaning that the insect or egg must be thoroughly covered to gain effective control. Since there is little residual effect, multiple applications may be necessary to keep insect populations under control.

INSECTS

Aphids are one-tenth- to one-eighth-inch, soft-bodied insects with or without wings. They can be green, black, pink, red, yellow, orange, or clear. They suck juices from succulent stems and leaves. Infested new growth is distorted and stunted, and the leaves eventually yellow and fall. As aphids draw fluids from the plant, they excrete a sticky, sugary sap called honeydew. The honeydew coats the

SENSITIVE PLANTS

Some plants are sensitive and may be harmed by some sprays, so read the label carefully. Apply to a small area of the plant and wait three to seven days to see that there are no adverse reactions. Be sure to note all precautions. Some plants may show some sensitivity to soaps (allowing the soap to sit on the plant for thirty minutes and then rinsing may help avoid damage). Some sensitive plants:
Angel's trumpet
Crown-of-thorns
Dracaena
Gardenia
Ivy
Jade
Peperomia
Poinsettia
Some orchids
Any succulent with a whitish, waxy surface
Some ferns

Mealybugs and ants on *Crassula falcata.*

leaves and supports the growth of an unsightly black sooty mold. Although the mold washes off with water, controlling the aphids will eliminate the entire problem.

Aphids multiply quickly and weaken a plant over time. Mature wingless females have the ability to give birth to live young without being fertilized. Once the populations are large and overcrowding occurs, winged aphids will develop and migrate to other plants. When male and females are both present, eggs will be laid after fertilization.

Generally, aphids are easy to keep in check by wiping or washing them off and pruning out damaged areas. Insecticidal soaps are very effective, making use of other insecticides unnecessary. Beneficials: *Aphidoletes aphidimyza, Chrysoperla carnea* (green lacewings), *Hippodamia convergens* (lady beetles), parasitic wasps.

Mealybugs are one-eighth- to one-fifth-inch soft-bodied insects covered with white, woolly, waxy filaments. These sucking insects feed in leaf axils and branch crotches, and their egg sacks appear as white, cottony fluff. Mealybugs also produce sticky honeydew, which can develop sooty mold (see aphids). Extended feeding weakens the plant and can deform plant parts.

Small infestations can be removed with a cotton swab. Larger infestations form dense colonies covered in waxy filaments, making penetration of insecticidal soaps and other controls difficult. Dislodge as much of the colony as possible by scraping off or spraying with a strong stream of water, and then apply the control. Horticultural oils are quite effective. Beneficials: *Cryptolaemus montrovzieri, Hippodamia convergens.*

Scale insects are soft-bodied and covered with an oval or hemispherical "shell." The waxy shell can vary in size and color depending on the species of scale. Brown is the most common color, and the insects appear as bumps along stems and leaves; they are often mistaken as part of the bark. Scales are sucking insects that excrete honeydew (see aphids).

Scales hatch from eggs laid under the shell covering of a mature female. These tiny crawlers (1/100-inch) are translucent with red eyes and wander over the plant until they find a spot to settle. Until the crawlers develop a protective covering, they are particularly vulnerable to controls. They are difficult to see without a hand lens or microscope at this stage. Once the crawlers settle and begin feeding, they lose their legs, grow, and develop a shell covering.

Scales are controlled easily with insecticidal soap or oil at the crawler stage, but are more difficult to control as adults–timing is critical. Lift an adult to see whether any crawlers have hatched. If so, the time is right to spray. The adults are impervious to soaps and insecticides but can sometimes be controlled by removing with a fingernail or soft cloth or by spraying with horticultural oil. Beneficials: predatory wasps, *Hippodamia convergens* (lady beetles).

Spider mites are 1/00 to 1/160 inch and generally are not obvious without a hand lens or microscope. They are not classified as a true insect but belong to the spider family. Most often plant damage or fine webbing is noticed instead of the actual mites. Either of these problems indicates high populations.

Mites tend to feed on the underside of the leaves, although in heavy infestations they will feed on all surfaces. Unfortunately, by the time mite populations are large enough to be noticed, the damage is quite severe. Damage appears as an overall dull color. Upon close inspection, tiny yellow stipple marks are obvious where mites have fed and injured the tissue. Severe leaf distortion and defoliation can occur. If mites are suspected, hold a piece of white paper under a leaf and tap the leaf. If the "dust" that falls on the paper moves, you probably have mites.

Mites proliferate in temperatures over 70° F. and in low humidity. During hot, dry periods, mites can complete an entire life cycle in five to seven days. Since mites multiply rapidly, control measures should be taken as soon as possible. Separate infested plants from clean plants to prevent the mites from spreading and clean off any nearby surfaces. Prune off any badly infested parts to remove a good portion of the mites. Rinse the plants to remove the majority of adults. Soaps may be somewhat effective; oils are highly effective, although several treatments may be necessary since eggs are not affected. In some cases, plants may be damaged enough to warrant replacement. Chemical miticides are available if greater control is needed. Beneficials: *Phytoseiulus persimilis*.

Whitefly adults are 1/25-inch white-winged insects that look like tiny white moths. Whiteflies dart around the plant when disturbed and then settle on the underside of the leaves. Honeydew and sooty mold may be present in whitefly infestations (see aphids). Whiteflies are sucking insects that cause stippled areas, stunting and eventually weaken the plant.

Small infestations of whiteflies can be controlled effectively by trapping the adults on sticky yellow cards that can be purchased or made (paint a four-inch-by-five-inch piece of yellow poster board with a light layer of three parts petroleum jelly and one part mineral oil. Stick the card in a clothespin and insert in the soil at canopy height.) Infested plants should be lightly shaken to cause adults to fly to the trap. Larger infestations can be controlled with repeat applications of soap or oil. Beneficials: *Encarsia formosa, Delphastus pusillus*.

Fungus gnats are one-eighth-inch dark gray or black flies, often mistaken for fruit flies. They can be seen running on the soil surface or flying around potted plants. The white larvae can sometimes be seen when a plant is watered and the water floats them to the surface. They are approximately one-quarter-inch and live in the soil. The adult gnats are merely a nuisance and cause no harm to plants. The larvae, however, feed on plant roots, and continued feeding results in slight stunting of the plant.

Fungus gnats reproduce in moist soils and can be controlled easily by allowing the soil mix to dry out slightly between waterings. Submerging the pot in water for fifteen minutes will suffocate and float away the larvae. In extreme cases, the plant can be removed from its pot, the soil removed, the roots washed, and the plant repotted into fresh soil mix. A chemical soil drench control should be the last resort. Beneficials: beneficial nematodes, *Bacillus thuringiensis*.

Thrips are 1/50-inch slender insects that are usually dark-colored. With a hand lens or microscope you can see two sets of narrow fringed wings. They leap or fly when disturbed. Thrips are not often seen, but their characteristic damage indicates their presence. Adult and nymph thrips feed primarily on young tissue in

Spider mites on adenium.

the bud or shoot apex by rasping or scraping the surface of the tissue and then sucking the fluids. Injured tissue dries out, giving a whitish or silver-flecked appearance. Flowers can become spotted or distorted and appear to have the color rubbed off. Growth is often stunted. Thrips secrete black tarlike droplets that can be seen on the leaves.

Eggs are inserted in the leaves and stems and emerge in one to two weeks as pale yellow wingless nymphs. The nymphs tend to cluster on the leaves. Eventually they form cocoons in the soil and emerge as adults to feed, mate, and lay more eggs. Control of thrips can be difficult, if not impossible. Soaps, oils, and predators can sometimes keep populations in check. Severe infestations may require the use of insecticides or warrant the disposal of the plant depending on its value. Beneficials: *Neoseiulus cucumeris* and other mites, *Orius insidiosus*, nematodes.

Root mealybugs are similar in appearance to typical mealybugs. They feed on the roots, and their continued feeding will weaken the plant and cause poor color and stunting. These insects can be lethal to cactus. Root mealybugs can be controlled with some effectiveness by removing the plant from its pot, shaking off the soil and rinsing the roots in soapy water. Then repot in new soil. Annual repotting is usually enough to control root mealybugs.

DISEASES

Diseases are uncommon on healthy plants, but stressed plants often have problems. Good culture and sanitation minimize disease-related problems. Pruning and pinching out infected areas as soon as they appear are good practices during regular grooming. Some diseases are recognizable; others require professional or lab diagnosis.

Infectious diseases

Powdery mildew is a fungal disease showing as a grayish white powdery coating on the leaf. It grows on the surface of the leaves, never entering the leaf tissue.

Powdery mildew is not a severe problem and generally is a sign of poor air circulation and too much moisture (air and soil). If powdery mildew persists and is allowed to spread, it may interfere with light reaching the leaf and result in poor color and leaf drop. Powdery mildew can be controlled effectively through pruning and improved culture. Remove all severely mildewed leaves and provide increased air circulation as well as allowing the soil to dry slightly between watering. Some susceptible plants, such as rosemary, will get it no matter what precautions you take. Keeping the temperature very cool and free air circulation may help alleviate the problem.

Root, stem, and crown rots Rots appear as a disintegration of tissue on the main stem, at the base or crown or in the roots. Plants will weaken, develop poor color, wilt, and become soft, smelly, and rotted at the described locations. The plant can collapse and die if the problem is not caught in time.

Many of the pathogens involved in rots develop when the soil is kept too wet. Allowing the soil to dry out somewhat will often alleviate the problem. If the plant is severely damaged, it should be discarded quickly to prevent the disease from spreading.

Leaf spots and blights appear as dry circular to irregular brown areas on the leaves. Infected leaves or flowers should be removed as soon as damage is noticed. Usually, this is enough to control the problem.

Botrytis, or gray mold, covers an infected plant with thick, gray, fuzzy mold. Infections occur on flowers and tender foliage under moist, cool conditions. Cool temperatures and moisture are required for spores to germinate and the disease to spread. Remove severely infected leaves and flowers and change the culture to prevent the disease from spreading further.

Viruses have no single symptom and are present in a dormant state in many plants. Stress from improper culture or insect infestation allows the virus to become active. They appear as stunted or distorted stems as well as irregular patterns in the leaf. Flowers can be streaked. Viruses are spread by insects, and once within the plant tissue, cannot be removed. Infected plants should be replaced and insects kept under control.

Non-infectious diseases

Oedema (or edema) appears as small blisters or callused raised spots on the leaves of overwatered plants or those grown under excessively high humidity. The plant cells literally expand and explode from too much water and then heal over as corky tissue. Oedema varies in appearance on different plants depending on the type of leaf. Some oedema spots dry and fall out leaving a hole or irregular open spot on the leaves. This disorder is not disease- or insect-related and is controlled by reducing watering and humidity.

Sooty mold is a gray or black fungus that grows on the sticky honeydew left on the leaf surface from sucking insects. It can inhibit light penetration, preventing photosynthesis and stressing the plant. Sooty mold rubs off or can be washed off with water but is eliminated only by controlling the insect that produces the honeydew.

Fluoride toxicity Fluoride salts can accumulate from watering, causing leaf tips and margins to brown and die. These symptoms are similar to and may often be confused with a low humidity or disease problem. Generally a review of the culture will reveal the actual problem. Fluoride toxicity can be alleviated by using distilled water on plants. Plants sensitive to fluoride are aspidistra, calathea, chamaedorea, chlorophytum, cordyline, dracaena, and maranta.

Salt build-up problems often show up as a white or yellowish encrustation around the pot edge and soil surface. Salts cause dry, brown edges on leaves of many plants. Excess salts come from water and from fertilizers. Salt build-up can burn fine root hairs, causing a plant to wilt from inability to take up water. Salt build-up can be alleviated by leaching pots regularly–pour fresh water through soil several times, letting pot drain thoroughly.

PLANTS FOR TERRARIUMS
Epicscia
Sinningia
Dionaea (Venus flytrap)
Drosera (sundew)
Hemigraphis 'Red Equator'
Adiantum (fern)
Pteris (fern)
Ceropegia
Begonia
Streptocarpus
Cryptanthus
Selaginella
Psilotum nudum
Muehlenbeckia complexa
Pilea
Euonymus japonica 'Microphylla'
Serissa foetida
Hoya engleriana
Cuphea hyssopifolia
Stenandrium lindenii
Chamaeranthemum venosum
Nerta grandensis
Microgramma vaccinifolia
Pyrossia psilosoides
Ophiopogon japonicus 'Kyoto Dwarf'
Saxifraga stolonifera
Peperomia dahlstedtii
Peperomia rotundifolia
Myrsine nummularia
Ficus pumila 'Quercifolia' (and other cultivars)
Pellonia

TERRARIUMS

Terrariums are miniature greenhouses made of glass or plastic for houseplants that flourish in very humid conditions. Terrariums can be sealed, in which case the garden within sustains itself by recycling oxygen, nutrients, and water; or terrariums can be left open, requiring some care by the gardener. Containers to house the terrarium run the gamut from aquariums to brandy snifters to glass jars to plastic ready-made terrariums. A well-planned terrarium uses all the elements of good garden design.

Terrariums may be planted with woodland plants, carnivorous plants, cactus, orchids, begonias, gesneriads, ferns and any other plants that are slow growing and small. There are even specialized terrariums called vivariums that have animals or insects living in them. Each type of community has special soil and care needs, depending upon not only the mix of plants, but also the container they are growing in. When choosing plants for a terrarium, it is essential to understand the plants' physical needs and to group plants with the same requirements. Otherwise, you may end up overwatering some or underwatering others.

A terrarium is usually constructed with a one-half- to two-inch layer of aquarium gravel in the bottom, topped by a thin layer of charcoal to keep out musty odors. A fine plastic screen, sheet moss, or soil cloth is then placed on top and sterile soil added to the level desired. Then the plants are added. Rocks, driftwood, or other design elements may be incorporated into the design, preferably before planting. There are special tools available to plant a terrarium in a bottle with a narrow neck. Bottles are somewhat difficult to clean, fill, and plant, but they are a conversation piece when finished.

After the terrarium is planted, it is watered in with a fine spray and placed in a bright spot. It should not be put in direct sun which would bake the plants. If the terrarium has no cover, the gardener will need to check it periodically for water. If it is sealed, it should be checked regularly for signs of mold. Terrariums are generally not fertilized because this will cause the plants to outgrow their home. Frequent pinching and removal of plants is necessary to keep some plants in bounds. If the conditions are right, a terrarium can last several years.

Right: Sinningia in terrarium.

BONSAI

Bonsai is an ancient Japanese art form in which a single tree or group of trees is grown in a shallow pot and trained as a miniature version of a plant or landscape found in nature. Bonsai involves elaborate and time-consuming pruning and training, beginning when a plant is very young. There are bonsai experts all over the world, bonsai societies in every city, and bonsai plants that are well over several hundred years old in museums and homes throughout the world. These plants are carefully tended by bonsai specialists or masters.

Bonsai may be deciduous or evergreen plants from tropical or temperate climates. Those from temperate climates, such as junipers, must be wintered outdoors to give the plant the conditions it requires. Tropical bonsai, such as serissa, on the other hand, can be kept indoors year-round or summered outdoors.

When purchasing a bonsai plant, be certain that you know its identity so that you may give it the conditions it requires. Be warned that bonsai take a considerable amount of time and care in order to have a healthy plant.

Placement Most bonsai, whether tropical or temperate, benefit from a summer outdoors. They should be placed where air can circulate freely all around the plant, including the container. Most thrive in full sun, but tropical bonsai should be carefully acclimated when brought outdoors in early summer. In order for bonsai to be viewed properly, they should be placed at eye level. Putting the plant on the ground is an invitation to disease and insect entry.

In winter, tropical bonsai must be brought indoors and given a place with high light and good air circulation. Temperate bonsai should be allowed to go naturally dormant through the fall, and then put into storage before cold weather hits. Plants are easily stored in a window well or cold frame with bark chips under and all around the plant. Water it well before putting it into storage. Temperatures of 25-32° F. are ideal–avoid extremes.

In spring, bring the plant gradually out of storage by moving it into an unheated garage or storage area. Water well and check often–plants coming out of dormancy may need water twice a day. This is also the time to do a spring pruning if necessary.

Watering Water bonsai with a can or syringe until water runs out the bottom of the container. In spring and summer, plants may need to be watered three or four times a day if they are in small containers. As with other plants, watering should not be done on a schedule, but rather when the plant needs it. This will vary depending on soil mix, type of plant, weather, and size of container. Incorrect watering is a common cause of bonsai death.

Fertilizing Fertilize bonsai spring through fall but not in winter. Fertilize with every watering with a solution that is one-quarter to one-eighth the strength recommended on the fertilizer label. Use a complete fertilizer, such as 10-10-10, unless you are growing the bonsai for flowers or fruit. In this case, choose a fertilizer that is high in phosphorus, such as 5-10-5. Do not be tempted to overfertilize. Bonsai roots are extremely susceptible to burning if too high a concentration of fertilizer is used.

GROOMING

Weekly grooming is a necessity to keep bonsai healthy and attractive. Inspect for disease and insect problems and remove any dead or discolored leaves or flowers. Use cuticle scissors for trimming instead of pulling. Rotate the container one-quarter turn every week to keep the plant full on all sides. Clip off any suckers or shoots arising from the main trunk and also remove any oversized leaves. Prune new growth by about one-half.

PRUNING

There are several styles of bonsai-- each with its own particular pruning style. Generally, pruning is done to miniaturize and give the illusion of old age. Sharp pruning tools are essential.

TOPIARY

There are three types of indoor topiary: pruned, hollow, and stuffed. The primary differences between these and the traditional outdoor forms of topiary are the use of indoor plants, the increased use of wire, the use of plants in containers rather than in-ground plantings, and the use of moss-stuffed, free-standing frames.

Pruned topiaries are container plants that are carefully trained, pruned, and pinched to create a particular design. The limit to the possible designs is defined by your imagination and creative vision. This type will take the longest time to achieve the desired shape but is long-lived and easy to maintain. Allow the plant you choose for this type of topiary to suggest a shape–don't try to turn an upright grower into an alligator!

Pruned topiary begins with a young container plant whose growth habit has the potential to become woody and ultimately support itself. Upright herbs, such as myrtle, rosemary, and santolina, are commonly used to make standards, spirals, cones, and other classic shapes as well as more whimsical designs. Once a plant and the desired shape are selected, a central stake may be used to control growth, and the plant is pruned and directed with the desired shape in mind. Copper wire is sometimes used to direct stems in directions other than a plant's natural tendency. Scissors, tweezers, and other small tools are used in pruning and grooming. No matter what the desired shape, pruning is essential to encourage a bushier plant in certain areas and to remove the foliage in other areas. As the plant becomes woody and holds its shape, the stake or wire may be removed. A completed topiary needs frequent trimming to maintain a clean shape. As the plant ages, root pruning may be necessary to keep the plant in prime health (this must be done in conjunction with top pruning–a delicate operation on a topiary that has been years in the making). Other suitable plants for pruned topiary include syzygium, serissa, lantana, plumbago, fuchsia, buddleia, tibouchina, malpighia, and ficus.

Hollow topiaries are container plants that twine onto and around the silhouette of a wire frame. A wire frame is placed in the pot to provide support, and vining plants such as English ivy or creeping fig are used. The vining plants are wound around or attached loosely with soft ties or copper wire to the wire frame as they grow. Once established on the frame, the ties are removed, and the plants are trimmed and pinched to maintain a smooth appearance. The frame is ultimately covered by the plant and is not removed. This type of topiary takes less time to complete than pruned topiary, but requires more maintenance.

Some common shapes are spheres, pyramids, wreaths, and animals. In addition to ivies (of which there are hundreds) and creeping fig, hoya, trachelospermum, and ceropegia are also popular. Crown of thorns trains beautifully, but wear gloves when pruning.

Stuffed topiaries are novel, free-standing units. These plants are not grown in a container of soil, but are grown in a moss-stuffed form. Creeping and vining plants are traditionally used, but can be combined with other plants to add interest. Wire frames can be hand-made or purchased in nearly any shape. The frame is stuffed with moistened long-fiber sphagnum moss and sometimes wrapped in sheet moss (that has been soaked and wrung out) and secured with fishing line or florist's wire. Small plants (two- to three-inch-pot size) are typically planted in the sphagnum moss. If the plants are used in sufficient numbers, they will cover the form quickly. As vines grow, they should be pinned to the moss with hairpins. The form must be submerged for ten to fifteen minutes in tepid water when it begins to dry out. Stuffed topiaries perform well for several years, although the interior moss will eventually deteriorate. This is often accompanied by rusting of the form, so a renovation is in order. Renovation generally means taking cuttings from the original topiary and starting with a new frame. Shamrock ivy makes a beautiful stuffed topiary—the leaves lie flat and the dark green lobes overlap. Scirpus makes great tufts of hair, as does ophiopogon. Ceropegia offers good color and it's easy to train its stems. Hoya, sedum, episcia, and many others offer interesting color and texture to create a topiary with personality.

Topiaries at Chicago Botanic Garden.

PLACEMENT

The chart below provides basic reference points for placement.

Low-light intensity

Place plants:
8 inches under two 20-watt tubes
 (24 inch long bulbs)
12 inches under two 40-watt tubes
 (48 inch long bulbs)
12-24 inches under four 40-watt tubes

Medium-light intensity

Place plants:
4-8 inches under two 20-watt tubes
6-12 inches under two 40-watt tubes
12-24 inches under four 40-watt
tubes

High-light intensity

Place plants:
8-15 inches under four 40-watt tubes

GROWING PLANTS WITH SUPPLEMENTAL LIGHT

When natural light is insufficient to promote healthy plant growth, fluorescent lights can be used as supplements or as the sole source of light for plants.
A plant's performance and appearance can often be greatly improved with the
addition of supplemental light, especially in rooms where natural light is lacking.

Plant collectors with special collections, such as African violets, often use
light carts, which enable them to control the quality and intensity of light.
These plants are usually removed from the light source only for display. On
the other hand, the home gardener who wants to start seeds and grow trans-
plants for the outdoor garden can easily hang inexpensive light fixtures over
growing areas. These single light supplements are also appropriate for African
violets, etc.

With the use of supplemental light, the gardener can maintain control of
the quality and intensity of light and can vary the day length according to
plant needs. However, the light bulbs can be expensive and must be replaced
annually to ensure good-quality light.

Although almost any plant can be grown under fluorescent lights, the best
candidates are small, slow-growers that need medium to low light. Plants
must be very close to the light, which limits plant collections to those of similar heights. Additionally, plants requiring similar culture make better partners
for sharing a single light source.

Ordinary incandescent bulbs are not suited for light gardening because
they generate too much heat. Fluorescent tube lighting is most commonly
used because it provides light without much heat, allowing plants to be
placed close to the light source. Fluorescent tubes are generally less expensive
and use less electricity than any other kind of light. A combination of cool
white and warm white tubes provides light that closely mimics the sun's color
spectrum. Lights sold specifically for plant growing are effective, but are
much more expensive than standard fluorescent tubes and do not necessarily
give better results.

Most lighting units are in use for fourteen to sixteen hours a day. Most
plants should be placed six to twelve inches from the light source (this differs
with seedlings). The length and wattage of the bulbs dictates the actual lighting duration and distance at which to place the plants from the light source.
It is also important to recognize that the plants on the outer edge of a light
cart or toward the end of the light tubes will receive less light than those near
the center. Rotate plants regularly or put the plants that require the highest
light where the light is greatest. Experience with a plant's response to the
placement will help refine your approach.

Plants need not only light, but they need darkness each night to rest and
respire. Timers are helpful in regulating the hours of light a plant receives,
especially when the gardener is away. Light fixtures should always have reflec-
tors on top to direct light where it is most needed.

Light intensity and quality decline as the bulbs age. To continue to grow high-quality plants, replace the tubes after 5,100 hours of use (generally a year) and on a staggered schedule so that the change in light levels is not terribly abrupt. (Mark the date at the end of each tube to keep track of changes.) Bulbs that still have some life can be used to light garages and utility rooms.

Although most care is the same for plants grown under lights as those grown in natural light, temperatures may be slightly warmer and the air slightly drier under lights. A small fan is useful to keep the air cool and circulating. A shallow tray of moist pebbles under the pots will increase humidity.

PLANTS THAT GROW WELL UNDER ARTIFICIAL LIGHT.

Achimenes (Magic flower)
Aeschynanthus javanicus (Lipstick plant)
Aloe (Medicine plant)
Asparagus densiflorus (Asparagus fern)
Begonia x *rex* (Begonia)
Bromeliads
Browallia speciosa (Browallia)
Chlorophytum (Spider plant)
Cissus rhombifolia (Grape ivy)
Coleus (Coleus)
Columnea (Goldfish plant)
Crassula argentea (Jade plant)
Crypthanthus (Earth star)
Episcia hybrids (Flame violet)
Fittonia verschaffeltii (Silver nerve plant)
Gynura aurantiaca (Velvet plant)
Haworthia (Window plant)
Hypoestes phyllostachya (Freckle face)
Maranta leuconeura (Prayer plant)
Nephrolepis (Boston fern)
Orchids (many species)
Pelargonium (Geranium)
Peperomia (Peperomia
Philodendron (Philodendron)
Pilea microphylla (Artillery plant)
Plectranthus australis (Swedish ivy)
Rosa chinensis var. *minima* (Miniature rose)
Saintpaulia (African violet)
Saxifraga stolonifera (Strawberry geranium)
Selaginella (Clubmoss)
Sinningia (Florist's gloxinia)
Streptocarpus (Cape primrose)
Tolmiea menziesii (Piggy-back plant)
Tradescantia (Wandering jew)
Zebrina (Wandering jew)

HERBS FOR INDOOR CULTURE
Basil
Bay
Chamomile
Chives
Lavender
Lemon balm
Mint
Oregano
Parsley
Rosemary
Sage
Sweet marjoram
Thyme

GROWING HERBS INDOORS

Some herbs can be grown indoors as houseplants, and. tender perennials that may not survive the winter outdoors can be overwintered indoors. Generally, herbs need a minimum of four to six hours of bright light each day or fourteen hours of supplemental light for ideal indoor growth. Herbs in insufficient light are extremely susceptible to insects. All herbs except basil perform best in a cold sunny window. Frequent pinching keeps them stocky and full.

Herbs grown indoors tend to lack some of the intense oils that give the flavor desired for cooking. The outdoor garden will produce herbs full of flavor, while indoor herbs are rather like hothouse tomatoes–they lack the color and some of the flavor, but will tide you over until spring.

And, as an added bonus, indoor herbs emit delicious scents when you brush up against them, filling a room with the scent of summer in midwinter.

Above, from left to right:
Aloe, parsley, rosemary, bay, chives.

GROWING ORCHIDS INDOORS

Orchids grace any room they inhabit with mystery and beauty—and contrary to popular opinion, they can be grown by just about everyone, not only eccentric millionaires. According to both Jerry Parsons at the University of California, Berkeley, and Robert Bowden of Harry P. Leu Botanical Gardens, orchids have an undeserved bad reputation as being hard to handle; most species can be grown successfully by home gardeners as long as conditions are right.

The secret to success with orchids varies with the individual varieties, but in general, orchids need a temperature of about 70° F. in summer and 60° F. in winter; it is imperative that nights be cooler by about ten degrees. Orchids need about ten to fifteen hours of strong light each day, but should be shielded from direct sunlight. Soil should be kept moist. Repot infrequently even if roots begin to grow outside the pot; repot only when plant begins to wilt, and be sure to use a potting mixture that is appropriate to the species. Chicago Botanic Garden suggests repotting every two years or so, as potting media tends to break down. Good aeration around roots is essential for good growth; when the media breaks down, the air spaces are lost, and the plants suffer.

The most important factor is humidity. A greenhouse is ideal, but humidity can be improved by misting or by placing humidifiers around the plants. Pebble trays are also beneficial. Fertilize with special orchid fertilizer at every second watering during growing season; most orchid fertilizers are water-soluble because salt buildup is detrimental to orchid roots.

There are over one hundred thousand known orchid species—more than any other type of plant. Some of these are indeed rare and temperamental. Others can be purchased for a few dollars and rebloom reliably in the right circumstances. See index for more information on the following orchids: cymbidium, cattleya, paphiopedilum, phalaenopsis, and laelia. Other types to consider are vandas (tall, single-stemmed, epiphytic orchids that produce five to ten large flowers), miltonias (which bear smaller flowers that resemble pansies, but are not eary to grow indoors), oncidiums (some of which produce masses of small bright flowers known as "dancing dolls), and dendrobiums (a genus which consists of many worthy species).

Orchid propagation is difficult for the amateur; try dividing plants when you repot them, but do not count on success.

Orchids react predictably if their needs are not met. Inadequate light will cause them to droop; direct sun will cause brown spots on the leaves. Orchids are also subject to mildew and fungus diseases because they are grown in humid conditions; impeccable sanitation is necessary.

Cattleya orchids.

acidic: having pH lower than 7.0

acclimate: process by which a plant adjusts to a new environment

aeration: supply with oxygen

aerial roots: roots formed along a stem above soil level

air layering: propagation process in which the top portion of the plant develops roots while still attached and nourished by the parent plant.

alkaline: having a pH greater than 7.0

anaerobic: without the presence of oxygen

anthers: the pollen-bearing structure of a flower

anthocyanins: red and blue pigments found in leaves, flowers and fruits

apex: growing point or tip

areole: hairy cushion-like spot unique to cactus from which spines and flowers grow

aroids: plants in the family *Araceae*

asexual propagation: reproduction by cuttings rather than seed

average household temperature: temperature that is comfortable for the average person

balanced fertilizer: fertilizer with an analysis in which the three major components have equal proportions: i.e., 10-10-10

beneficial insects: predatory or parasitic insects that attack pests

binomial nomenclature: system of scientific naming of plants; each species name is made up of a genus and specific epithet

biodegradable: decomposes easily by natural means

biological control: pest control by naturally occurring means, usually by predatory or parasitic insect, virus or bacteria

bipinnate: compound leaf that is twice divided

bloom: waxy covering sometimes occurring on leaves, stems and fruits

bottom watering: setting a plant in a

container of water to let the water be naturally wicked up into the soil

bracts: modified leaf that is usually highly colored and long-lasting

bulbous: arising from a bulb

bud: a growth point

bulbules: immature bulbs or plantlets forming on a parent plant

calcined clay: clay treated with heat (common example is cat litter)

calyx : the outer protective covering of a flower, made up of green or other colored sepals

canes: stiff stems

carotenoids: yellow and orange pigments found in leaves, flowers and fruits

caudex: thickened axis of a plant, consisting of stem and root

chlorophyll: green pigment that is necessary for photosynthesis

chlorotic: yellowing of leaves or stems due to nutrient deficiency or pest problem

cloning: process of reproducing a plant by asexual reproduction; making an exact genetic duplicate of the parent plant

compound leaf: leaf that is divided into several leaflets

cooling period: certain number of weeks or months in which a bulb or plant must be cooled in order to produce flowers

corm: an underground storage organ formed from a thickened stem

crawlers: immature stage of scale insects

crown: the area of a plant from which shoots and roots arise

cultivar: a cultivated variety, i.e., human-created

cuticle: the outer covering of a leaf or stem

cuttings: stem, tip, leaf and root sections used in asexual propagation

cyathium: whorl of bracts that are fused together

deciduous: goes into dormant period (usually drops leaves)

defoliation: loss of leaves

desiccation: drying out

differentiate: process in which unspecialized cells undergo specialization: i.e., cells on a leaf cutting differentiate to produce root cells.

dilute solution: fertilizer mixed at lower-concentration than recommended on the label

dioecious: having male and female reproductive parts located on separate plants–hence two plants (male and female) are required for seed production

division: propagation by separating the crown of the plant into more than one piece

dormancy: period of arrested growth in which a plant shuts down many metabolic processes

dorsal sepal: main sepal on orchid, usually has different appearance than the other sepals

double potting: using a draining pot inside a non-draining, usually decorative pot; done for aesthetics or stabilization

ecosystem: an ecological community together with its physical setting; considered a single unit

elongation: stretching of a stem

epiphyte: a plant that obtains its nutrients and water from the atmosphere or small pockets of decaying material in crevices of rocks or other plants; non-parasitic

ethylene gas: natural plant growth substance given off by ripening fruit; used to stimulate flowering

etiolation: lack of light causes plant cells to expand rapidly, making a stem elongate and become pale

eye: growing point from which a stem will emerge; i.e., a bud. A distinct coloration at the center of a flower

fertilizer analysis: the composition of nitrogen, phosphorus and potassium; designated as X-X-X on the fertilizer label

fibrous-rooted: plant has stringy mass of fine roots

filaments: wire-like structures that hold the anthers in a flower

flagging: point just before damaging

wilting when a plant lacks turgidity; leaves hang down slightly

floriferous: bearing many flowers

forcing: procedure in which a bulb is taken through a regime that mimicks its natural cycle in order to make it flower indoors

fronds: the leaves of ferns

genus: taxonomic name that designates a group of plants that have more in common with each other than any other group

germination: beginning growth by a spore or seed

glochids: tiny barbed hair found on cactus

growth regulators: plant hormones used in the commercial plant industry to influence plant growth

habit: a plant's natural outline or shape

herbaceous plants: plants that do not have woody stems

honeydew: sticky secretion from pests such as aphids, scale and whiteflies

horticultural oil: highly refined oils that kill pests by smothering the insect or egg, or by interfering with an insect's metabolism

humidity: moisture in the air

hybrid: plant that arises from the cross-fertilization of two dissimilar parents

hydroponics: method of growing plants in water containing all the nutrients they need

incised: deeply notched

indolebutyric acid (IBA): plant hormone used to speed the rooting process

inflorescence: flower or group of flowers

insecticidal soap: soap solution containing fatty acids that disrupt membrane and cell functions in insects, killing them

insectivorous: consumes insects

Integrated Pest Management (IPM): system of evaluating all the factors in a growing situation and providing options to keep pest populations at a low enough level to avoid unacceptable or irreparable damage

keel: V-shaped ridge on the lower side of a leaf

keikii: plantlets that form along the flower stems of certain orchids; used for propagation (Hawaiian for baby)

layering: propagation by pinning a trailing stem on top of the soil or burying it slightly under the soil where it will form roots; once roots have formed, the new plant can be severed from the old

leach: ridding soil of fertilizer salt build-up by letting water run through the soil and drain away several times

leaf axils: joints where leaves are joined to stems

leaf blades: the wide part of the leaf

leaf cuttings: propagation by using only leaves to form roots and shoots

leaf scars: indentations or marks left on a stem by leaves that have fallen

leaf shine products: commercial formulations that are used to clean and give a shine to leaves

leaf-bud cuttings: propagation by using a leaf attached to a short piece of stem with a bud

leaflets: segment of a compound leaf

lip: a petal or flower lobe that is distinctly different than the rest of the petals; found on all orchids

lobe: rounded projection of a leaf or flower

macronutrients: essential nutrients needed in greatest quantities by plants for growth; including nitrogen, phosphorus, potassium, calcium, carbon, hydrogen, magnesium, oxygen and sulfur

margin: the edge of a leaf

medium: material in which a plant is grown–usually soil or soil-less potting mixture

microclimates: climate of a specific area within a larger area of different climate

micronutrients: trace elements used in small amounts by a plant for growth; including boron, chlorine, copper, iron, manganese, molybdenum and zinc

midrib: center vein of a leaf

mutant: plant that differs genetically from the parent due to gene mutation

naphthalene acetic acid (NAA): plant hormone that is used to speed the rooting process

nitrogen: one of the essential nutrients need for leaf growth

nocturnal flowers: flowers that bloom in the evening or at night

node: point on the stem where leaves and buds arise

nomenclature: taxonomic naming system

nymph: immature stage of an insect

offsets: plantlets arising from the base of the mother plant; used for propagation

offshoots: synonym for offset

organic fertilizers: fertilizers derived from natural sources

ovule: structure which becomes seed after fertilization

palmate: compound leaf with leaflets attached to petiole at a single point; lobes that resemble fingers

peat moss: carbonized sphagnum moss; brown and crumbly in texture; used as major component in soil-less potting mixes

pedicel: stalk that attaches a flower to the main axis of the inflorescence

pendent: drooping

perlite: white volcanic material that is heated for expansion; component of potting mixes to improve drainage; desirable due to its light weight

pesticide: fungicide, herbicide or insecticide

petiole: stalk that attaches a leaf to a stem

phosphorus: one of the essential nutrients needed for plant growth, important for flowering

photoperiodic: flowering response dependent upon the number of hours of darkness and daylight

photosynthesis: process by which a plant uses light energy to produce carbohydrates from water and carbon dioxide

pinch: to remove the growing tip of a stem

pinna (pinnae): single leaflet on a fern frond

pith: tissue in the center of a stem

plantlets: immature plants arising from leaves, stems or roots of a mother plant

pollen: powder-like substance produced from the anthers of a flower, providing the male element in sexual reproduction

pollination: transfer of the pollen to the ovary to accomplish fertilization

porous: well-aerated potting mix with ample pore spaces for oxygen and water, drains well

pot bound: state in which plant roots fill a pot

potassium: a major nutrient necessary for plant growth; important for fruits and flowers

propagate: to create new plants by sexual or asexual methods

pseudobulb: thickened stems that emerge from creeping ground stems or rhizomes; function to store moisture and food; used for propagation

pubescent: covered with soft, fine hairs

raceme: elongate inflorescence

recurve: bend or curve backward or downward

reflexed: to turn backward

respiration: the process of breaking down sugar and other carbon compounds into carbon dioxide and water

rhizomatous: derived from a rhizome

rhizome: a fleshy horizontal stem that usually occurs underground; gives rise to roots and shoots

root cuttings: propagation method in which pieces of a root are planted to give rise to new plants

root hairs: tiny tender structures on roots that absorb water and nutrients from the soil

root pruning: trimming off roots during the process of repotting a plant

rooting powder (hormone): powder or liquid made of plant hormones that is used to increase the quantity and quality of roots from cuttings

rosette: group of leaves that grows directly from the crown of a plant (without stems)

runner: aboveground horizontal stem that produces buds at the nodes from which roots and shoots form

scarification: process of physically scratching a seed coat so that water can enter and germination can begin

seed coat: the hard covering of a seed that prevents germination at inopportune times

self-watering containers: specialized pots that keep a plant watered by means of a reservoir and any number of water-moving methods

sepals: outermost flower structures that usually enclose a bud; can be highly colored

simple leaf: an undivided leaf (as compared with a compound leaf)

sleeve: paper or plastic wrapping to protect plants from the weather or physical damage, used in transportation of plants

slow-release fertilizer: fertilizer that is encapsulated in gelatin or clay pellet that releases nutrients slowly and is usually incorporated into soil

soil-less potting mix: potting soil composed of sterile elements such as peat moss, vermiculite, perlite and shredded bark, but does not include "black dirt"

sooty mold: black fungus that grows on honeydew excreted by insects such as aphids and mealybugs

sori (singular is sorus): fruiting bodies of ferns–hold the spores

spadix: flowering structure of aroid plants such as spathiphyllum; tiny florets are embedded in a fleshy spike

spathe: leafy protective covering around a spadix; sometimes brightly colored as with anthurium

species: plant name consisting of the genus and specific epithet

specific epithet: the second word in a scientific name; usually descriptive of the individual plant

spine: thorny prickle found on many types of cactus

spore: dustlike single-celled reproductive body of ferns and mosses

sport: branch or leaf that has different characteristics from the parent plant

stamen: male reproductive organ of a flower

standard: a plant that is trained into a tree-like form

stem cutting: reproductive sections made of a portion of the stem and some leaves

stolon: a horizontal stem that creeps along the ground and roots wherever it touches soil

stomate: microscopic openings on leaves and stems that allow air and water exchange

stratification: alternating temperature regimes in order to break dormancy of a seed

taxonomy: the science of classifying organisms

temperate: climate with distinct hot and cold periods (as opposed to tropical)

terminal stem cutting: stem cutting made of the end of a stem that includes the growing tip

terrarium: partially or completely enclosed growing environment

tissue culture: the use of single cells from a plant to generate new plants

topiary: plants clipped, shaped, and trained into various forms not normally associated with that plant

trace elements: minor nutrients that a plant must have, but used in very small amounts

tubercles: a wartlike swelling on the stems of plants, particularly cactus

turgid: filled with water, rigid

variation: markings or patterns on leaves, stems or flowers in various colors

variety: naturally occurring variation which is indicated by the term "var."

vegetative propagation: asexually reproducing a plant by methods other than seed

vein: conducting tissue in a leaf; usually strandlike

vermiculite: mineral that is heated for expansion and water retention; major component of potting mixes

whorled: three or more leaves or flowers occurring at a single node

woody: having stems above ground that retain live buds even if the leaves die

The following list is intended to provide readers with sources for plant materials. Inclusion on this list does not indicate endorsement of the company, and there are many fine sources that have not been included.

Abbey Garden Cactus and Succulents
4620 Carpinteria Avenue
Carpinteria, California 93013
805-684-5112/1595

Arid Lands Greenhouses
3560 West Bilby Road
Tucson, Arizona 85746
602-883-9404
Fax: 602-883-8874

The Banana Tree, Inc. (seeds)
715 Northampton Street
Easton, Pennsylvania 18042
215-253-9589
Fax: 215-253-4864

Everglades Orchids
1101 Tabit Road
Belle Glade, Florida 33430
407-996-9600
Fax: 407-996-2601

Glasshouse Works Greenhouses (exotics)
Church Street
PO Box 97
Stewart, Ohio 45778-0097
614-662-2142

Grigsby Cactus Gardens
2354 Belle Vista Drive
Vista, California 92084
619-727-1578

Highland Succulents
1446 Bear Run Road
Gallipolis, Ohio 45631

Jerry Horne (ferns)
10195 Southwest 70th Street
Miami, Florida 33173
305-270-1235

Klehm Growers, Inc. (Orchids)
44W637 State Route 72
Hampshire, Illinois 60140-9801
708-683-4766

Living Stones Nursery
2936 North Stone Avenue
Tucson, Arizona 85705

Logees Greenhouses
141 North Street
Danielson, Connecticut 06239
203-774-8038

Oakhill Gardens (orchids and supplies)
PO Box 25
Binnie Road
West Dundee, Illinois 60118
708-428-8500

Rhapis Gardens
PO Box 287
Gregory, Texas 78359
512-643-2061/5814

Stewart Orchids
3376 Foothill Road
PO Box 550
Carpinteria, California 93014
805-684-5448

CONTRIBUTORS

Main Garden:
Wanda Supanich and
  Meegan McCarthy-Bilow
Chicago Botanic Garden
Post Office Box 400
Lake Cook and Eden Roads
Glencoe, IL 60022

Robert Bowden
Harry P. Leu Botanical Gardens
1730 North Forest Avenue
Orlando, FL 32803

Deborah Lalumondier
Missouri Botanical Garden
PO Box 299
St. Louis, MO 63166

Julie Morris
Blithewold Mansion and Gardens
Box 417, Ferry Road
Bristol, RI 02809

Jerry Parsons
University of California
  Botanical Garden, Berkeley
Centennial Drive
Berkeley, CA 94720

Francisca Planchard-Coelho
The New York Botanical Garden
Bronx, New York 10458

PHOTO CREDITS

All photographs ©Cliff Zenor with the following exceptions:

  ©Dr. Thomas Antonio: pp. 129TL, TR; 153; 213.

  ©Elvin McDonald: pp. 26BR; 34TL; 38; 43TR; 49TR, BR; 50; 53TR; 54; 55; 60; 64BR; 73TL, TR; 82BR; 89Tl; 91; 95TL; 97; 99TR; 103TR; 108BL; 110; 11; 11BR; 119BL; 131BR; 141TR; 145TR, BR; 149TL; 159BR; 150, 162, 168, 206.

  ©Steve and Sylvia Sharnoff: p. 73BL

  ©Albert Squillace: pp. 20-21; 29; 31BR; 46TR; 53TL; 60BR; 71TL, BL, BR; 75BL; 80, 81, 83, 84TL; 95BR; 111TL; 113TL; 117TR, BL; 127; 128TR, BL, 134BR; 136; 137TR, BR; 147BL; 155BR; 169R.

  ©John Trager: pp. 31TL; 39TL; 40; 63BL; 67TL; 163.

  ©Chani Yammer: pp. 13B; 24TL; 26TR; 37BL; 43TL; 48; 60BL; 62; 92TR; 105TL; 114; 140; 147BR; 207T.

  llustrations on endpapers and on pages 16-17 by Delores Bego; all other illustrations by Eric Marshall

  T=Top; B=Bottom; R=Right; L=Left

LEAF SHAPES

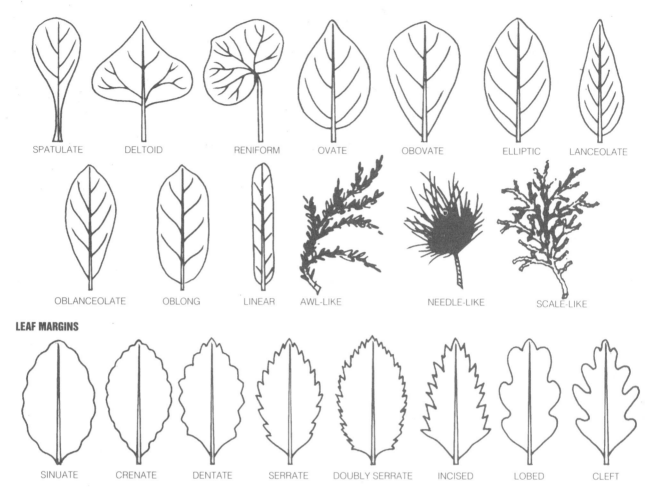

SPATULATE · DELTOID · RENIFORM · OVATE · OBOVATE · ELLIPTIC · LANCEOLATE

OBLANCEOLATE · OBLONG · LINEAR · AWL-LIKE · NEEDLE-LIKE · SCALE-LIKE

LEAF MARGINS

SINUATE · CRENATE · DENTATE · SERRATE · DOUBLY SERRATE · INCISED · LOBED · CLEFT

LEAF ARRANGEMENTS AND STRUCTURES

SIMPLE · PALMATE · COMPOUND BIPINNATE

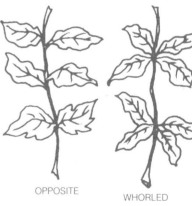

ALTERNATE

OPPOSITE

WHORLED